Lecture Notes
in Business Information Processing 497

LNBIP reports state-of-the-art results in areas related to business information systems and industrial application software development – timely, at a high level, and in both printed and electronic form.

The type of material published includes

- Proceedings (published in time for the respective event)
- Postproceedings (consisting of thoroughly revised and/or extended final papers)
- Other edited monographs (such as, for example, project reports or invited volumes)
- Tutorials (coherently integrated collections of lectures given at advanced courses, seminars, schools, etc.)
- Award-winning or exceptional theses

LNBIP is abstracted/indexed in DBLP, EI and Scopus. LNBIP volumes are also submitted for the inclusion in ISI Proceedings.

João Paulo A. Almeida ·
Monika Kaczmarek-Heß · Agnes Koschmider ·
Henderik A. Proper
Editors

The Practice of Enterprise Modeling

16th IFIP Working Conference, PoEM 2023
Vienna, Austria, November 28 – December 1, 2023
Proceedings

Springer

Editors
João Paulo A. Almeida (ID)
Federal University of Espírito Santo
Vitória, Brazil

Monika Kaczmarek-Heß (ID)
University of Duisburg-Essen
Essen, Germany

Agnes Koschmider (ID)
University of Bayreuth
Bayreuth, Germany

Henderik A. Proper (ID)
TU Wien
Vienna, Austria

ISSN 1865-1348   ISSN 1865-1356 (electronic)
Lecture Notes in Business Information Processing
ISBN 978-3-031-48582-4   ISBN 978-3-031-48583-1 (eBook)
https://doi.org/10.1007/978-3-031-48583-1

This Springer imprint is published by the registered company Springer Nature Switzerland AG
The registered company address is: Gewerbestrasse 11, 6330 Cham, Switzerland

Paper in this product is recyclable.

Preface

This volume of the *Lecture Notes in Business Information Processing* series contains the proceedings of the 16th IFIP WG 8.1 Working Conference on the Practice of Enterprise Modeling (PoEM), held in Vienna, Austria, during November 28th to December 1st, 2023. The PoEM working conference aims to improve the understanding of the practice of Enterprise Modeling (EM) by offering a forum for sharing experiences and knowledge between the academic community and practitioners from industry and the public sector.

These proceedings include 12 full papers selected out of 34 full papers sent for peer review (35.3% acceptance rate). All submissions have been thoroughly reviewed in a single-blind process by three program committee members. The review process was led by the program committee chairs João Paulo A. Almeida and Monika Kaczmarek-Heß overseen by the general chairs Henderik A. Proper and Agnes Koschmider. The selected papers cover topical areas such as *Enterprise Modeling and Artificial Intelligence*, *Enterprise Modeling and Emerging Architectures*, *Enterprise Modeling and Digital Transformation*, *Enterprise Modeling Tools and Approaches*, etc. We would like to show our greatest appreciation to the submitting authors and the members of the program committee as well as additional reviewers for their hard work.

This year, the theme of the conference is *Enterprise Modeling in the Circular Economy*. The theme reflects the importance of enterprise modeling methods, techniques, and tools to enable enterprises to move to more sustainable practices. We are glad to see in these proceedings papers that are aligned with this theme.

The proceedings further include abstracts of the invited talks of our keynote speakers: Anna-Vera Deinhammer, Professor for Sustainable Real Estate Development at Vienna University of Applied Sciences for Management and Communication, and Iva Kovacic, Professor for Integrated Planning and Head of Institute for Building and Industrial Construction at the Faculty of Civil and Environmental Engineering, Vienna University of Technology. We would like to express our sincere gratitude for their presentations and attendance at our event.

This year's PoEM was collocated with the 13th Enterprise Design & Engineering Working Conference (EDEWC). We would like to thank the EDEWC PC chairs Cristine Gritto, Monika Malinova Mandelburger, and Sérgio Guerreiro for their collaboration; the week's program reflects the synergy of the communities involved in the two conferences. Separate proceedings for the collocated conference are to appear also in the Springer LNBIP series as post-proceedings.

Part of the program of PoEM (and jointly EDEWC) is devoted to the PoEM/EDEWC Forum, which was designed to offer a platform for discussing emerging ideas, challenges, methods, techniques, and tools relevant for Enterprise Modeling. The Forum aims at a high level of interactivity between presenters and participants. Companion post-conference proceedings are published separately and include papers selected for the PoEM/EDEWC Forum, the Enterprise Modeling Tools Forum, and satellite workshops of PoEM 2023.

We would like to thank the PoEM steering committee for entrusting us with the responsibility of organizing this year's conference. We would like to thank PoEM/EDEWC Forum chairs Sérgio Guerreiro and Sybren de Kinderen, as well as the workshop chairs David Aveiro and Tiago Prince Sales, and Enterprise Modeling Tools Forum chairs Dominik Bork and Mark Mulder for their work. We would like to express our gratitude to the local organization committee, including Angela Edlinger, Aleksandar Gavric, and Marianne Schnellmann. We would like to thank the Business Informatics Group of the Technical University of Vienna for hosting the conference.

Finally, there can be no conference without engaged participation: we would like to express our deep gratitude to all who contributed with their insights to make our conference program interesting and all those who came to Vienna for PoEM 2023.

October 2023

João Paulo A. Almeida
Monika Kaczmarek-Heß
Agnes Koschmider
Henderik A. Proper

Organization

General Chairs

Henderik A. Proper   TU Wien, Austria
Agnes Koschmider   University of Bayreuth, Germany

Program Chairs

João Paulo A. Almeida   Federal University of Espírito Santo, Brazil
Monika Kaczmarek-Heß   University of Duisburg-Essen, Germany

Workshop and Working Sessions Chairs

David Aveiro   University of Madeira, Portugal
Tiago Prince Sales   University of Twente, The Netherlands

Joint EDEWC and PoEM Forum Chairs

Sérgio Guerreiro   Instituto Superior Técnico, Portugal
Sybren de Kinderen   TU Eindhoven, The Netherlands

Enterprise Modeling Tools Forum

Dominik Bork   TU Wien, Austria
Mark Mulder   TEEC2, The Netherlands

Local Organization Committee

Angela Edlinger   TU Wien, Austria
Aleksandar Gavric   TU Wien, Austria
Marianne Schnellmann   TU Wien, Austria

Steering Committee

Anne Persson   University of Skövde, Sweden
Janis Stirna   Stockholm University, Sweden
Kurt Sandkuhl   University of Rostock, Germany

Program Committee

Raian Ali   Hamad Bin Khalifa University, Qatar
Souvik Barat   Tata Consultancy Services Research, India
Balbir Barn   Middlesex University, UK
Judith Barrios Albornoz   University of Los Andes, Venezuela
Dominik Bork   TU Wien, Austria
Robert Andrei Buchmann   Babeş-Bolyai University of Cluj Napoca,
                               Romania
Rimantas Butleris   Kaunas University of Technology, Lithuania
Tony Clark   Aston University, UK
Sybren de Kinderen   TU Eindhoven, The Netherlands
Paul Drews   Leuphana University of Lüneburg, Germany
Michael Fellmann   University of Rostock, Germany
Hans-Georg Fill   University of Fribourg, Switzerland
Ana-Maria Ghiran   Babes-Bolyai University of Cluj-Napoca,
                               Romania
Jaap Gordijn   Vrije Universiteit Amsterdam, The Netherlands
Jānis Grabis   Riga Technical University, Latvia
Giancarlo Guizzardi   University of Twente, The Netherlands
Jens Gulden   Utrecht University, The Netherlands
Simon Hacks   Stockholm University, Sweden
Martin Henkel   Stockholm University, Sweden
Knut Hinkelmann   FHNW, Switzerland
Stijn Hoppenbrouwers   HAN Univ. of Applied Sciences, The Netherlands
Jennifer Horkoff   Chalmers University of Technology, Sweden
Manfred Jeusfeld   University of Skövde, Sweden
John Krogstie   Norwegian University of Science and Technology,
                               Norway
Ulrike Lechner   Universität der Bundeswehr München, Germany
Beatriz Marín   Universitat Politècnica de València, Spain
Andreas L. Opdahl   University of Bergen, Norway
Jose Ignacio Panach   Universitat de València, Spain
Oscar Pastor   Universidad Politècnica de Valencia, Spain
Luca Piras   Middlesex University, UK

Rūta Pirta	Riga Technical University, Latvia
Geert Poels	Ghent University, Belgium
Andrea Polini	University of Camerino, Italy
Jolita Ralyté	University of Geneva, Switzerland
Ben Roelens	Open Universiteit, The Netherlands and Ghent University, Belgium
Kristina Rosenthal	FernUniversität in Hagen, Germany
Kurt Sandkuhl	University of Rostock, Germany
Estefanía Serral	KU Leuven, Belgium
Nikolay Shilov	SPC RAS, Russia
Monique Snoeck	KU Leuven, Belgium
Janis Stirna	Stockholm University, Sweden
Darijus Strasunskas	HEMIT, Norway
Stefan Strecker	University of Hagen, Germany
Yves Wautelet	Katholieke Universiteit Leuven, Belgium
Hans Weigand	Tilburg University, The Netherlands
Robert Woitsch	BOC Products & Services AG, Austria
Jelena Zdravkovic	Stockholm University, Sweden
Steffen Zschaler	King's College London, UK

Additional Reviewers

Christ, Sven
Fedeli, Arianna
Kapočius, Kęstutis
Reiz, Achim
Winkler, Philip

Keynotes

The Butterfly Potential: The DNA of the Transformation to a Regenerative Circular Economy is a Quadruple Helix

Anna-Vera Deinhammer

Sustainable Real Estate Development, Vienna University of Applied Sciences for
Management and Communication, Austria
Anna-Vera.Deinhammer@fh-wien.ac.at

The fundamental preconditions for climate protection are decided at city level because cities are responsible for around 75% of global greenhouse gas emissions. Thus, it is becoming ever more widely understood that climate protection can only succeed in the context of a just transition to a circular economy.

At this point the Quadruple Helix Approach comes into play, which is a concept defining the collaboration of academia, industry, government, and society as necessary to ensure that innovative solutions are relevant, feasible and sustainable. Of course, it is not possible to always discuss all aspects in a grassroots approach with all stakeholders. But that's not necessary if we identify possible contributors from the other strands of the Quadruple Helix as we develop content or concepts for transformation and prioritize the focus groups as part of a knowledge web.

Aspects of research and development should, on the one hand, be integrated into cultural-social habits and, on the other hand, into economic and regulatory capabilities for implementation. Even if we make the transformation somehow happen by solely updating the regulatory frameworks or constantly adding particles for pseudo-business-novelties just for demonstrating action, a transformed built environment as well as economy cannot function under outdated frameworks.

These two assumptions lead to only one logical conclusion: change is no longer enough; we need to transform our economy! Instantly, we are wondering *"What is the difference between change and transformation?"* The answer might be given with the parable of the caterpillar, which lives a ground-bound life, but needs a completely different system when it has transformed into a butterfly – specifically, the aerial one.

This lecture will showcase the three innovation-fields which are interconnected together through the Quadruple Helix approach for the new paradigm of transformation towards a circular economy, focusing on real estate as an example: (1) governance and building culture, (2) economics and sustainable finance, and (3) integrated engineering sciences.

Digital Tools for Circular Construction – BIM and Beyond

Iva Kovacic

Institute for Building and Industrial Construction, Faculty of Civil
and Environmental Engineering, TU Wien, Austria
Iva.Kovacic@tuwien.ac.at

The strong population growth and urbanization are increasing the global resources and energy consumption. The AEC (architecture, engineering and construction) industry is responsible for 60% of the extracted raw materials and generates 40% of the energy-related CO_2 emissions. In Austria, the AEC sector is responsible for 70% of total annual waste – facts that are underlining the importance of implementing strategies for enhancement of resources efficiency through strategies for circularity. Circular construction aims, next to achievement of long life duration, to maximize reusability and recyclability. The building stock has great potential to serve as raw material reservoir, however currently there is a lack of comprehensive knowledge about the actual building stock, which is the largest obstacle for reusing and recycling of materials and elements. Further, in order to enhance circular construction, strategies along the value chain along the lifecycle are needed, addressing all of the stakeholders through joint and accessible models and knowledge bases.

At the Department for Integrated Planning and Industrial Building we are developing a comprehensive Digital Platform for Circular AEC – an ecosystem of digital tools and processes for enhancement of circularity along the lifecycle – from design, over operation, deconstruction and finally second life of buildings.

The platform unifies several supplementary tools and concepts, developed in a number of funded cooperative research projects – BIM-based Material Passports, as fundament of digital cadaster; integrated BIM-based methods for assessment of both resources and energy performance (project SCI_BIM), and finally a concept for a digital urban mining platform for Vienna within research project **BIMstocks**. This approach represents the continuation of the framework developed in SCI_BIM, which investigated an integrated determination of geometry and material by coupling laser scanning and Ground Penetrating Radar (GPR) technology for the semi-automated BIM-Model generation. SCI_BIM demonstrated that GPR technology needs further testing to a) apply it to different building structures and b) build up a material database, which would significantly increase the efficiency of material determination.

BIMstocks proposes a method for generation of consistent digital documentation of the material composition of existing building stock; and for modeling of the secondary raw materials cadaster combining top-down and bottom-up approaches.

In the bottom-up approach, we analyzed and scanned 10 different use cases, as representative types of Viennese buildings according to their function and age. Upon the assessment via inspection, invasive methods and finally GPR a catalogue of BIM-Objects for types was generated, which enabled us to create BIM models for all of the buildings of the same typology on the city level. In the top-down approach, such material-informed BIM models were allocated in a GIS model of the city of Vienna, which enabled generation of a GIS-based Urban Mining Platform, which embeds the obtained material and geometry information of the use cases and predicts the recycling potential, the material flow and waste mass.

The *innovation* of the project is the coupling of different technologies, which enable upscaling from component-level to city-level: scanning technology using Ground Penetrating Radar, application of machine learning for the automated determination of material compositions, and predictive modelling at city level in the digital urban mining platform. For the first time the uncertainties resulting from the use case samples, the measured values and the extrapolation are estimated.

The result is a *concept* for the publicly accessible GIS-based Urban Mining Platform, based on a building catalogue of typical Viennese buildings, built with GPR scans and subsequent machine learning algorithms, upscaled to the city level, which should increase the knowledge of the material composition of the existing stock and increase recycling rates. As future outlook, new buildings planned in BIM could also easily be integrated into the platform.

Contents

Enterprise Modeling at Work

Enterprise Modeling and Artificial Intelligence

Adaptation of Enterprise Modeling Methods for Large Language Models

Balbir S. Barn[1], Souvik Barat[2], and Kurt Sandkuhl[3]

[1] Middlesex University, London, UK
b.barn@mdx.ac.uk
[2] Tata Consultancy Services Research, Pune, India
souvik.barat@tcs.com
[3] The University of Rostock, Rostock, Germany
kurt.sandkuhl@uni-rostock.de

Abstract. Large language models (LLM) are considered by many researchers as promising technology for automating routine tasks. Results from applying LLM in engineering disciplines such as Enterprise Modeling also indicate potential for the support of modeling activities. LLMs are fine-tuned for specific tasks using chat based interaction through the use of prompts. This paper aims at a detailed investigation of the potential of LLMs in Enterprise Modeling (EM) by taking the perspective of EM method adaptation of selected parts of the modeling process within the context of using prompts to interrogate the LLM. The research question addressed is: What adaptations in EM methods have to be made to exploit the potential of prompt based interaction with LLMs? The main contributions are (1) a meta-model for prompt engineering that integrates the concepts of the modeling domain under consideration with the notation of the modeling language applied and the input and output of prompts, (2) an investigation into the general potential of LLM in EM methods and its application in the 4EM method, and (3) implications for enterprise modeling methods.

Keywords: Enterprise Modeling · Large Language Model · Modeling Method · ChatGPT · Prompt meta-model

1 Introduction

Language technologies, large language models (LLM) and neural text generators, such as OpenAI's ChatGPT, are considered by many business analysts and researchers as promising technology for automating routine tasks leading to substantial improvement of productivity (see, e.g., [12,22]). First results from applying LLM in engineering disciplines also indicate the potential of this technology for the support of modeling processes. Examples are the use of ChatGPT in software engineering for UML modeling [8] and in design and manufacturing [34].

Our own previous work in this area [27] indicates that ChatGPT can be used to support Enterprise Modeling by substituting the domain expert in some

© IFIP International Federation for Information Processing 2024
Published by Springer Nature Switzerland AG 2024
J. P. A. Almeida et al. (Eds.): PoEM 2023, LNBIP 497, pp. 3–18, 2024.
https://doi.org/10.1007/978-3-031-48583-1_1

of the preparatory tasks for early modeling phases or in the development of
models for the general situation in an application domain. Encouraged by these
results, this paper aims at a more detailed investigation of the potential of LLMs
in Enterprise Modeling (EM) by taking the perspective of EM methods. More
concretely, our conjectures are that (a) a meta-model for prompt engineering
integrating relevant domain concepts and the modeling language's meta-model
would ease the use of LLMs in EM and (b) an adaptation of selected parts of
the modeling procedure is required. The primary research question for our work
is: *In the context of LLM use, what adaptations in EM methods have to be made
to exploit the potential of this technology?*

The main contributions of our work are (1) a meta-model for prompt engineering that integrates the concepts of the modeling domain under consideration
with the notation of the modeling language applied and the input and output
of prompts, (2) an investigation into the general potential of LLM in EM methods and its application in the 4EM method, and (3) implication for enterprise
modeling methods.

The paper is structured as follows: Sect. 2 introduces the background for
our work from large language models, enterprise modeling and method engineering. Section 3 introduces the research approach applied. Section 4 focuses on
the development of the method-aware prompt engineering meta-model. Section 5
discusses effects of LLM use on organisational aspects of EM method. Section 6
discusses implications for Enterprise Modeling and future work.

2 Background and Related Work

2.1 Large Language Models and Prompt Engineering

The OpenAI public release of ChatGPT in November 2022 represents a key transition in the mainstream use of AI as an aid to solving many types of problems.
It has captured the imagination of both researchers and the public at large.

GPT-3 uses 175 billion parameters and is trained on data from the Common Crawl data set[1] comprising nearly a trillion words. The development in
large language models and their evolution has been widely documented and the
reader is directed to key texts such as [5]. The pre-training of LLMs is task-
agnostic [19]. The training is based on string prediction tasks: that is, predicting
the probability of the next token (character, word or string) given either its pre-
ceding context or its surrounding context. GPT-3 is capable of generating novel
sequences of words never observed previously by the model, but that represent
plausible sequences based on natural human language [19]. The pre-training is
task-agnostic.

LLMs present new opportunities for experimentation and prototyping with
Artificial Intelligence (AI) as pre-training ensures that enough information is
encoded such that customisation is possible, in-context and at run-time, to enable
handling of new tasks through prompts expressed in natural language [37].

---

[1] https://commoncrawl.org/the-data/.

GPT-3 with its Chatbot frontend - ChatGPT[2] can solve a variety of tasks that have so far included summarisation, translation, grammar correction, email composition and others [15]. The so-far free availability of ChatGPT and the very simple and powerful prompt based front-end to GPT-3 has led to many domains of application. In higher (tertiary) education, there is a fulsome debate about the potential of academic misconduct as well as the opportunities such as that described in [3, 20, 26].

Prompt engineering as a term, originated from an online post about GPT3 and creative writing by Gwern Branwen who suggested anthropomorphising LLMs through prompting the model to elicit required knowledge[3]. Prompting in this way could be seen as form of prompt programming where the "prompt is now a "program" which programs GPT-3 to do new things.". Prompting is the practice of representing a task as a natural language utterance in order to query a language model for a response [21].

A comprehensive review of prompting methods is available in [21]. Prompts are often described as zero-shot or few-shot. A zero-shot prompt describes the intention of the task requirement in natural language. E.g. a prompt asking ChatGPT to ask if a Volkswagen Beetle is a car forms a simple classification task. Few-shot prompts are those that demonstrate to the LLM the required pattern (desirable inputs and outputs) to follow in order to fine tune the LLM to produce the desired prediction. An example typically has a context and a desired completion (for example an English sentence and the French translation).

The fluid response of LLMs to prompts given to the system means that prompt based prototyping allows non-Machine Learning (ML) experts to prototype ML functionality at lower cost and without the need to train models up front. Effectively, augmenting input with answered prompts becomes in-context learning. Against that, however, is a lack of clear guidance, techniques, and supporting tools for prompt design. Research literature in the text to image generation field also indicates that prompt engineering is a non-intuitive skill that is learned from extensive experimentation and trial and error [23].

The core of this paper is the exploration of the use of LLM and their effectiveness as "modeling assistants". Our experience to date and our earlier work reported in 2023 [27] indicate that the conversational style of using prompts to construct models is promising. However, the conversational style of using prompts to interrogate a LLM is lacking guidelines, strategies and an engineering approach and therefore supporting the findings in [23]. Other analysis is reported in [14] where Fill et al. indicate similar concerns. The experiments reported in that paper hint at a meta model through the use of informal guided prompts developed for conducting simple experiments in entity modeling, business process design and other conceptual modeling approaches. They also assert the need for the development of domain specific languages for few shot prompts to support the complex descriptions necessary for formal frameworks used in conceptual modeling. This is also the subject of this section. A recent paper by

---

[2] https://chat.openai.com/.
[3] https://gwern.net/gpt-3.

Camara et al. [8] reports on experiments in evaluating the use of LLMs for software modeling (UML and OCL constraints). Their findings indicate that there is success in producing syntactically correct UML models but semantic errors are frequent.

The literature on prompt engineering highlights the following observations: Firstly, there is a lack of language/meta-model support underpinning prompt design. For many domains such as law [30], healthcare [33], generative art [23], and systems design (such as business process modeling [7] and OCL specification [1] the focus is on using examples derived from the prompt template approach advocated by Liu et al. [21]. Formal descriptions such as a meta model or a modeling language are absent.

Secondly, related to the idea of an under-pinning meta model, is the use of software tools for designing and managing the use of prompts. Fiannaca et al. identify the concern that that prompts are used to solve complex problems but lack the strict grammar of traditional programming languages. They propose methods for extracting a semantically meaningful structure of natural language prompts but stop short of producing a description of that structure [13]. Others have proposed the need to have prompt catalogues that contain specifications of prompts that can be re-used in different contexts [36]. Again, there is an implicit meta model underpinning these specifications. There are several examples of software tools for supporting prompt design that exist in the literature.

PromptChainer [37] provides a visual programming model/metaphor to support prompt chain authoring with a focus on transforming data between chain elements and for debugging prompt chains. Rapsai [10] like PromptChainer provides a visual programming platform featuring a node-graph editor to facilitate streamlining of end-end prototyping of multimedia applications that use ML. PromptSapper [9] is an AI Chain no-code interactive development environment that utilises block-based visual programming to support AI chain (c.f. prompt chain) design, testing and deployment. PromptSource [2] is a web-based system for creating, sharing and using natural language prompts. The environment offers a templating language and interface for defining data-linked prompts. The system is not specifically designed for a LLM such as GPT3.0.

The third important observation is the lack of comprehensive support for methods for prompt design and usage. The literature provides an example of the provision of cookbook-style guidelines for prompts, such as that reported in [11]. Despite the technical advances, particularly in tool development using visual modeling paradigms, the approaches taken are method-agnostic. Our proposal is part of a journey to similar tool environments but with one notable difference. Future tools need to be built around existing methods and practice to benefit from expert knowledge and therefore address some of the issues around validation of outcomes from an interaction session with a LLM. In particular, we think that a method driven use of LLMs would be a promising route to addressing the semantics concerns reported by Camara et al.

In Sect. 4, we present a meta model for prompt design that is integrated with the 4EM method. Our intention is that such a model can contribute to the basis of future tools that will support prompt design for enterprise modeling using the 4EM method. With such a proposition, prompt chaining, for example, then becomes a method dependent activity.

2.2 Enterprise Modeling

EM is addressing the "systematic analysis and modeling of processes, organisation structures, product structures, IT-systems or any other perspective relevant for the modeling purpose" [32]. The variety of methods, languages and tools supporting EM is visible in work on research roadmaps and future directions from the information systems community (see, e.g., [28]) and from industrial organisation (e.g., [31]).

Enterprise Modeling (EM) is meant to support organisations in coping with a broad range of challenges, including managing organisational change in dynamic market environments, aligning of organizational goals and information systems to support these goals, as well as explicating and consolidating knowledge from various stakeholder groups thus facilitating organisational learning. The role of EM usually is to provide methods, tools, and practices for capturing and visualising the current ("as-is") situation and to develop the future ("to-be") situation. In particular, a model of the current situation forms one of the fundamentals for supporting future development of organisations. Given the complexity of enterprises, there seems to be an agreement in the academic literature related to enterprise modeling that a key feature of an enterprise model is that it includes various perspectives. Among the most prominent ones is [6,24] to use EM as a problem-solving tool. Here, EM is only used for supporting the discussion among a group of stakeholders trying to analyse a specific problem at hand.

For illustrating effects of LLM use in EM in Sects. 4 and 5 with a concrete example, we selected 4EM [29], a multi-perspective EM language used in many universities for teaching EM. 4EM distinguishes several modeling perspectives that are summarized with their focus, issues to model and main components in Fig. 1.

2.3 Constituents of Modeling Methods

Modeling methods and their constituents have been subject of research in the field of information systems development and, in particular, in method engineering since at least two decades. Method engineering (ME) is *the engineering discipline to design, construct and adapt methods, techniques and tools for the development of information systems* [4]. The need to adapt methods and tools according to organizational needs has been addressed by Situational Method Engineering (SME) [18]. SME is an ME approach that includes designing method parts supporting the realization of some specific IS development activity as well as tailoring them based on local situational factors (e.g. the business sector, or size of the business). Each method part is represented according to a same template and adheres to a unique meta-model. Another practicable ME approach was proposed in [17]; it sets a high attention on the elaboration of method parts

	Goals Model (GM)	Business Rules Model (BRM)	Concepts Model (CM)	Business Process Model (BPM)	Actors and Recourses Model (ARM)	Product/Service (P/S)	Technical Components Model (TCRM)
Focus	Vision and strategy	Policies and rules	Business ontology	Business operations	Organizational structure	Products and Services	Information system needs
Issues to model	What does the organization want to achieve or to avoid and why?	What are the business rules, how do they support organization's goals?	What are the things and "phenomena" addressed in other sub-models?	What are the business processes? How do they handle information? and material?	Who are responsible for goals and process? How are the actors interrelated?	What product and services components exist? What are core features?	What are the business requirements to the IS? How are they related to other models?
Components	Goal, problem, external constraint, opportunity	Business rule	Concept, attribute	Process, external proc., information set, material set	Actor, role, organizational unit, individual	Product, service, component, feature	IS goal, IS problem, IS requirement, IS component

Fig. 1. 4EM perspectives and method components

such as the procedures for meta-modeling, i.e. for choosing appropriate concepts for inclusion.

Since this paper aims at investigating the different constituents of methods, the core concern was to correctly identify the main method parts and their relevant concepts. For that reason, the approach described in [17] by Goldkuhl et al. has been chosen. It proposes that methods are to be described in terms of the following aspects: Goldkuhl et al. state that a comprehensive method description should describe the perspective, framework, cooperation principles and all method components. Figure 2 illustrates how these elements of the method conceptualization are related.

- Method components: A method component should consist of concepts, a procedure and a notation. The concepts specify what aspects of reality are regarded as relevant in the modeling process, i.e. what is important and what should be captured a model. These relevant concepts should be named in the method component and explained if necessary. The procedure describes in concrete terms how to identify the relevant concepts in a method component. It may also cover prerequisites and resources. The notation specifies how the result of the procedure should be documented. As a rule, this must provide appropriate expressions for each concept and for the potential relationships between them. In graphic notations, these are the symbols to be used.
- Framework: the method framework describes the relationships between the individual method components, i.e. which components are to be used and under what conditions, as well as the sequence of the method components (if any).

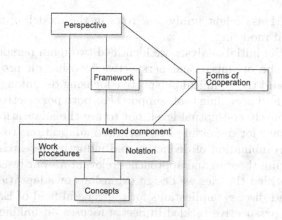

Fig. 2. Components of Methods according to [17]

- Forms of cooperation: many modeling tasks require a range of specialist skills or cooperation between different roles. These necessary skills and roles must be described, along with the division of responsibilities between the roles and the form of cooperation. The cooperation form also includes who will take responsibility for each task or method component, and how the collaboration will be organized.
- Perspective: every method describes the procedure for the modeling process from a particular perspective, which influences what is considered important when developing a model. This perspective often is related to the aims and purpose of the method.

3   Research Approach

Starting from the research question presented in the introduction and using the method conceptualisation discussed in section 2.3, we performed an initial analysis of what elements of methods could be affected by using LLM. This initial analysis had the purpose of structuring and planning the research process.

The perspective of a method is not affected by LLM use. LLMs are supposed to be a tool or aid to support the method, but the intention of the method, viewpoints to be taken, or concerns to be considered have to remain stable. Method components might change by using LLMs, primarily because the procedure to be performed is expected to need adaptation. In contrast, the concepts in focus and the notation for capturing the results of the method components remain unchanged. Concepts and notation are both expected to be an important input to LLM use as they indicate the subject of LLM prompts and how the output should be structured. If the method components have to be adapted, this might also affect the framework. Furthermore, we have to investigate if LLM use requires an additional method component to prepare LLM use, which would affect the framework again. We expect the cooperation principles to require an adaptation as LLM use might imply new roles in the modeling team and new tools for the actual modeling.

As a result of the initial analysis, we identified two main perspectives for the research process: the organisational perspective focusing on procedures, roles and cooperation, and the technical perspective focusing on linking concepts and notations to LLM and providing tools support. For both perspectives, we decided not to stay on a purely conceptual level, but to use the adaptation of the 4EM method as a use case for discussing LLM-oriented adaptations to EM methods. This results in a combination of deductive and inductive research. We start by investigating existing theories and approaches relevant for our research question; based on the identified theories we design extensions or adaptations, apply our results to 4EM and discuss implications for the general field of EM.

The technical perspective tackled in Sect. 4 focuses on linking the concepts and notations of method components to prompts for large language models. We propose a meta-model for prompt engineering for this purpose. The organisational perspective is addressed in Sect. 5 and uses in a first step the general approach of enterprise modeling to identify potential for LLM use and in a second step the specific procedures of 4EM method components to make this general potential more concrete.

4   Method-Aware Meta-model for Prompt Engineering

Enterprise modeling has tended to be method-agnostic and generally guided by various meta models. In the context of integrating enterprise modeling practice with the use of LLM, we believe that enterprise modeling activities should be tailored to existing methods and practices to harness the expert knowledge embedded within the methodologies. In this section we propose a meta-model-based method-aware approach for enterprise modeling using LLMs. In addition to the proposed meta-model for defining a structural approach to use LLM, our approach utilizes the core concept of a meta-modeling framework to interoperate with any modeling technique in a seamless manner. In the case shown, we employ the 4EM method for underlying methodological support, and leverage the approach proposed by Goldkuhl et al. [17] to integrate meta-modeling techniques, 4EM methodology and LLM-based modeling.

Fig. 3 first presents the overall package structure and introduces the base meta-models representing existing knowledge in terms of meta-modeling and the 4EM method. The Package *MDE* (shown top right) illustrates the bare minimum meta model for describing any model. Package EM-4EM describes the core concepts of the 4EM method. The point to be noted here is that the Package*EM-4EM* interoperates with Package *MDE*, as the 4EM methodology is a specialized methodology focusing on enterprise modeling activities.

The Prompt Model Package, shown in the lower part of Fig. 3, is our primary contribution. White et al. [36] propose a pattern modeling language similar to that found in software patterns [16]. Accordingly, we propose a concept *Prompt Pattern*. Prompt patterns can be collected into domain specific catalogues which

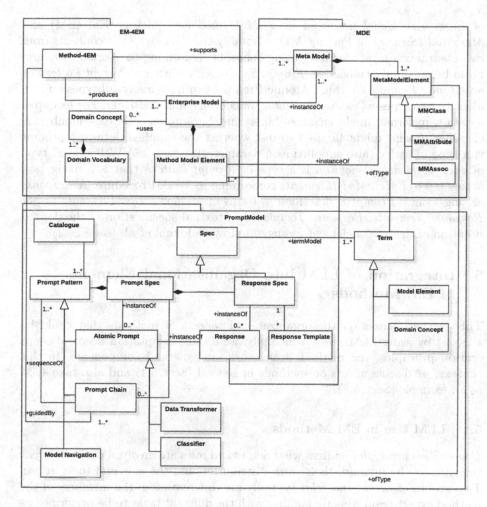

Fig. 3. Method Driven Prompt Meta Model

support classification of patterns into categories conforming to the underlying method. In this case, the catalogue is typically derived based on the concept *Perspective* as described by Goldkuhl et al. [17] (see Fig. 2). We establish the relationship of LLM based modeling activity with 4EM methodology through PromptChain and ModelNavigation. The PromptChain guides how to explore concepts (i.e., Work Procedure component proposed by Goldkuhl et al.) and the ModelNavigation focuses on what to capture, i.e., Concepts.

Our *Prompt Spec* captures concepts (i.e., data) conforming to work procedure (i.e., behaviour). We adopt the pattern language proposed by White et al. to capture these behavior and data specification. The data specification is expressed as a set of *Term* queries that are built from a Term model that derives from *Model Elements* and *Domain Concepts*. Model Elements include *Method Model Element* of *Enterprise Model* produced by *4EM Method* (see Package EM-4EM) and *MetaModelElement* of Package MDE. Notably the *Term* uses the concepts from two abstraction layers for navigating concepts conforming to Work Procedure. From behavioural perspective, *Prompt Spec* specifies either a *Prompt Pattern* or an *Atomic Prompt*. We think Atomic Prompts can have many subtypes and we identify two types as examples: *Data Transformer* and *Classifier*. For example, a data transformer might change a binary number into an octal base number. A classifier prompt might be used to test whether the supplied data in a prompt is a type of entity (also supplied as a parameter), e.g., is a"VW beetle a" type of car?. A *Model Navigation* is a type of *Prompt Pattern* that is a navigation across a set of *MetaModelElements* conforming to Work Procedure. A *Response* arising from a *Prompt* is described in terms of *Method Model Elements* as per *Response Template*. *Response Template* is a textual specification of the desired notation of the model element as suggested by Goldkuhl et al. (see Fig. 2).

5   Integration of LLM into Organisational Elements of EM Methods

This section focuses on the organizational aspects of methods that could be affected by using LLM. More concretely, we discuss adaptation needs of cooperation principles, the methods framework, and method components. In this context, we discuss effects on methods in general (Sect. 5.1) and also take 4EM as an example (Sect. 5.2).

5.1   LLM Use in EM Methods

Cooperation principles address what actors and roles are involved in the different activities of the method, their work distribution and the aids and tools in use. Two groups of actors and roles typically are differentiated: the members of the method expert team who are familiar with the different tasks to be performed as recommended in the method, and the actors from the organisation or application domain under consideration who are experts in the domain or familiar with the organization. The use of LLM requires a good understanding of this relatively new technology, for example when it comes to the formulation and chaining of prompts. Thus, the method expert team should be extended with an LLM expert or, alternatively, one of the other team members has to develop/provide this competence. The role of LLM expert is expected to select the concrete LLM platform to be used, provide or acquire licences, prepare prompts and prompt chains, check the results for soundness and provide them to the team. The only other role also affected by the LLM use would be the head of the method expert team who often also acts as project manager. The person having this role should understand the potential of LLM and its effects on the process of performing the method tasks for being able to take this into account when planning the time and activities for the method use.

As for the *tool support*, the LLM obviously can be considered as additional tool. The discussion about the prompt meta-model in Sect. 4 already indicated the probability to develop tool support beyond the actual neural text generators, for example for generating enterprise models from the output of LLMs or validating the generated models.

The *framework* of a method basically describes the sequence the method components should be used in or preconditions for using them. When using LLM, some method components may be affected (see below) but their sequence of usage is expected to remain stable, with the exception of the initial phase of the method. Here, LLM use has to be prepared, for example by designing prompts that inform the LLM about the modeling language used or the scope of the modeling. These prompts can be expected to be used as elements in prompt chains in some of the following method components as defined by the framework. The preparatory work for the LLM use could either motivate an additional *method component*, or, if a general method component for the preparation phase exists, an extension of this preparation task. The new role of LLM expert should be made responsible for this new task and the project manager should participate.

Table 1. Features of new Method Component prepare LLM use

MC Name	Preparation of LLM use
Input	meta-model of modeling language; scope of modeling project
Responsible	LLM expert
Tasks	to select suitable neural text generator and acquire licences
	to prepare prompt elements that inform the neural text generate
	about meta-model for expected output
	to prepare prompt elements for the scope of modeling
	to inform affected method components and prepare element
	for prompt chains
Output	reusable prompt chain elements

Furthermore, it might be advisable to inform the project team from the organisation under consideration (i.e., the "client") that LLM will be used, for what purpose or tasks, and how this affects the LLM process. In some application domains very sensitive for data protection issues, it might even be advisable to get the consent of the client to use LLMs. The ethics of using LLMs is also an area of significant study. For example a taxonomy of risks has been proposed, such as discrimination, information hazards (privacy, leaking of sensitive information), malicious use, and socio-economic harms [35]. A particular concern relevent to enterprise modeling is the idea of credit-blame asymmetry - assigning responsibility to outcomes [25]. Questions that the project team will need to consider include: how reliable is the model? What about changes in employment patterns arising from the use of LLMs. Further work in this area will be required.

The *method components* define the actual modeling task in detail with the procedure, notation and concepts to focus on. Concepts and notation of method components in general are not affected by the use of LLMs, as LLM is not applied for the development of notations and does not change the purpose or focus of the modeling activity that is reflected in the concepts. If the procedure of a method component has to be adapted to LLM use or not, from our perspective has to be investigated for every method component individually, as this depends on the actual purpose of the method component. In earlier work, we used the different phases of EM projects (scoping, model the current situation, identify change needs, develop alternatives for addressing change needs, model future situation) and the tasks of domain experts in this process (supply of domain knowledge, integrate modeling results, evaluate results) to identify possibilities for LLM use to partially substitute the domain expert. The result was that mainly tasks in the early phases, like building up domain knowledge in the method experts team, and tasks related to the general problem domain (like modeling widely established processes similar at most of the organizations in the domain) could be supported by LLM whereas tasks requiring specific information for the organization under consideration were not suitable. This finding is considered as relevant even for this work. Thus, our recommendation is to investigate method components for LLM usage potential addressing early phases of EM and requiring general information in the domain.

5.2   4EM Adaptation for LLM Use

The previous section identified the need to introduce the new role of LLM expert, changes in the framework, a new method component to prepare LLM use, and potential changes in different method components depending on their purpose. This section investigates if these changes are relevant for 4EM and how to implement them in the 4EM method.

Introducing a new role as LLM expert is also relevant for 4EM. The 4EM method recommends that all EM be organized in projects. This includes defined roles to be established in a project. The LLM expert is a new role in the modeling team and should take over the tasks described in the previous section. 4EM's equivalence to the framework is a recommendation on how to conduct modeling projects that is documented as a process description. This process description has to be extended by the preparatory tasks described in Sect. 5.1. Although all the tasks are relevant and required, this cannot be considered as new method component from a 4EM perspective. Method components in 4EM are dedicated to different EM perspectives, such as business process or product/service modeling. As for the different 4EM method components, various adaptations could be made (see below) that address - as discussed in Sect. 5.1 – only the procedure of the method component and concern mainly the earlier phases of EM projects and general information from the domain:

- Goal/Problem Modeling: general threats and opportunities for organizations in the modeling domain can be identified by LLMs as potential input to the first modeling phase,

- Business Process Modeling: LLM can be used to get an overview to typical processes in the domain and their input and output information,
- Concept Modeling: when the first version of the concept model has been developed, LLM can be used to explore potential dependencies and relationships between the domain concepts to check with the enterprise stakeholders,
- Actors and Resource Modeling: LLM can be used to explore the existence and tasks of typical roles in the domain,
- Business Rule Modeling, technical components and requirements modeling and product/service Modeling: we do not expect substantial potential for LLM use as all address largely enterprise-specific topics.

It should be noted that all the application potentials listed above are related to preparations for modeling the current situation in the different method components. We do not consider generating as-is models from LLM output as an option as these models most likely do not correspond to the reality in the enterprise and also would prejudice the enterprise stakeholders.

When the goal modeling has been completed in an EM project, there might be additional application potential for LLM in collecting inspiration on how specific goals can be reached, i.e., generating additional alternatives for the future situations to be discussed with the enterprise stakeholders might make sense. For these future-oriented tasks the proposed meta-model in Sect. 4 is of particular importance as the goals to be achieved will be expressed in domain concepts that have to be included in prompt chains and the results of the LLM use have to mapped on the 4EM meta-model to be able to generate actual 4EM models. For the procedures in the 4EM method components, this means that the way to present, discuss and amend the LLM results has to be integrated into the current way of deciding on the best alternative for change.

6   Concluding Remarks

The research presented in this paper had the aim to investigate the research question what adaptations in EM methods have to be made to exploit the potential of LLM. Starting from the different constituents of methods identified by [17], we separated between organizational and technical aspects. From the organizational perspective, we see the need to add a new role to the method expert team having LLM competences and taking care of all LLM-related issues. Furthermore, we see the need to add activities in the method framework, or even a new method component, to systematically prepare the LLM use within the method. On the technical side, our view is that no modifications in notations or tools of EM methods are required. Further experiments might expose such a requirement. Critically, we think that a **formal link** between modeling language, the domain under consideration and prompt engineering would be beneficial. This paper has provided a prompt meta-model that basically is method-agnostic but can be the basis of future endeavours to construct this formal link.

The main limitation of our work is that the organisational and technical results so far only have been applied for a single EM method: 4EM. The package structure proposed in this work provides a means of separating concerns such that other methods can be incorporated. Future work will have to include investigation of other methods as part of the validation. Meaningful validation of the prompt meta model is feasible through the our envisioned development of tool support.

References

1. Abukhalaf, S., Hamdaqa, M., Khomh, F.: On codex prompt engineering for OCL generation: an empirical study. arXiv preprint arXiv:2303.16244 (2023)
2. Bach, S.H., et al.: PromptSource: an integrated development environment and repository for natural language prompts. arXiv preprint arXiv:2202.01279 (2022)
3. Barn, B.: ChatGPT could be your ally - really! (2023). https://doi.org/10.1007/s12055-023-01507-6
4. Brinkkemper, S.: Method engineering: engineering of information systems development methods and tools. Inf. Softw. Technol. **38**(4), 275–280 (1996)
5. Tom, B.B., et al.: Language models are few-shot learners. In: H. Larochelle, M. Ranzato, R. Hadsell, M.F. Balcan, and H. Lin, editors, Advances in Neural Information Processing Systems, vol.33, pp1877–1901. Curran Associates Inc (2020)
6. Bubenko, J., Persson, A., Stirna, J.: An intentional perspective on enterprise modeling. In: Nurcan, S., Salinesi, C., Souveyet, C., Ralyté, J. (eds.) Intentional Perspectives on Information Systems Engineering, pp. 215–237. Springer, Berlin, Heidelberg (2010). https://doi.org/10.1007/978-3-642-12544-7_12
7. Busch, K., Rochlitzer, A., Sola, D., Leopold, H.: Just tell me: prompt engineering in business process management. In: van der Aa, H., Bork, D., Proper, H.A., Schmidt, R. (eds.) Enterprise, Business-Process and Information Systems Modeling: 24th International Conference, BPMDS 2023, and 28th International Conference, EMMSAD 2023, Zaragoza, Spain, June 12–13, 2023, Proceedings, pp. 3–11. Springer, Cham (2023). https://doi.org/10.1007/978-3-031-34241-7_1
8. Cámara, J., Troya, J., Burgueño, L., Vallecillo, A.: On the assessment of generative AI in modeling tasks: an experience report with ChatGPT and UML. Softw. Syst. Model. **22**(3), 781–793 (2023). https://doi.org/10.1007/s10270-023-01105-5
9. Cheng, Y., Chen, J., Huang, H., Xing, Z., Xu, X., Lu, Q.: Prompt sapper: a LLM-empowered production tool for building AI chains. arXiv preprint arXiv:2306.12028 (2023)
10. Du, R., et al.: Rapsai: accelerating machine learning prototyping of multimedia applications through visual programming. In: Proceedings of the 2023 CHI Conference on Human Factors in Computing Systems, pp. 1–23 (2023)
11. Ekin, S.: Prompt engineering for chatGPT: a quick guide to techniques, tips, and best practices (2023)
12. Eloundou, T., Manning, S., Mishkin, P., Rock, D.: GPTs are gpts: an early look at the labor market impact potential of large language models. arXiv preprint arXiv:2303.10130 (2023)
13. Fiannaca, A.J., Kulkarni, C., Cai, C.J., Terry, M.: Programming without a programming language: Challenges and opportunities for designing developer tools for prompt programming. In: Extended Abstracts of the 2023 CHI Conference on Human Factors in Computing Systems, pp. 1–7 (2023)
14. Fill, H.-G., Fettke, P., Köpke, J.: Conceptual modeling and large language models: impressions from first experiments with ChatGPT. Enterp. Model. Inf. Syst. Architectures (EMISAJ) **18**, 1–15 (2023)

15. Floridi, L.: Chiriatti, Massimo: Gpt-3: Its nature, scope, limits, and consequences. Mind. Mach. **30**, 681–694 (2020)
16. Gamma, E., Helm, R., Johnson, R., Vlissides, J.: Design patterns: elements of reusable object-oriented software. Pearson Deutschland GmbH (1995)
17. Goldkuhl, G., Lind, M., Seigerroth, Ulf, S.: Method integration: the need for a learning perspective. IEE Proc. Softw. **145**(4), 113–118 (1998)
18. Henderson-Sellers, B., Ralyté, J., Ågerfalk, P.J., Rossi, M.: Situational Method Engineering. Springer, Berlin, Heidelberg (2014). https://doi.org/10.1007/978-3-642-41467-1
19. Huang, W., Abbeel, P., Pathak, D., Mordatch, I.: Language models as zero-shot planners: Extracting actionable knowledge for embodied agents. In: International Conference on Machine Learning, pp 9118–9147. PMLR (2022)
20. Kasneci, E., et al.: ChatGPT for good? on opportunities and challenges of large language models for education. Learn. Individ. Differ. **103**, 102274 (2023)
21. Liu, P., Yuan, W., Jinlan, F., Jiang, Z., Hayashi, H., Neubig, G.: Pre-train, prompt, and predict: a systematic survey of prompting methods in natural language processing. ACM Comput. Surv. **55**(9), 1–35 (2023)
22. Makridakis, S.: The forthcoming artificial intelligence (AI) revolution: its impact on society and firms. Futures **90**, 46–60 (2017)
23. Oppenlaender, J.: Prompt engineering for text-based generative art. arXiv preprint arXiv:2204.13988 (2022)
24. Persson, A., Stirna, J.: An explorative study into the influence of business goals on the practical use of enterprise modelling methods and tools. In: Harindranath, G., et al. (eds.) New Perspectives on Information Systems Development, pp. 275–287. Springer US, Boston, MA (2002). https://doi.org/10.1007/978-1-4615-0595-2_22
25. Mann, S.P., et al. Generative AI entails a credit-blame asymmetry. Nature Machine Intelligence, pp. 1–4 (2023)
26. Rudolph, J., Tan, S., Tan, S.: ChatGPT: bullshit spewer or the end of traditional assessments in higher education? J. Appl. Learn. Teach. **6**(1) (2023)
27. Sandkuhl, K., Barn, B., Barat, S.: Neural text generators in enterprise modeling: can ChatGPT be used as proxy domain expert? Accepted for publication. In: Proceedings ISD 2023 conference (2023)
28. Sandkuhl, K., et al.: From expert discipline to common practice: a vision and research agenda for extending the reach of enterprise modeling. Bus. Inf. Syst. Eng. **60**, 69–80 (2018)
29. Sandkuhl, K., Stirna, J., Persson, A., Wißotzki, M.: Enterprise Modeling: Tackling Business Challenges with the 4EM Method. Springer, Berlin, Heidelberg (2014)
30. Trautmann, D., Petrova, A., Schilder, F.: Legal prompt engineering for multilingual legal judgement prediction. arXiv preprint arXiv:2212.02199 (2022)
31. Vernadat, F.: Enterprise modelling: research review and outlook. Comput. Ind. **122**, 103265 (2020)
32. Vernadat, F.B.: Enterprise modelling and integration. In: Kosanke, K., Jochem, R., Nell, J.G., Bas, A.O. (eds.) Enterprise Inter- and Intra-Organizational Integration. ITIFIP, vol. 108, pp. 25–33. Springer, Boston, MA (2003). https://doi.org/10.1007/978-0-387-35621-1_4
33. Wang, J., et al.: Prompt engineering for healthcare: methodologies and applications. arXiv preprint arXiv:2304.14670 (2023)
34. Wang, X.: Anwer, Nabil, Dai, Yun, Liu, Ang: Chatgpt for design, manufacturing, and education. Procedia CIRP **119**, 7–14 (2023)

35. Weidinger, L., et al.: Taxonomy of risks posed by language models. In: Proceedings of the 2022 ACM Conference on Fairness, Accountability, and Transparency, pp. 214–229 (2022)
36. White, J., et al.: A prompt pattern catalog to enhance prompt engineering with chatgpt. arXiv preprint arXiv:2302.11382 (2023)
37. Tongshuang Wu, T., et al.: Promptchainer: chaining large language model prompts through visual programming. In: CHI Conference on Human Factors in Computing Systems Extended Abstracts, pp. 1–10 (2022)

EA ModelSet – A FAIR Dataset for Machine Learning in Enterprise Modeling

Philipp-Lorenz Glaser[1]([✉])(iD), Emanuel Sallinger[2](iD), and Dominik Bork[1](iD)

[1] Business Informatics Group, TU Wien, Vienna, Austria
{philipp-lorenz.glaser,dominik.bork}@tuwien.ac.at
[2] Database and Artificial Intelligence Group, TU Wien, Vienna, Austria
emanuel.sallinger@tuwien.ac.at

Abstract. The conceptual modeling community and its subdivisions of enterprise modeling are increasingly investigating the potentials of applying artificial intelligence, in particular machine learning (ML), to tasks like model creation, model analysis, and model processing. A prerequisite—and currently a limiting factor for the community—to conduct research involving ML is the scarcity of openly available models of adequate quality and quantity. With the paper at hand, we aim to tackle this limitation by introducing an EA ModelSet, i.e., a curated and FAIR repository of enterprise architecture models that can be used by the community. We report on our efforts in building this data set and elaborate on the possibilities of conducting ML-based modeling research with it. We hope this paper sparks a community effort toward the development of a FAIR, large model set that enables ML research with conceptual models.

Keywords: Enterprise modeling · Machine learning · FAIR · Enterprise architecture · Data set

1 Introduction

In recent years, the field of conceptual modeling, particularly enterprise modeling, has seen an increasing interest in exploring the promising applications of artificial intelligence, specifically machine learning (ML), to various tasks such as model creation, analysis, processing, and transformation [2,6,20]. Leveraging ML has the potential to revolutionize the way enterprise modeling is approached and implemented. However, a significant challenge hindering progress in this domain is the scarcity of readily available data, specifically high-quality and diverse models in sufficient quantities.

The success of ML approaches heavily relies on large and diverse datasets that capture the intricacies and complexities of real-world scenarios. For the conceptual modeling community, access to an extensive repository of models is crucial to enable robust and data-driven research. Unfortunately, the lack of publicly available, free-to-access datasets has emerged as a major bottleneck in advancing ML research in this domain. Without access to a substantial collection

J. P. A. Almeida et al. (Eds.): PoEM 2023, LNBIP 497, pp. 19–36, 2024.
https://doi.org/10.1007/978-3-031-48583-1_2

of models, researchers face significant challenges in developing and evaluating ML algorithms, hindering progress and innovation.

To address the challenges mentioned at the outset, researchers recognize the importance of adhering to the principles of Findable, Accessible, Interoperable, and Reusable (F.A.I.R.) [23] data management. A FAIR dataset ensures that data is discoverable and accessible to all interested researchers, fostering collaboration and enabling the reproducibility of results. Additionally, a FAIR dataset is designed to be interoperable, facilitating seamless integration with various ML tools and techniques. Moreover, by making the dataset reusable, researchers can build upon existing work and accelerate the development of innovative solutions.

A FAIR dataset of enterprise architecture (EA) models is essential for several reasons. Firstly, it addresses the issue of data scarcity by collating a comprehensive collection of diverse and high-quality EA models from various domains and industries. Secondly, adhering to the principles of FAIR ensures that the dataset is openly available to the conceptual modeling community, breaking down barriers and encouraging active engagement and contribution from researchers worldwide. The introduction of a FAIR EA ModelSet unlocks a plethora of possibilities for ML-based research in the domain of conceptual modeling. Researchers can now leverage this curated repository to train and validate ML models, enabling automated tasks such as generating new EA models, analyzing complex relationships within models, processing large volumes of data efficiently, and transforming models to adapt to evolving business requirements.

Furthermore, the availability of a FAIR dataset fosters the growth of a collaborative and innovative research community dedicated to exploring the potential applications of ML in EA management. By providing a common foundation for experiments and evaluations, the FAIR EA ModelSet empowers researchers to benchmark their methods against existing approaches, driving continuous improvement and development in the field. Eventually, this research holds immense significance for the conceptual modeling community by not only addressing data scarcity but also paving the way for a more collaborative and dynamic research landscape. Through this research, we aim to inspire and encourage a collective effort toward the development of a comprehensive and freely available dataset, sparking new avenues of exploration and innovation at the intersection of artificial intelligence and conceptual modeling (for an overview, see [6]).

FAIR datasets have garnered significant attention in various research domains. In the field of **conceptual and enterprise modeling**, researchers have focused on creating FAIR datasets that encompass various domain-specific models, such as data models, ontology models [3], and domain models. These datasets aim to enhance the accessibility and reusability of conceptual models for research and practical applications and to enable insights into the actual use of modeling languages. Additionally, efforts have been made to standardize metadata annotation and representation to improve the findability and interoperability of the datasets [4,21]. In **software engineering and software modeling** research, the development of FAIR datasets has been crucial for advancing the state of software development, testing, and maintenance. Researchers have built datasets that comprise software architecture models [17], UML diagrams, and source code representations [12–14,18]. These datasets enable software engineers to leverage ML and data-driven techniques to automate and/or improve software development tasks. Within the **process modeling** community, there have been efforts to curate datasets containing various types of process models [8,19,22]. The sub-discipline of **process mining** is also heavily engaged in the creation and use of publicly available datasets (see [9]). These datasets facilitate the empirical analysis of business process management and the evaluation and comparison of process mining algorithms and tools.

In this paper, we report our efforts of creating an open, curated repository of EA models following the FAIR principles. In total, we were able to collect, harmonize, integrate, and publicize a total of 863 ArchiMate models. Moreover, we contribute means of efficiently exploiting the EA ModelSet by providing a Webpage, a Java Command Line Interface, and a Python library.

In the remainder of this paper, we discuss the method we applied to collect, process, and manage the ModelSet in Sect. 2. Section 3 then introduces the characteristics of the EA ModelSet. An evaluation of the ModelSet according to the FAIR principles is presented in Sect. 4. A number of enabled usage scenarios by our EA ModelSet are discussed in Sect. 5 before we conclude this paper in Sect. 6.

2 Method for Creating the Model Set

Next, we describe the three stages of the method we followed while creating the EA ModelSet dataset.

2.1 Dataset Collection

The data collection process (see Fig. 1) revolves around retrieving and storing EA models from diverse data sources. These models serve as the raw data input for subsequent processing activities. In our process, we identified *GitHub* and *Gen-MyModel* as valuable data sources due to their extensive collections of ArchiMate models, which can also be retrieved with reasonable effort. GitHub, a popular platform for hosting and sharing code repositories, hosts numerous open-source projects and provides a Search API for searching code globally across all indexed repositories. Utilizing the provided search functionality, we formulated specific queries to retrieve ArchiMate models in different formats commonly used by the community.

We obtained models in: *i*) The Open Group Standard ArchiMate Model Exchange File Format - a standard XML format allowing for model exchange between tools[1], *ii*) Archi model storage format - used by the Archi modeling tool[2], and *iii*) Git Friendly Archi File Collection (GRAFICO) format - mostly

---

[1] https://www.opengroup.org/xsd/archimate/.
[2] https://www.archimatetool.com/.

used by the model collaboration Archi plugin coArchi[3], which is also in XML format. These formats were queried by including the respective file extensions (i.e., *.xml and *.archimate).

The collection process is partly automated, by downloading the individual files from the search results through a browser script. At a later stage, we used the Python library PyGithub[4] to automatically retrieve models from GitHub, associate them with their respective repositories, and if present, link the corresponding license information. Models in GRAFICO format were transformed into format ii) using the Archi Command-Line Interface (CLI) tool to not introduce any additional complexity for later activities (e.g., not requiring an additional parser). In total, we collected 922 models from GitHub, stored in the raw-data/github/ directory.

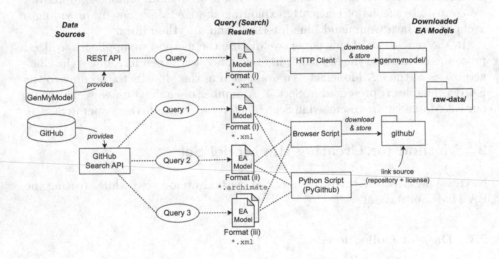

Fig. 1. Data collection workflow

GenMyModel, an online modeling platform supporting a variety of modeling languages, serves as another data source. Through its REST API[5], we filtered for public ArchiMate projects and retrieved the models in the standard model exchange XML format (format i) from above). We collected 287 models from GenMyModel, stored in the raw-data/genmymodel/ directory.

In addition to GitHub and GenMyModel, we manually collected models from other sources, including forums, publications, and project/company websites. These models were obtained through targeted web searches. We collected 15 models from other sources, stored in the raw-data/other/ directory.

---

[3] https://github.com/archimatetool/archi-modelrepository-plugin.

[4] https://github.com/PyGithub/PyGithub.

[5] https://app.genmymodel.com/api/projects/public.

2.2 Dataset Processing

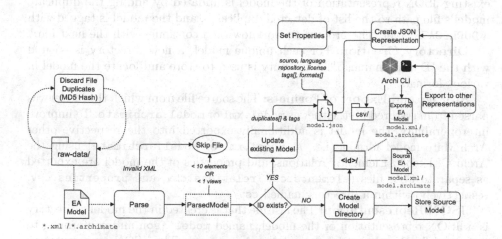

Fig. 2. Data processing workflow

With a substantial collection of almost 1,000 ArchiMate models in different formats, the subsequent step in our method involves processing these models to transform them into a standardized format suitable for advanced analysis and ML tasks. The data processing phase (Fig. 2) is initiated by receiving the collected models from the `raw-data/` directory as input, with file duplicates discarded beforehand by comparing their MD5 file hashes. Each raw ArchiMate model is processed as follows:

Parsing: The file is parsed to extract relevant information and to create an intermediate `ParsedModel` representation. Since all our input files are either in format *i*) or *ii*), two separate XML parsers are used. Although the formats differ in their hierarchical structure and naming schemes, they contain the same information and, therefore, can be parsed into a unified representation (i.e., a `ParsedModel`). If any major errors occur during parsing or the number of elements in the parsed model is less than 10 (indicating a model with insufficient complexity), the file is skipped.

Duplicate Detection: The parsed model's ID is checked against existing IDs of models that have already been processed. If a duplicate is found, the existing JSON representation of the model is updated by adding the duplicate model's file path to the list of detected duplicates, and the model is tagged with a `DUPLICATE` label. The processing workflow then continues with the next file.

Directory Creation: For each unique model, a new directory is created with the ID as its name. This directory is used to store and locate the model in various formats.

Storage and Export of Formats: The source file from which the model was parsed from is stored first, either as `model.xml` or `model.archimate`. To improve interoperability, the model is additionally exported into the respective other ArchiMate model format (i.e., as `model.xml` or `model.archimate`) using the Archi CLI tool[6]. Elements, relations, and properties of the model are exported as separate CSV files (`elements.csv`, `relations.csv`, and `properties.csv`, respectively) within a directory named `csv/`.

JSON Representation: The last file that is created in the model's directory is a JSON representation of the model, named `model.json` and conforming to a defined JSON schema in `ea-model.schema.json`. The JSON representation includes additional properties to further classify certain characteristics of the model in the dataset, in addition to common ArchiMate model properties already present in the parsed source file (see Sect. 3.1 for more information regarding the JSON schema). For the first release of the dataset, we relied on simple mechanisms to set the properties: The `source` property is set to the path of the parsed source file, for warnings during the parsing process (e.g., a relationship could not be parsed due to invalid source/target ID) we added a `WARNING` label to the list of `tags`, a corresponding `repository` URL and `license` is linked, the list of `formats` is based on the successfully exported formats of the previous step, and at last we set the `language` property by merging the names of a model's elements into a single textual representation to serve as input for the language detection Java library Lingua[7] that provides us an estimate of a suitable language.

After data processing, a total of 863 unique models remained, which are stored in the `processed-models/` directory. Each model has its own subdirectory, denoted by the model's ID, and contains the different representations of the model created during the processing stage (i.e. JSON, XML, ARCHIMATE, CSV).

---

[6] https://github.com/archimatetool/archi/wiki/Archi-Command-Line-Interface.
[7] https://github.com/pemistahl/lingua.

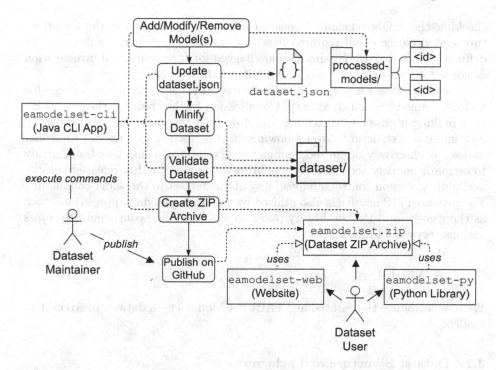

Fig. 3. Dataset management and publishing workflow

2.3 Dataset Management and Publishing

The final stage of our method focuses on managing and publishing the EA ModelSet dataset with its accompanying services (Fig. 3). The dataset is stored within the `EAModelSet` GitHub repository (see Footnote 9) in a central directory called `dataset/`. This directory includes the `processed-models/` directory from the previous stage and a `dataset.json` file which adheres to the JSON schema specified in `ea-dataset.schema.json` (see Sect. 3.1) containing metadata and computed data about the dataset itself. It also includes brief information about each model and a subset of its characteristics, facilitating model search. The `dataset.json` is further used by the website for model search and the Python library for searching within the pandas dataframe.

Dataset management activities are primarily performed using the accompanying *Java CLI application* (see Footnote 9), enabling maintainers to add, modify, or remove models from the dataset. When preparing for a new release, the `dataset.json` file is updated to reflect the changes made to the dataset. Following the update, the processed models undergo a *minification* process to reduce their file size and optimize storage efficiency. Minification involves removing unnecessary white spaces, comments, and other non-essential elements from the model files, further improving their compactness. The dataset then undergoes a validation process to ensure its quality and consistency. Validation includes checking the JSON schema to ensure conformity and verifying the file structure and presence of all required files. Any models that do not adhere to the defined schema or have missing files are flagged for further manual investigation or correction, ensuring the overall integrity of the data.

Once the dataset is prepared and validated, it is compressed into a single file archive, named `ea-modelset.zip`. Compression further reduces the overall file size, making it easier to distribute and download the dataset while preserving its content and structure. After following the described stages, the EA ModelSet dataset is effectively organized, summarized, validated, compressed, and ready to be made publicly accessible. It is published as a new GitHub release to ensure availability, version control, and visibility of the dataset to the wider community. The prepared ZIP archive is also utilized by the accompanying applications, such as the website and Python library (see Sect. 3.3), enabling consistent use across various services and interfaces.

3   EA ModelSet

We now introduce the curated and FAIR EA ModelSet—a dataset of ArchiMate models.

3.1   Dataset Structure and Schema

EA ModelSet follows a well-defined structure and leverages JSON schemas [15] to facilitate efficient data management and to provide a FAIR dataset of EA models. The relevant directories and files within the dataset are structured as follows:

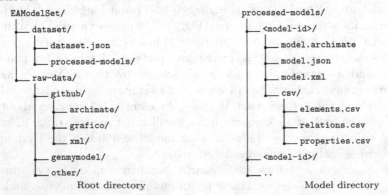

Root directory   Model directory

The `raw-data/` directory holds the collected raw data models that were used for data processing. It includes subdirectories for different data sources, such as `github/` (i.e., from GitHub), `genmymodel/` (i.e., from GenMyModel), and `other/` (i.e., from miscellaneous sources). The models from GitHub are further organized in three sub-directories `archimate/`, `grafico/`, and `xml/` based on their respective file format.

The main directory for the dataset is the `dataset/` directory, which contains the `dataset.json` file. Within the `processed-models/` directory, each processed model has its own subdirectory and follows a consistent format. A model directory contains the primary JSON model file (`model.json`) and two ArchiMate XML model files (`model.archimate` or `model.xml`). Additionally, models and their contents are stored in separate CSV files within the `csv/` directory.

Figure 4 illustrates how the JSON schemas are positioned in relation to the dataset to ensure consistency of metadata and data. The `ea-modelset.schema.json` and `ea-model.schema.json` schema files define the structure and validation rules for content in the `dataset.json` and `model.json` files, respectively.

The *Dataset* object contains the dataset metadata and includes information such as the title, version, lastUpdated date, repository URL, homepage URL, distribution details (including distribution title, download URL, media type, and byte size), model count, and an array of *ModelInfo* objects that provide a reduced subset of metadata and computed properties of each individual model. The *EA Model* object provides comprehensive information about each model including its elements, relationships, and views.

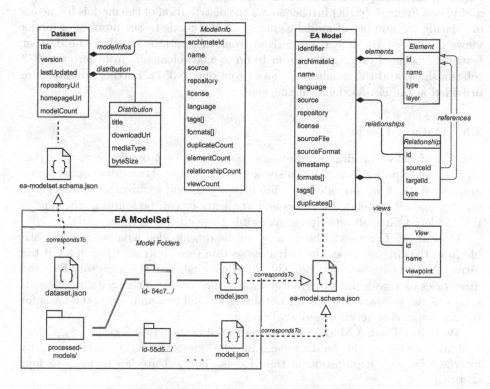

Fig. 4. JSON Schemas used in EA ModelSet

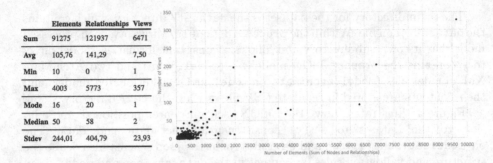

	Elements	Relationships	Views
Sum	91275	121937	6471
Avg	105,76	141,29	7,50
Min	10	0	1
Max	4003	5773	357
Mode	16	20	1
Median	50	58	2
Stdev	244,01	404,79	23,93

Fig. 5. Descriptive statistics of the EA ModelSet models (left) and distribution of the models with respect to number of model elements and views (right).

3.2   Dataset Description and Statistics

The final EA ModelSet dataset is composed of 863 unique ArchiMate models. The table in Fig. 5 (left) provides some descriptive statistics of the dataset including the sum, average, minimal, and maximum number of elements, relationships, and views. Figure 5 (right) further shows the distribution of the models by means of relating the number of model elements on the x-axis to the number of model views on the y-axis. It can be derived from these statistics, that the dataset features models of varying size (from 10 up to 4,003 elements, from zero to 5,773 relationships) and the number of views (from one to 357). Further statistics are provided at the EA ModelSet homepage[8].

3.3   Dataset Usage

The EA ModelSet facilitates various usage scenarios by providing accompanying services and applications. In this section, we describe these different scenarios and the support we provided to efficiently access and utilize the dataset. The dataset and all its related services and applications can be found in the central EA ModelSet GitHub repository, accessible through the assigned pURL[9].

Download Dataset: The dataset can be downloaded as a compressed ZIP file from the GitHub repository's release section (see Footnote 9) with a Git tag introduced for each new version. The ZIP file contains all the necessary files and directories to access and explore the dataset locally (except `raw-data/` files). It serves as the primary method for obtaining the dataset and forms the basis for the accompanying services and applications.

Website: The EA ModelSet has a dedicated website (see Footnote 8) (Fig. 6) that also serves as the landing page for the dataset, offering a user-friendly interface for easy exploration of the models. The website is divided into four sections:

---

[8] https://me-big-tuwien-ac-at.github.io/EAModelSet/home.
[9] https://purl.org/eamodelset.

Fig. 6. Search tab of the EA ModelSet homepage

i) Home: The home section serves as the dataset's landing page and as a starting point for users to get acquainted with the dataset. It lists the dataset's metadata, which is read from the `dataset.json` file, ensuring that the information can be easily updated in subsequent releases. The home section also includes a button to download the dataset as a ZIP file (also linked through the JSON file to the released distribution on GitHub).

ii) Search: The search interface enables efficient exploration and retrieval of relevant models in the dataset (see Fig. 6). Users can search for specific models based on various criteria, such as model ID, name, tags, language, source, license, or the minimum/maximum number of elements, relationships, or views. The search functionality supports arbitrary combinations of filtering criteria, sorting columns, and a "global search" feature to filter all fields.

iii) Model Details: This page allows in-depth analysis of each model. It can be accessed by navigating from the search section or by following the URL of the model's identifier (https://me-big-tuwien-ac-at.github.io/EAModelSet/model/<id>). The details page lists all information related to a specific model, including its metadata, elements, relationships, and views, which are extracted from the respective `model.json` file. Additionally, the associated files of a model (e.g., .json, .xml, .archimate, .csv) can be downloaded directly from this page.

iv) Statistics: The statistics page provides insights into the dataset's composition, complexity, and characteristics through the presentation of key statistics and metrics. Users can explore charts showing the usage of specific languages, layers, element/relationship types, or concrete values for the total number of models, as well as the total, minimum, maximum, and average number of elements, relationships, and views.

Python Library: A dedicated Python library is provided to facilitate programmatic access and analysis of the dataset within a Python environment. The library offers convenient methods to interact with the dataset using a pandas dataframe representation. Users can display the data in a tabular format and use additional filtering functionality to filter models based on various attributes such as source, language, or the minimum/maximum number of elements, relationships, or views. The complete JSON or CSV representation of a model (with all its elements/relationships/views) can then be accessed by passing the model's ID property obtained from the dataframe to a provided method. An example showcasing the functionality of the EA ModelSet Python library can be found in the provided Jupyter Notebook[10] in the repository.

Java CLI: For managing and maintaining the dataset, a Java Command-Line Interface (CLI) was realized. The CLI enables users to issue command line commands to perform operations on the dataset like adding or removing models, updating metadata, generating statistics, or validating the dataset's integrity (cf. Sect. 2.3). The Java CLI also provides the option to connect and load the data into a MongoDB document database or a Neo4j Graph Database for advanced querying and analysis. The use of the functionality of the Java CLI is demonstrated in the Github repository[11].

4   Evaluation Against the FAIR Principles

The FAIR principles provide guidelines to improve the **F**indability, **A**ccessibility, **I**nteroperability, and **R**euse of digital assets [23]. The FAIR principles further emphasize machine-actionability in scientific data management to support dealing with increased volume, complexity, and creation speed of data. In the following, we evaluate the compliance of `EAModelSet` in regard to each FAIR principle.

Findability *F1: "(meta)data are assigned a globally unique and persistent identifier"*. The EAModelSet meets this requirement by assigning a Persistent Uniform Resource Locator (pURL) to access the (meta)data stored in the GitHub repository (see Footnote 9). Furthermore, the dataset is accessible via a globally unique DOI (10.5281/*zenodo*.8192011) and uses ORCID for author identification. Within the dataset, each model has a unique URI, in the form of https://me-big-tuwien-ac-at.github.io/EAModelSet/model/<id>, where <id> represents a tool-generated Universally Unique Identifier (UUID) or a similar type of identifier for the model. The unique identifier allows direct access to each model and guarantees global uniqueness and unambiguous identification.

F2: "data are described with rich metadata". The dataset provides comprehensive information about each model, capturing e.g., its name, description, source, license, language, and various other attributes (see Fig. 4). The metadata defined in the JSON schema richly describes the data through additional characteristics.

F3: "metadata clearly and explicitly include the identifier of the data it describes". In the JSON representation of the EA Model, the metadata explicitly

---

includes the identifier of the data it describes. Each model is associated with a unique URI identifier that incorporates its ID, providing a clear reference to a model. The ID is based on the `archimateId` property which is also included in the metadata and is an auto-generated UUID already present in the collected data, which is reused.

F4: "(meta)data are registered or indexed in a searchable resource". The EAModelSet is hosted in a public GitHub repository, providing e.g., search functionality and version control to locate and access the dataset. The dedicated website and Python library offer additional functionalities, including search- and filter capabilities to find models based on certain characteristics (e.g., language, views, number of elements).

Accessibility *A1: "(meta)data are retrievable by their identifier using a standardized communications protocol".* Metadata and data are retrievable on GitHub, and also using the identifier URI leading to the website, which is accessible using an open, free, and universally implementable communications protocol *(A1.1)*, e.g., through the HTTP(S) protocol by using a common web browser. The protocol thereby enables free access for use but requires an authentication and authorization procedure for updating the dataset *(A1.2)* (i.e., a GitHub account with the required permissions on the repository).

A2: "metadata are accessible, even when the data are no longer available". The dataset includes an additional JSON file for each model, providing descriptive metadata for each model. This metadata remains accessible even if the actual data associated with the model are no longer available. We further publish the repository releases on persistent data storage via Zenodo [10] to ensure accessibility even if the GitHub repository would not be available anymore.

Interoperability *I1: "(meta)data use a formal, accessible, shared, and broadly applicable language for knowledge representation".* The metadata and data are stored in JSON files as the main method for knowledge representation. JSON is a widely adopted format for structuring data in a human-readable and machine-readable manner, and the files correspond to a JSON Schema that provides a formal and standardized syntax. Furthermore, we enable additional data formats, including XML and CSV.

I2: "(meta)data use vocabularies that follow FAIR principles". The dataset employs a customized and adapted meta(data) description that partly reuse subsets of FAIR vocabularies. The dataset reuses vocabularies, e.g., from Data Catalog Vocabulary (DCAT)[12] or Dublin Core Terms (DCT)[13], by translating relevant properties into JSON schema[14]. Relevant datatypes are also translated, e.g., dates are formatted according to the provided datatypes in the JSON schema language (i.e. `date` and `date-time`), and for language codes, the two-letter ISO-6391-1 format is used.

I3: "(meta)data include qualified references to other (meta)data". The dataset itself includes `ModelInfo` objects, which are a lightweight representa-

---

[12] www.w3.org/TR/vocab-dcat-2/.

[13] www.dublincore.org/specifications/dublin-core/dcmi-terms/.

[14] https://json-schema.org/specification.html.

tion of models and include an explicit reference to the actual model. Also, the metadata of each model contains explicit references to related models (e.g. duplicates) or internal (e.g. source file) and external resources (e.g. repository).

Reusability *R1: "(meta)data are richly described with a plurality of accurate and relevant attributes".* Each JSON file contains the (meta)data derived from the source model, together with other relevant properties to richly describe a model (e.g. source, timestamp, language, tags). While the dataset already includes many relevant attributes, there is still room for improvement in terms of enriching the metadata. For instance, additional properties such as categories or more descriptive tags could be incorporated to enhance the richness of the metadata, precise filtering, and analysis.

R1.1: "(meta)data are released with a clear and accessible data usage license". The majority of models in the dataset have their source repository attached as an entry in the JSON file, including information about the license. The repository and license were automatically retrieved during data collection (see Sect. 2.1) and the results were manually re-checked to ensure accuracy. The data usage license is clearly associated with each model, providing information on how to legally use the data.

R1.2: "(meta)data are associated with detailed provenance". The JSON files in each model's folder include properties to present the original source and associated information. The properties provide a level of provenance and include, e.g., source, repository, license, or the parsed source file, allowing to trace back the origin of a model. While the current provenance information offers valuable insights, there is potential for more detailed provenance to be included. For example, associating publications or providing diagrams (e.g., as PNG files) could further enhance the dataset's provenance.

R1.3: "(meta)data meet domain-relevant community standards". The EAModelSet provides models in domain-relevant formats such as ArchiMate XML (two different formats) and CSV. The formats are widely accepted and align with the community's standards, promoting interoperability with existing tools. Furthermore, the newly introduced JSON schema maintains well-established structures and adheres to recognized naming conventions. The introduction of the JSON schema does not add unnecessary complexity, but rather provides clarity and consistency to ensure the metadata is understandable within the EA domain. The CSV formats further ease the execution of ML techniques on the EA ModelSet.

5   EA ModelSet Applications, Reflection, and Future Work

The EA ModelSet dataset provides a rich collection of EA models, unlocking new possibilities for research and practical applications. In this section, we critically reflect on our efforts to establish a FAIR dataset of EA models and discuss potential applications and directions for future research.

Researchers can explore the dataset to gain insights into different modeling approaches, applications, and patterns. By analyzing the models within the dataset, researchers can identify best practices and discover common modeling patterns, which can significantly contribute to advancing the field of EA.

The dataset's availability in different formats, including JSON, XML, and CSV, makes it applicable for a range of ML tasks that extract valuable insights from the data. Some potential applications of ML using EAModelSet include *Natural Language Processing* (NLP) and *Recommender Systems*. The dataset's textual information, e.g., names, documentation, languages, or tags, can be used to develop NLP models that extract meaningful information from unstructured text. This can support tasks such as *automatic model annotation* [1] and *semantic search*. The EA ModelSet dataset can also assist in building recommender systems tailored to EA [16,24]. By analyzing patterns and similarities among EA models, ML algorithms can provide context-based recommendations for specific modeling scenarios. These recommendations can guide architects by suggesting architectural decisions based on historical data, which can enhance productivity and support informed decision-making [5].

While the current EA ModelSet dataset is valuable, there are some limitations and areas for future improvement. One current limitation is its ability to process ArchiMate models in the .archimate and .xml formats. To broaden its applicability in the future, we aim to incorporate EA models that *i*) conform to other EA modeling languages, and which were *ii*) created with different EA modeling tools. Of course, such an extension will require additional research with respect to data harmonization and integration. Even transforming images of models created with other tools to our format is an interesting research challenge.

An additional current shortcoming we aim to address in the future is the fully automated data collection process and to ensure correct record linkage of the source. The current process involving GitHub downloads poses challenges due to authentication, rate limits, and API constraints (e.g., limited file size).

Maintaining data quality and integrity is essential for the EA ModelSet's adoption. Aside from our initial efforts to detect and flag duplicates (based on identifiers and MD5 file hashes) we plan to research and develop more advanced similarity metrics [7] that would help to further clean the data. In terms of data maintenance and publishing, we aim to enhance the dataset's interoperability and operationalizability using an RDF ontology (e.g. [11]). We also aspire to enrich the classification of models by incorporating semantic domain classification (e.g., hotel, banking, insurance). However, such a classification process requires significant manual effort and thus necessitates community engagement.

For all future considerations, we invite and hope to actively engage the enterprise modeling research community. The EA ModelSet is open source, and we plan to realize functionalities that enable efficient contributions from the community, especially with respect to curating the existing dataset and extending the dataset with new models. In conclusion, the EA ModelSet dataset not only empowers current research but also presents a promising platform for future endeavors. With continuous community engagement and improvement efforts, we aspire to make the EA ModelSet a valuable and comprehensive resource for researchers in the enterprise modeling domain.

6   Conclusion

In the paper at hand, we proposed the EA ModelSet, the first FAIR dataset that allows machine learning research in enterprise modeling. The EA ModelSet is a curated dataset that currently contains 863 enterprise architecture models represented by ArchiMate. We believe the EA ModelSet can be an important asset for sparking research at the intersection of machine learning and enterprise modeling. We invite the modeling research community to help further curate and extend the dataset, and also tool vendors to explore their interest in sharing some of their models. The scarcity of models in adequate quantity and quality is a huge barrier to conducting cutting-edge machine learning research in modeling. We hope that the EA ModelSet becomes the central point for FAIR model data which can be freely used to conduct this kind of research.

Acknowledgements. This work has been partially funded through the Erasmus+ KA220-HED project "Digital Platform Enterprise" (project no. 2021-1-RO01-KA220-HED-000027576) and the Vienna Science and Technology Fund (WWTF) (10.47379/VRG18013).

References

1. Ali, S.J., Guizzardi, G., Bork, D.: Enabling representation learning in ontology-driven conceptual modeling using graph neural networks. In: Indulska, M., Reinhartz-Berger, I., Cetina, C., Pastor, O. (eds.) Advanced Information Systems Engineering - 35th International Conference, CAiSE 2023, Zaragoza, Spain, 12–16 June 2023, Proceedings. LNCS, vol. 13901, pp. 278–294. Springer, Cham (2023). https://doi.org/10.1007/978-3-031-34560-9_17
2. Barbosa, A.O., Santana, A., Hacks, S., von Stein, N.: A taxonomy for enterprise architecture analysis research. In: 21st International Conference on Enterprise Information Systems, ICEIS 2019, pp. 493–504. SciTePress (2019). https://doi.org/10.5220/0007692304930504
3. Barcelos, P.P.F., Sales, T.P., Fumagalli, M., et al.: A FAIR model catalog for ontology-driven conceptual modeling research. In: Ralyté, J., Chakravarthy, S., Mohania, M., Jeusfeld, M.A., Karlapalem, K. (eds.) 41st International Conference on Conceptual Modeling, ER 2022. LNCS, vol. 13607, pp. 3–17. Springer, Cham (2022). https://doi.org/10.1007/978-3-031-17995-2_1

4. Bernabé, C., Sales, T.P., Schultes, E., et al.: A goal-oriented method for FAIRification planning (2023). https://doi.org/10.21203/rs.3.rs-3092538/v1
5. Bork, D., Ali, S.J., Dinev, G.M.: AI-enhanced hybrid decision management. Bus. Inf. Syst. Eng. **65**(2), 179–199 (2023). https://doi.org/10.1007/s12599-023-00790-2
6. Bork, D., Ali, S.J., Roelens, B.: Conceptual modeling and artificial intelligence: a systematic mapping study. CoRR abs/2303.06758 (2023). https://doi.org/10.48550/arXiv.2303.06758
7. Borozanov, V., Hacks, S., Silva, N.: Using machine learning techniques for evaluating the similarity of enterprise architecture models - technical paper. In: Advanced Information Systems Engineering - 31st International Conference, pp. 563–578 (2019)
8. Corradini, F., Fornari, F., Polini, A., et al.: RePROSitory: a repository platform for sharing business process models and logs. In: Proceedings of the 1st Italian Forum on Business Process Management, pp. 13–18. CEUR-WS.org (2021)
9. Dumas, M., Rosa, M.L., Mendling, J., Reijers, H.A.: Fundamentals of BPM: model collections. http://fundamentals-of-bpm.org/process-model-collections/. Accessed 24 July 2023
10. Glaser, P.L., Sallinger, E., Bork, D.: EA ModelSet, July 2023. https://doi.org/10.5281/zenodo.8192011
11. Hinkelmann, K., Laurenzi, E., Martin, A., et al.: ArchiMEO: a standardized enterprise ontology based on the ArchiMate conceptual model. In: Proceedings of the 8th International Conference on Model-Driven Engineering and Software Development, MODELSWARD 2020, pp. 417–424. SCITEPRESS (2020). https://doi.org/10.5220/0009000204170424
12. López, J.A.H., Cuadrado, J.S.: An efficient and scalable search engine for models. Softw. Syst. Model. **21**(5), 1715–1737 (2022). https://doi.org/10.1007/s10270-021-00960-4
13. López, J.A.H., Izquierdo, J.L.C., Cuadrado, J.S.: ModelSet: a dataset for machine learning in model-driven engineering. Softw. Syst. Model. **21**(3), 967–986 (2022). https://doi.org/10.1007/s10270-021-00929-3
14. López, J.A.H., Izquierdo, J.L.C., Cuadrado, J.S.: Using the ModelSet dataset to support machine learning in model-driven engineering. In: Kühn, T., Sousa, V. (eds.) 25th International Conference on Model Driven Engineering Languages and Systems: Companion Proceedings, MODELS 2022, pp. 66–70. ACM (2022). https://doi.org/10.1145/3550356.3559096
15. Pezoa, F., Reutter, J.L., Suárez, F., et al.: Foundations of JSON schema. In: 25th International Conference on World Wide Web, WWW 2016, pp. 263–273. ACM (2016)
16. Raavikanti, S., Hacks, S., Katsikeas, S.: A recommender plug-in for enterprise architecture models. In: 25th International Conference on Enterprise Information Systems, ICEIS 2023, pp. 474–480. SCITEPRESS (2023). https://doi.org/10.5220/0011709000003467
17. Rahman, M.I., Panichella, S., Taibi, D.: A curated dataset of microservices-based systems. CoRR abs/1909.03249 (2019). http://arxiv.org/abs/1909.03249
18. Robles, G., Ho-Quang, T., Hebig, R., et al.: An extensive dataset of UML models in GitHub. In: 14th International Conference on Mining Software Repositories, MSR 2017, pp. 519–522. IEEE Computer Society (2017). https://doi.org/10.1109/MSR.2017.48

19. Schäfer, B., van der Aa, H., Leopold, H., Stuckenschmidt, H.: Sketch2BPMN: automatic recognition of hand-drawn BPMN models. In: La Rosa, M., Sadiq, S., Teniente, E. (eds.) CAiSE 2021. LNCS, vol. 12751, pp. 344–360. Springer, Cham (2021). https://doi.org/10.1007/978-3-030-79382-1_21

20. Shilov, N., Othman, W., Fellmann, M., Sandkuhl, K.: Machine learning for enterprise modeling assistance: an investigation of the potential and proof of concept. Softw. Syst. Model. **22**(2), 619–646 (2023). https://doi.org/10.1007/s10270-022-01077-y

21. da Silva Santos, L.O.B., Sales, T.P., Fonseca, C.M., Guizzardi, G.: Towards a conceptual model for the FAIR digital object framework. CoRR abs/2302.11894 (2023). https://doi.org/10.48550/arXiv.2302.11894

22. Sola, D., Warmuth, C., Schäfer, B., et al.: SAP Signavio Academic Models: a large process model dataset. In: Montali, M., Senderovich, A., Weidlich, M. (eds.) Process Mining Workshops - ICPM 2022 International Workshops. LNBIP, vol. 468, pp. 453–465. Springer, Cham (2022). https://doi.org/10.1007/978-3-031-27815-0_33

23. Wilkinson, M.D., Dumontier, M., Aalbersberg, I.J., et al.: The FAIR guiding principles for scientific data management and stewardship. Sci. Data **3**(1), 160018 (2016). https://doi.org/10.1038/sdata.2016.18

24. Zhi, Q., Zhou, Z.: Empirically modeling enterprise architecture using ArchiMate. Comput. Syst. Sci. Eng. **40**(1), 357–374 (2022). https://doi.org/10.32604/csse.2022.018759

Towards AI as a Service for Small and Medium-Sized Enterprises (SME)

Leon Griesch[1(⊠)], Jack Rittelmeyer[1], and Kurt Sandkuhl[1,2]

[1] Rostock University, 18051 Rostock, Germany
{leon.griesch,jack.rittemeyer,kurt.sandkuhl}@uni-rostock.de
[2] Jönköping University, 55111 Jönköping, Sweden

Abstract. AI-as-a-Service (AIaaS) combines Artificial Intelligence (AI) and cloud computing to make AI accessible to enterprises without implementing complex solutions or technologies on-premise. Many small and medium-sized enterprises (SME) that lack competencies in the AI and technology sector consider AIaaS as a promising option to implement AI solutions. However, the differences between AIaaS and AI on-premise have not attracted much research. The intention of this paper is to contribute to this area by analysing the literature in the field and investigating a concrete example in more detail. Exploring AIaaS is crucial to better understand the opportunities and limitations of AI services. The contributions of the paper are (a) an analysis of the literature on AIaaS to identify factors affecting AI implementation and how AIaaS solutions differ from on-premise solutions when introducing AI in a company, (b) a case study of an SME that compares AIaaS and AI on-premise in practice, and (c) the application potential of a morphological box to compare AIaaS and AI on-premise.

Keywords: AI-as-a-Service · SME · AI · AI introduction

1 Introduction

Artificial intelligence (AI) has made significant progress in recent years, offering innovative solutions to various problems in business, society, medicine, and many other areas. One of the growing trends in AI is "AI as a Service" (AIaaS), where companies offer AI solutions as a service. AIaaS combines AI and cloud computing to make AI accessible to users without implementing complex algorithms [4].

This development is supposed to enable small and medium-sized enterprises (SMEs) to reap the benefits of AI without the need for extensive in-house resources and expertise. However, research in the area of AI introduction to enterprises observed that organizations usually have to change to become "AI-ready" [11] and that AI often causes modifications in the business, application, and data architecture of a company [21]. In this context, it should be investigated if there are differences between AIaaS and AI on-premise concerning required organizational changes or readiness factors. So far, this topic has not attracted much research. This paper intends to contribute to this area by

© IFIP International Federation for Information Processing 2024
Published by Springer Nature Switzerland AG 2024
J. P. A. Almeida et al. (Eds.): PoEM 2023, LNBIP 497, pp. 37–53, 2024.
https://doi.org/10.1007/978-3-031-48583-1_3

analyzing the literature in the field and investigating a concrete example in more detail. Exploring AIaaS is crucial to understanding the opportunities and limitations of AI services. More concretely, this paper focuses on AIaaS and the current research knowledge state by conducting a Systematic Literature Review (SLA), especially for SMEs. In doing so, the following research questions are examined in more detail: What scientific literature already exists on "AI as a Service"? (RQ1); which already known factors are relevant when introducing new technologies from the perspective of an SME (RQ2), and to what extent do AI as a service solutions differ from on-premise solutions when introducing AI in the company? (RQ3). The third research question compares AI as a service and AI on-premise solutions to investigate the differences arising when companies purchase AI solutions as an external service or develop them in-house. To answer these questions, the current literature is examined first (see Sect. 4). This is realized with the help of a Systematic Literature Analysis, aiming to map and evaluate the current state of published research papers on this topic. In addition, a case study of an SME is used to compare AI as a service and AI on-premise solutions, reflecting the differences from a practical point of view. This case study analysis investigates the conjecture that purchasing existing AIaaS solutions makes more sense for most SMEs than developing AI solutions in-house. This conjecture results from previous experiences in research projects (see, e.g., [6]) that support SMEs in their AI introduction process. We observed that most SMEs lack substantial resources for AI implementation, such as IT know-how, time, and financial resources to cover the implementation costs. Among the reasons are the high complexity of developing the algorithms and the personnel requirements for the realization. It can be assumed that in-house developments are not attractive for every company due to the lack of feasibility and cost efficiency. Consequently, SMEs should instead focus on sufficient expertise and highly qualified workforce for organizational integration and application of AI solutions rather than on AI solution development and operation.

2 Theoretical Background

This chapter will present the background and related work relevant to this paper. First, the term AI will be explained briefly to get a shared understanding of what we mean when we talk about AI (see Sect. 2.1). This will be followed by the presentation of a morphological box developed as a guideline not to miss any relevant aspects when considering implementing an AI solution (see Sect. 2.2). Finally, we briefly introduce Enterprise Architecture Management (EAM), which will later be used to sort the papers found in the SLA according to the different EAM layers (see Sect. 2.3).

2.1 Artificial Intelligence (AI)

AI was defined by John McCarthy, one of the AI pioneers, in 1955 as "the science and engineering of making intelligent machines" [16]. Furthermore, AI can be distinguished into various technologies such as Machine Learning (ML), Deep Learning (DL), ontologies, support vector machines, and probabilistic or multiagent systems. The application possibilities of AI can range from text, image, or speech recognition to text generation, problem-solving, or decision-making, to name a few [23]. In public discussions about AI, AI is often reduced to ML or DL, the currently most prominent areas of AI. ML often uses statistical methods to search for patterns in large datasets. In contrast, DL simulates the human brain, often requiring more data than ML, training, testing, and using the developed neural networks [24].

2.2 Morphological Box for AI Solutions

This research aims to contrast the differences between AI on-premise and AIaaS solutions. To be able to do that, we were searching for factors of AI solution implementation that influence the success of the implementation. Our focus was especially not only on technology factors regarding the software solution itself, but we also wanted to include factors that are important for the introduction process, precisely because the main differences between AI on-premise and AIaaS come from the fact that there is a need to develop the first one yourself, you need employees and knowledge who can do that and maintain it. The second option, on the other hand, could come with other restrictions regarding flexibility, adaptability, suitability, or cost structure. Because of that, we chose the morphological box for AI solutions by Rittelmeyer & Sandkuhl [6] as a framework for our comparison. Other approaches like maturity models or AI readiness factors exist, but no framework deals with the implementation itself. They mainly only consider the technological side of AI solutions. The morphological box, on the other side, is intended to assist in planning and implementing an AI solution. It should support engineering requirements, especially for practitioners, and it should help to make a decision when considering the usage of AI. It offers 17 different features of AI with several possible values each (see Table 1). When planning the development, use, or introduction of an AI

Table 1. Morphological box for AI solution development

Feature	Values					
AI Focus	Processing input		Generating output		Computing task	
End-User	IT-Expert		IT-Savvy		No IT-Knowledge	
Computing Source	Cloud		Local computing center	End-Device	Hybrid	
Time to Decision	Real-time		Near Real-Time	Several Hours	Later	
Special Hardware Required	Computing		Data Capture	Data Visualization	Data Output	
Reliability and Precision of Results	~99,9 % Required		Defined by Enterprise	Defined by Domain	Defined by Competitors	
Point in Time of AI Use in Solution Development	Design-Time		Runtime	Accompanying runtime	Hybrid	
Primary Purpose	Assistance	Decision Making	Forecasting	Classification	Anomaly Detection	
Data Source	Own Data	Augmented Data	Open Data	Commercial Collection	Synthetic Data	
Data Quantity	Very High	High	Moderate	Low	Very Low	
Maturity	COTS	Commercial Components	Open Source Components	Prototype	Individual	
Data and Model Update Frequency	Continuously	In Case of Changes in Regulation	In Case of New Documents/Data	In case of Changes in Customer Behavior	In Case of Quality Problems	
Extent of Effect on Enterprise	Isolated Solution	Single Process	Workflow	Work System	Business Model	
Communication	Frequent & detailed, active collaboration	Regular, some collaboration	Minimal, min. collaboration	Specific moments	None	
Primary Data Type	Audio	Video	Raster Image	Vector Image	Transaction Records	Time Series Data
Data Quality	Inconsistent	Duplicate	Incomplete	Outdated	Biased	Noisy	Corrupted
Data Security	Compliance	Data Encryption	Access Control	Data Integrity	Data Privacy	Incident Management	Audit & Monitoring

solution in a company, it is suggested to use it in the planning or requirements engineering phase to make sure that no critical aspect of the AI development and introduction process will be forgotten that could negatively impact the adoption because it was realized too late. In Sect. 6, the different features of the box will be used to compare AI on-premise and AIaaS solutions.

2.3 Enterprise Architecture Management (EAM)

Enterprise Architecture Management (EAM) is a system approach that offers a variety of methodologies, principals, practices, tools, and notations that can be used to increase efficiency and reduce redundancies by aligning company's business goals and IT with EA models. It further offers guidance for the planning, development, and coordination of an EA [1].

An EA is a model of a company, depicting its most essential structures and principles grouped by different layers to get a compromised overview of a company. The TOGAF framework differentiates between motivation, business, application, and technology layers. Each layer offers different modeling elements, like business roles and processes on the business layer and application components or services on the application layer [26].

3 Research Method

This paper is part of a research project aiming at technological and methodical support for implementing AI-as-a-Service solutions in SMEs. It follows the paradigm of design science research (DSR) [7], the envisioned artefact being a method including tool support for the selection and organizational integration of AIaaS components and solutions. Work presented in the paper focuses on one of the first phases in DSR, investigating and confirming problem relevance, and the first steps towards requirements analysis for the envisioned artifact. The research questions in the focus of this paper were already described in the introduction.

Investigation of problem relevance in DSR has to address relevance for businesses and relevance for scientific community. Thus, with the intention to address both aspects of relevance, the research approach selected for the paper combines literature analysis, descriptive case study, and argumentative-deductive work. We start with a systematic literature analysis to identify the existing scientific work on AI as a service. The purpose of the analysis was to find existing theories, approaches, or technologies which could support the implementation process in SMEs in all phases, from requirement and decision-making to operation and maintenance. The research method used for the literature analysis and its results is described in detail in Sect. 4. The core result of the literature work is that there is a need for more scientific research on AI-as-a-Service. This motivates the collection of additional empirical data using a case study, which at the same time addresses the aspect of business relevance. We need to explore the nature and phenomenon of AI-as-a-Service in real-world environments applying AI, which is possible in case studies.

Based on the research question, we identified an industrial case study suitable to illuminate AI usage in SMEs. Yin differentiates various case studies [30] explanatory, exploratory, and descriptive. The case study presented in Sect. 5 must be considered descriptive, as it describes the phenomenon of AI-as-a-Service and the real-life context in which it occurs. Based on the case study results, there is a need to support AIaaS implementation methodically. In this context, tools that help to structure decision processes and reduce complexity, such as the morphological box for AI, are relevant. This argumentative-deductive part of our work is discussed in Sect. 6.

4 Structured Literature Review

A systematic literature analysis is carried out to review the existing work. The following subsections describe the exact procedure of the literature analysis and presents the results. The structured literature analysis is based on Kitchenham's approach to obtaining an overview of AI as a service approach in introducing such solutions [12]. Among other things, gaps in current research in this area should be identified.

4.1 Search Process

After we have defined the theoretical background and the research questions in more detail, we start with the literature analysis. For the literature search, we exclusively used the search engine Scopus. In order to find a more extensive range of papers, the search strings were developed independently at the beginning and merged afterward.

First, we started with a population and used Scopus to analyze in more detail all scientific publications that exist in general on the main keyword "AI as a service." The initial search term we developed is as follows:

TITLE-ABS-KEY

(*AIaaS* **OR** *"AI as a service"* **OR** *"Artificial Intelligence as a service"*)

The first search query produced 62 papers that can be found under this term. It turned out that there is a significant overlap in content with the main topics of "cloud computing" and "edge computing," which increasingly relate to the provision and processing location of the service. Out of 62 scientific articles, 12 papers were sorted out because their content had nothing to do with Ai as a Service or the synonym AIaaS had a different meaning. For example, "Anti-impulsive aggression agents" was found more frequently in the sorted-out articles under the search term "AIaaS," which occurs in the pharmacotherapy study.

From the collected research papers, we have noted down all the resulting keywords from the analysis of the scientific articles. The listing of all keywords from the 50 papers can be found in Table 2. For a simplified representation, the synonyms such as "Artificial Intelligence" and "AI," as well as "AIaaS" and "AI-as-a-service" were summarized from the total 148 keywords found. Only the keywords mentioned in at least two different articles are listed.

Based on this finding, we have formed three upper categories for the closer search string development: The first category refers to AI as a general service. The second category is "technology innovation," which includes keywords related to introducing AI systems. The third category refers to the place of the service and how the AI solution as a service can be provided and used by the companies. Examples include whether the AI as

Table 2. Identified keywords from the main search query

Keywords	Number of mentions
Artificial intelligence	23
AI-as-a-service	18
Machine Learning	6
Cloud Computing	6
Edge Computing	5
Convolutional neural network	3
accountability	3
metric learning, 5G, Deep Learning, cloud, PaaS, Machine Learning as a Service, misuse, monitoring, audit, compliance, image processing	2 for every keyword

a service solution can be accessed via the cloud or locally on hardware. These keywords can be found under the category "Service Access." In addition, we have also assigned synonyms of suitable approaches to technology innovation that fit the introduction of such AI solutions. The selected keywords for the search string development can be found in Table 3.

Table 3. Selected search terms for the SLR

AI as a service	Technology innovation	Service Access
AIaaS	innovation	cloud computing
AI as a service	implementation	edge computing
Artificial intelligence as a service	adoption	on-premise computing
Machine Learning as a Service	approach	fog computing
Deep Learning as a Service	framework	AI on-demand
	strategy	
	model	
	process	

Below, we used the keywords to develop multiple searches, starting with the first two basic ones, and then added synonyms to compare how the results changed. The publications found were very general.

4.2 Search String Development

In this subsection, we devote ourselves to developing an effective search string for our systematic literature review. Our primary focus is on the topic "AI as a Service." The search string was created in several steps to ensure that we identified the most relevant and informative scientific papers in our research area.

In the first step, we relied on the findings from our initial search terms. Based on the main keyword "AI as a Service" and the most frequently mentioned keywords analyzed from it, we could filter out initial relevant papers. This process allowed us to get a first overview of the research field and to identify the most critical topics and trends. In the second step, we expanded and refined our search string. We have added "Machine Learning as a Service" and "Deep Learning as a Service" to the service terms. This expansion allowed us to cover a broader range of literature and ensure we covered all relevant aspects of AI as a Service. In the third step, we expanded our search string to include the concepts of cloud computing and implementation approaches. This allowed us to gain a broader perspective on the topic and identify papers addressing theoretical and practical aspects of AI as a Service. The identified papers from the developed search strings are listed in the table below. This selection represents the most relevant papers for us in this research area. They were selected based on their relevance to our topic, methodological strength, and contributions to the existing literature. In the next section, we discuss these relevant papers in more detail. We detail the inclusion criteria we used to select these papers and explain why the papers are particularly relevant to our literature review.

Table 4. Final search strings of the SLR

Search String	No. of Results	Identified Papers
TITLE-ABS-KEY (aiaas OR "AI as a service" OR "Artificial Intelligence as a service")	62	[2, 5, 8–10, 13–15, 18, 25, 31]
TITLE-ABS-KEY (aiaas OR "AI as a service" OR "Artificial Intelligence as a service" OR "Machine Learning as a service" OR "Deep Learning as a service")	293	[2, 5, 6, 8–10, 13, 13–15, 18, 20, 25, 27, 29, 31]
TITLE-ABS-KEY ((aiaas OR "AI as a service" OR "Artificial Intelligence as a service" OR "Machine Learning as a service" OR "Deep Learning as a service") AND ("cloud-computing" OR "edge computing" OR "on-premise" OR "fog computing" OR "AI on-demand"))	59	[8, 9, 13, 14, 18, 19, 29]

(*continued*)

44 L. Griesch et al.

Table 4. (*continued*)

Search String	No. of Results	Identified Papers
TITLE-ABS-KEY ((aiaas OR "AI as a service" OR "Artificial Intelligence as a service" OR "Machine Learning as a service" OR "Deep Learning as a service") AND ("cloud-computing" OR "edge computing" OR "on-premise" OR "fog computing" OR "AI on-demand") AND (implementation OR adoption))	9	[3, 8, 9]
TITLE-ABS-KEY ((aiaas OR "AI as a service" OR "Artificial Intelligence as a service" OR "Machine Learning as a service" OR "Deep Learning as a service") AND ("cloud-computing" OR "edge computing" OR "on-premise" OR "fog computing" OR "AI on-demand") AND (implementation OR adoption OR approach OR framework OR strategy OR model OR process))	51	[3, 8, 9, 13, 17, 18, 29]

The results relate to different industries and consider different use cases in AI as a service. The range of topics is extensive, from architectural models and diagnostics in medicine to the energy sector and the use of 5 G or 6 G networks. Interestingly, adding the third dimension, "technology innovation," reduces the number of hits enormously, indicating that there are few scientific studies on introducing AI as a service.

For further consideration, we are guided by the definition of the paper [14] that defines "AIaaS as cloud-based systems providing on-demand services to organizations and individuals to deploy, develop, train, and manage AI models.". Beyond that we excluded papers for reasons that either did not deal with the specific introduction of AI as a service or if the service concept did not correspond to the definition – some of the papers dealt with aspects related to ethical or security issues. We also excluded papers that were too specific to certain industries, such as medical, automotive, or AI systems in intelligent grid networks in the power sector. In the following, we probed the most relevant papers from the search strings in the next chapter and assigned inclusion criteria with a thematic focus.

4.3   Paper Selection and Inclusion

A total of 18 papers were identified from the analyzed search strings relevant to the topic "Introduction of Ai as a service."It was found that some of the search strings have overlaps in their hit set, as shown in Table 4. For further investigation and justification of the relevance to the proximity to the research topic, we have subsequently set up inclusion criteria in Table 5 in order to classify the identified papers thematically. From the first perspective, we have analyzed the papers in their underlying research methods. To classify the research papers and the associated methods, we refer in the analysis to the primary paper by Hess and Wilde and their empirical investigation of research methods in information systems [28]. An assignment of the research methods to the papers can be found in Table 5.

The findings from the research methods of the 18 relevant papers coincide with the findings from our primary source on research methods in business informatics. Most papers examined AI as a service using deductive analysis as a research method. They frequently substantiated their research findings in the context of a case study in the context of use cases or case studies. Many of the papers in this research area have developed a reference architecture model, particularly on data distribution. This justifies the previously identified issue that there is a solid link to cloud computing in the area of AI as a service, and the search term machine learning as a service can be found more frequently in the research papers. This often involves the question of the extent to which the AI service can be used as a service and via which paths or how the service can be accessed. The research methods "grounded theory" and "laboratory/field experiment" were not applied to the analysed papers, for which reason they have not been included in Table 5.

The second perspective deals with the content of the considered papers. For this purpose, the papers were examined concerning the following main content points:

1) **Challenges and opportunities of AIaaS** [3, 5, 6, 10, 14]

Many of the papers reviewed relate to the challenges and opportunities of AI as a service. AIaaS can help run AI in an enterprise more efficiently and cost-effectively by providing access to advanced AI technology without requiring in-depth knowledge. However, managing such services is a challenge, as it requires careful monitoring and maintenance [3]. The development of new types of AIaaS is resulting in a concentration of control and power among a few large providers. This can inhibit innovation in the design of novel solutions. At the same time, there is an opportunity for companies to improve the accessibility and usability of AI through the proliferation of these dominant designs [5]. The term Machine Learning as a service is often mentioned, which can be assigned to the umbrella topic of AIaaS. Here, advantages are mentioned for scalability and accessibility, but also significant challenges concerning data privacy and security [6]. The privacy challenges are also addressed in the paper "Monitoring AI Services for Misuse" [10], emphasizing the need to monitor AI services to prevent misuse. This creates the challenge of balancing monitoring and privacy. However, it also allows to create trust in AIaaS by establishing transparent and secure processes. Finally, the paper [14] emphasizes that a precise classification

Table 5. Overview of inclusion criteria applied to the most relevant papers.

Criteria/Paper	[2]	[3]	[5]	[6]	[8]	[9]	[10]	[13]	[14]	[15]	[17]	[18]	[19]	[20]	[25]	[27]	[29]	[31]
Formal/conceptual and Argumentative-deductive analysis		×	×	×			×		×				×	×	×			×
Simulation	×						×									×	×	
Reference modeling		×			×	×		×	×	×		×	×	×		×		
Action-research		×																
Prototyping	×					×								×		×		
Case study			×	×	×	×				×	×	×		×	×		×	
Qualitative/Quantitative Cross-sectional analysis															×			×

and taxonomy of AIaaS services helps reduce the field's complexity and thus facilitates access to these technologies. However, challenges related to standardization and interoperability are also mentioned.

In summary, AIaaS presents both opportunities and challenges. It gives companies access to advanced AI technologies but also requires careful monitoring and management to ensure privacy, security, and fairness. There is a need for more research and development to address these challenges and realize the full potential of AIaaS.

2) **Development of an architecture reference model** [8, 9, 13, 14, 18, 20, 27]

When analyzing the scientific papers, it was noticed that many of the papers either developed their architecture reference model on the research topic of AIaaS or MLaaS or made a proposal for the distribution of data processing. For example, many of the papers examined take a closer look at technical aspects, such as the application of AI in future network environments such as the Internet of Everything (IoE) and 6G networks [8]. Within the scope of two case studies, the method of cloud computing is combined with the method from IoE via Fog and edge computing for data processing at an intelligent airport and in the area of a smart city in a defined district. A proposed architecture model discusses the performance, energy consumption, and costs in various scenarios in more detail. Also, in this area, [9] presents a reference architecture for distributed AI services for skin disease diagnosis, whose architecture leverages cloud, Fog, and edge computing approaches. Also, the paper by [13] focuses on the architecture of AI services specifically for edge devices, which focuses more on the technical aspect of AIaaS. The paper "Artificial Intelligence as a Service - Classification and Research Directions"[14] provides a classification and investigation of the research directions related to AIaaS, where this paper takes a closer look at the whole ecosystem of an enterprise and includes possible stakeholders on this topic. Compared to the other research papers, this paper tries to comprehensively classify the whole topic around AIaaS and not only examine the technical component in their proposed AIaaS stack. In addition, the papers of [18] and [20] explore both a paradigm for providing AIaaS on software-defined infrastructures, indicating the integration of AI into existing technical infrastructures and the provision of machine learning as a service in the application of AI in data extraction. Finally, [27] describes the implementation and evaluation of an MLaaS for document classification using continuous deep learning models, demonstrating a practical use case of MLaaS.

Many of the reviewed papers show different perspectives on developing architecture reference models. In contrast, the papers focusing on MLaaS rather deal with the technical aspects, such as the increased focus on the machine pipeline for the creation as well as the configuration of AI models. The focus of AIaaS as an overarching topic additionally deals with questions regarding the organizational factors such as the Inclusion of relevant stakeholders or investigations of necessary business processes to connect the service performance of pre-trained AI models.

3) **Performance Evaluation/Adoption** [6, 27, 29] [31]

With the growth of cloud services, MLaaS has evolved, providing complex ML models that can also handle big data. These applications are used in systems, production models, and business processes. In analyzing the research area, it was noticed that some of the papers focused on the performance of the ML algorithms and, in an evaluation, investigated which different scenarios and application areas the performance of different ML algorithms vary. Aspects such as the accuracy of the models, resource consumption such as energy consumption, and cost and training time aspects were examined. In the paper "Machine Learning as a Service (MLaaS)-An Enterprise Perspective" [6], GPU performance versus price was evaluated in addition to professional changes as well as requirements that have changed over time due to technological trends. In another paper [27], three models were investigated in the area of text classification, in which, on the one hand, user feedback was not considered in training (model 1 as a base model), in the second model, which builds on the first model, user feedback was supplemented by active learning in the form of data augmentation (model 2), and the third model, as in the second model, user feedback was augmented by data simulation. The parameters used to investigate performance included accuracy, recall, F1 score, and losses in both the training and data sets. It was found that active learning through user feedback can increase accuracy and make the document classification process more efficient. In the research paper "Complexity vs. Performance:" [29], a comprehensive investigation of the effectiveness of Machine Learning as a Service (MLaaS) systems were undertaken, in which the auto-ren conducted experiments with different configurations of the ML pipeline, including feature selection, classifiers, and parameters. They found that increasing the complexity of the platform leads to better performance and significant performance degradation with poor configuration choices. In the last research paper studied [31], the preconditions and performance implications of using AI frontier resources were analyzed. A panel data analysis from S&P 500 index for 2010 to 2018 was conducted to investigate these aspects. The analysis took a closer look at, on the one hand, the AI capabilities stocked in an Un-enterprise and external market pressure on the impact of AI frontier resources. It was found that companies with high internal AI capabilities are particularly likely to use AI frontier resources for process improvement. In addition, companies with high external market pressure are positively associated with using AI frontier resources for customer service solutions.

4) **Application** [15]

One paper in AIaaS stood out from the literature review as the application for a particular use case scenario. The paper "Mobile Real-time Facial Expression Tracking with the Assistant of Public AI-as-a-Service" [15] focuses on developing a real-time facial expression tracking framework that combines AIaaS and mobile local assistance computation. Here, a photo of the face in terms of position and facial expression is captured on the mobile device, evaluated via an AIaaS, and fed back to the system via a tracking module. The results showed that their method has good real-time performance and efficient power saving. The time delay between cloud/edge servers and end users is challenging for real-time mobile AI applications. In addition, according to the authors, the potential service cost of AIaaS must also be considered. It is difficult to accomplish the task on the mobile side independently and quickly, and it is also difficult to meet the real-time requirements using only AIaaS. However, from the paper, a technical application by supplementing it with AIaaS can positively impact performance and reduce costs through lower power consumption.

5) **Focus on SMEs** [25]

From the overall review of the literature analysis, it was found that only one paper focused on SMEs on the research topic of AIaaS. In this regard, the authors of the paper [25] conducted a web-based survey of small and medium-sized enterprises (SMEs) in Northwest Germany to determine the level of AI adoption in these enterprises and to identify the barriers and concerns in implementing industrial AI applications. In doing so, the survey of over 357 SMEs revealed that 90% of the companies surveyed do not use AI, but 22% plan to introduce AI in the medium term. The research found that companies implementing AIaaS are more likely to have implemented a more advanced AI application than companies without AIaaS, even though the sample was tiny in terms of companies using AIaaS. In addition to these points, the study shows that many SMEs believe they need to master digital transformation before they can engage with AI.

Since the SME aspect was only addressed in one of the 18 relevant papers, we took this finding as an opportunity to take up the case study on a real SME company example in the following chapter to illustrate better the differentiation of the impact of AI on-premise solutions to AIaaS solutions.

5 Case Study: AI on-premise and as AIaaS Solution

The subject of the case study is a company with 58 employees from the north of Germany offering back-office services to insurance agents and financial product brokers. These back-office services generally include administrative and operational tasks supporting the agents' and brokers' sales and client service activities. Examples of typical services are administrative support (managing paperwork, organizing client records), policy processing (handling policy endorsements, cancellations, and renewals), premium collection from clients (incl. Maintaining records of premiums received), commission processing (tracking and processing agent commissions, verifying policy information) processing commission statements), and assistance with claims processing (claim information, claim handling, claim tracking).

In the case company, the business process to be supported by an AI solution is the registration of incoming business documents. The main tasks in this process are to document the arrival of documents (registration for tracking purposes), decide on the agent or broker to receive and process the document and extract the essential information required. The case company receives, on average, 2.500 documents per week, including insurance contracts, insurance claims, account statements, invoices, notices about overdue payments, commission statements, notices about fee increases, changes in insurance conditions, etc. After deciding what kind of document arrived and what agent or broker the addressee is, the insurance and/or client numbers should be extracted.

These documents arrive via different channels. One channel is surface mail which requires scanning the physical letters before processing them. The second channel is an electronic message exchange in the BIPro format, an agreement among insurance companies. BIPro messages include the actual documents and meta-data describing document type and content. The third channel is e-mail with attachments, including the document either as generated or scanned PDF file.

The IT support currently in place at the case company consists of a transformation of input from all channels to the same PDF format, OCR processing (if necessary), and search for keywords in the resulting text document (for example, "account statement," "contract," "commission," "insurance number" or "client" number) that can be used for document classification and information extraction. A rule set is applied to classify the document using the extracted keyword. Depending on the document type, a second rule set is used to extract additional information for specific keywords (for example, the actual "insurance number" number), resulting in key-value pairs.

With this procedure, on average, 58% of all documents can be classified automatically. However, extracting required information works only for less than 20% and often has to be done manually. The case company aims to improve document classification and information extraction using machine learning approaches. Two approaches were implemented in parallel: installing a machine learning approach on-premise and using a service in the cloud.

For the on-premise AI solution, the software Rapidminer was installed, and a data processing toolchain was implemented. A corpus of 1,200 documents was created to train the machine learning approach, including documents related to three groups of business processes: claims handling, premium collection, and new policies. For each group, documents from different insurance companies were included to represent the different content layouts, structures, and wordings. Keyword and stopword lists were created to support the document classification process. The AI approaches used were Naïve Bayes Classifier (NBC) and k-Nearest-Neigbours (kNN). After training the machine learning models with 80% of the document corpus (randomly selected), the remaining documents were used to test the document classification quality.

For the AI-as-a-Service solution, the machine learning platform of PlanetAI was used. PlanetAI offers the Intelligent Document Analysis (IDA) suite as a software-as-a-service solution. Like the on-premise approach, the IDA suite also needs training to establish the "ground truth." For this purpose, the training set of documents had to be uploaded, and the IDA extraction assistant could be used to prepare the documents. Based on an agreement with PlanetAI regarding data protection and confidentiality, the case company could use the same document corpus as the on-premise version.

6   Contrasting on-premise and AIaaS

The case study showed aspects of using AI on-premise and AIaaS solutions that are similar and different. We used the morphological box presented in Sect. 2.2 with its features and values as a framework to further compare the two approaches on an abstract level. We compared the two approaches for each feature and checked if they were similar or different. The different features were the following: computing source, maturity, hardware, data source, security, the extent of the effect on enterprise, and communication. In our case study, the computing source of the on-premise solution was established locally in their computing center while using a cloud solution for the AIaaS case. The remaining features were also considered but no difference between AIaaS and on-premise solutions could be found for them. Hence, only the features that should significant differences will be discussed further in this section.

Regarding the maturity in the on-premise case, a new individual solution was developed, but they also used open-source components. This shows that it is also possible to choose several values for a feature for one solution. For the AIaaS case, a ready commercial-of-the-shelf (COTS) solution was bought from the provider. For the on-premise solution, it was necessary to have its hardware available, while for the AIaaS solution, the company did not have to acquire hardware. The data source also differs between the two solutions. While for an on-premise solution, own data is needed, the AIaaS solution already offers commercial collections in the form of pre-made data sets.

Nevertheless, also in the AIaaS, the data sets of the provider were combined with the data from the company that will be using the solution. Regarding the data security aspect, it highly depends on the specific case, but what could be shown overall is that AIaaS must be General Data Protection Regulation (GDPR) compliant, especially when the AIaaS provide itself sources something. Lastly, the extent of the effect on the enterprise and communication features can be reviewed together because, for both, the main difference is that in the on-premise case, you have to manage the development of your solution yourself in your company, and everything that is included in this development process. On the other hand, in the AIaaS case, you only have to manage the contact, collaboration, and communication with your service provider and, depending on the service, also the maintenance later. Overall, the box itself cannot help directly with integrating the AI solution in a company, but it can help show essential aspects in advance so that they can be planned thoroughly. For the integration itself, it can only show that there will be some effects and communication that must be done to succeed at the end of the integration process.

7 Summary and Future Work

In this work, the concept of AI as a Service (AIaaS) was studied in depth, particularly in the context of small and medium-sized enterprises (SMEs). The study showed that AIaaS has the potential to facilitate the implementation of AI solutions in SMEs, which often need more skills in AI and technology.

The literature review revealed a link between AIaaS and cloud computing, and these two concepts are closely related. AIaaS uses cloud computing to deliver AI solutions in an accessible and cost-effective manner. This opens up new opportunities for SMEs by allowing them to access advanced AI technologies without implementing complex technologies on-premise.

Since only one paper was found from the literature review that explicitly addresses AIaaS for SMEs, the distinction between AI on-premise solutions and AIaaS solutions became apparent during the case study and with the help of the morphological box. In future work, several exciting avenues could take this research topic further. It is worthwhile to conduct further case studies in SMEs to gain a deeper understanding of the practical challenges and benefits of AIaaS. Research into the security aspects of AIaaS will also contribute to the literature, as security is a key concern when using cloud-based services.

References

1. Ahlemann, F., et al.: Strategic Enterprise Architecture Management: Challenges, Best Practices, and Future Developments. 2012nd edn. Management for Professionals. Springer, Berlin (2012)
2. Bordini, R.H., et al.: Agent programming in the cognitive era. Auton. Agent. Multi-Agent Syst. **34**, 1–34 (2020). https://doi.org/10.1007/s10458-020-09453-y
3. Casati, F., et al.: Operating enterprise AI as a service. In: Service-Oriented Computing: 17th International Conference, ICSOC 2019, pp. 331–344.https://doi.org/10.1007/978-3-030-33702-5_25
4. Elshawi, R., et al.: Big data systems meet machine learning challenges: towards big data science as a service. Big Data Res. **14**, 1–11 (2018). https://doi.org/10.1016/j.bdr.2018.04.004
5. Ferràs-Hernández, X., Nylund, P.A., Brem, A.: The emergence of dominant designs in artificial intelligence. California Manage. Rev., 000812562311643 (2023). https://doi.org/10.1177/000812562311164362
6. Grigoriadis, I., Vrochidou, E., Tsiatsiou, I., Papakostas, G.A.: Machine learning as a service (MLaaS)—an enterprise perspective. In: Saraswat, M., Chowdhury, C., Kumar Mandal, C., Gandomi, A.H. (eds.) Proceedings of International Conference on Data Science and Applications. Lecture Notes in Networks and Systems, vol. 552, pp. 261–273. Springer, Singapore (2023). https://doi.org/10.1007/978-981-19-6634-7_19
7. Hevner, A.R., et al.: Design science in information systems research. MIS Q. **28**, 75 (2004). https://doi.org/10.2307/25148625
8. Janbi, N., et al.: Distributed artificial intelligence-as-a-service (DAIaaS) for smarter IoE and 6G environments. Sensors (Basel) **20**, 5796 (2020). https://doi.org/10.3390/s20205796
9. Janbi, N., et al.: Imtidad: a reference architecture and a case study on developing distributed AI services for skin disease diagnosis over cloud fog and edge. Sensors (Basel) **22**, 1854 (2022). https://doi.org/10.3390/s22051854
10. Javadi, S.A., et al.: Monitoring AI Services for Misuse. In: Proceedings of the 2021 AAAI/ACM Conference on AI, Ethics, and Society, AIES '21, pp. 597–607 (2021). https://doi.org/10.1145/3461702.3462566
11. Jöhnk, J., Weißert, M., Wyrtki, K.: Ready or not, AI comes— an interview study of organizational AI readiness factors. Bus. Inf. Syst. Eng. **63**, 5–20 (2021). https://doi.org/10.1007/s12599-020-00676-7
12. Kitchenham, B., Charters, S.: Guidelines for performing systematic literature reviews in software engineering. EBSE Technical Report 2 (2007)
13. Kum, S., et al.: Artificial intelligence service architecture for edge device, pp. 1–3. https://doi.org/10.1109/ICCE-Berlin50680.2020.9352184
14. Lins, S., et al.: Artificial intelligence as a service: classification and research directions. Bus. Inf. Syst. Eng. **63**, 441–456 (2021). https://doi.org/10.1007/s12599-021-00708-w
15. Liu, X., et al.: Mobile real-time facial expression tracking with the assistant of public AI-as-a-service, pp. 648–654. https://doi.org/10.1109/HPCC-SmartCity-DSS50907.2020.00083
16. McCarthy, J.: What is artificial intelligence (2007). https://www.diochnos.com/about/McCarthyWhatisAI.pdf. Accessed 27 Sep 2023
17. Noshiri, N., Khorramfar, M., Halabi, T.: Machine learning-as-a-service performance evaluation on multi-class datasets. In: 2021 IEEE International Conference on Smart Internet of Things (SmartIoT). IEEE (2021)
18. Parsaeefard, S., Tabrizian, I., Leon-Garcia, A.: Artificial intelligence as a service (AI-aaS) on software-defined infrastructure. In: 2019 IEEE Conference on Standards for Communications and Networking (CSCN). 2019 IEEE Conference on Standards for Communications and Networking (CSCN) took place 28–30 October 2019 in Granada, Spain, pp 1–7. IEEE, Piscataway (2019)

19. Pop, D., Iuhasz, G., Petcu, D.: Distributed platforms and cloud services: enabling machine learning for big data, 139–159. https://doi.org/10.1007/978-3-319-31861-5_7

20. Ribeiro, M., Grolinger, K., Capretz, M.A.: MLaaS: machine learning as a service. In: 2015 IEEE 14th International Conference on Machine Learning and Applications. ICMLA 2015, 9–11 December 2015, Miami, Florida, USA: proceedings, pp 896–902. IEEE, Piscataway (2015)

21. Rittelmeyer, J.D., Sandkuhl, K.: Effects of artificial intelligence on enterprise architectures - a structured literature review. In: IEEE 25th International Enterprise Distributed Object Computing Workshop (EDOCW), pp. 130–137 (2021). https://doi.org/10.1109/EDOCW5 2865.2021.00042

22. Rittelmeyer, J.D., Sandkuhl, K.: Morphological box for AI solutions: evaluation and refinement with a taxonomy development method. In: Hinkelmann, K., López-Pellicer, F.J., Polini, A. (eds.) Perspectives in Business Informatics Research. BIR 2023. Lecture Notes in Business Information Processing, vol. 493145–157. Springer, Cham (2023). https://doi.org/10.1007/978-3-031-43126-5_11

23. Russell, S.J., Norvig, P.: Artificial Intelligence: A Modern Approach. Fourth edition, global edition. Pearson Series in Artificial Intelligence. Pearson, Harlow (2022)

24. Schmidt, R., et al.: Towards engineering artificial intelligence-based applications. In: IEEE 24th International Enterprise Distributed Object Computing Workshop (EDOCW), pp. 54–62. IEEE (2020). https://doi.org/10.1109/EDOCW49879.2020.00020

25. Szedlak, C., Poetters, P., Leyendecker, B.: Application of artificial intelligence in small and medium-sized enterprises. In: (2020) Proceedings of the International Conference on Industrial Engineering and Operations (2020)

26. Haren, V.: TOGAF Version 9.1. 10th. Togaf series. Van Haren Publishing, Zaltbommel (2011)

27. Walter-Tscharf, F.F.W.V.: Implementation and evaluation of a MLaaS for document classification with continuous deep learning models. In: Altan, H., et al. (eds.) Advances in Architecture, Engineering and Technology. Advances in Science, Technology & Innovation229–239. Springer, Cham (2022). https://doi.org/10.1007/978-3-031-11232-4_20

28. Wilde, T., Hess, T.: Forschungsmethoden der Wirtschaftsinformatik. Wirtschaftsinformatik 4(49), 280–287 (2007). https://doi.org/10.1007/s11576-007-0064-z

29. Yao, Y., et al.: Complexity vs. performance: empirical analysis of machine learning as a service. In: Uhlig, S. (ed.) Proceedings of the 2017 Internet Measurement Conference, pp 384–397. ACM, New York (2017)

30. Yin, R.K.: Case Study Research: Design and Methods, 3rd ed., 9th print. Applied social research methods series, vol. 5. SAGE Publications, Thousand Oaks (2007)

31. Zapadka, P., Hanelt, A., Firk, S., Oehmichen, J.: Leveraging "AI-as-a-Service"–antecedents and consequences of using artificial intelligence boundary resources (2020)

Emerging Architectures and Digital Transformation

Evaluating ArchiMate for Modelling IoT Systems

Yara Verhasselt[1], Janis Stirna[2](✉) (iD), and Estefanía Serral[1] (iD)

[1] KU Leuven, Warmoesberg 26, 1000 Brussel, Belgium
yara.verhasselt@student.kuleuven.be,
estefania.serralasensio@kuleuven.be
[2] Stockholm University, Stockholm, Sweden
js@dsv.su.se

Abstract. The Internet of Things (IoT) is a disruptive technology that allows connecting physical objects with the digital world. This challenges organizations in adjusting their Enterprise Architecture (EA) for adopting the IoT technology to improve their operations and maximize their value. Considering the complexity of such changes, a suitable modelling language must be used for EA design and documentation. ArchiMate, being a de facto standard for EA modelling, has already been used for modelling IoT systems, however, it is not used in a consistent manner and different extensions have been proposed to address limitations identified in specific domains. Based on the most common practices reported in the literature, we propose and evaluate a set of guidelines for modelling IoT elements in ArchiMate. The guidelines are evaluated by performing qualitative research based on case studies. The evaluation shows that ArchiMate is suitable for modelling IoT systems, but only at the conceptual level. When technical details are required, extensions to the standard may be needed. In addition, domain-specific limitations such as the lack of showing time-based communication and redundancy in an industry context are identified.

Keywords: Enterprise Architecture · Enterprise Modeling · IoT · Internet of Things

1 Introduction

The Internet of Things (IoT) facilitates innovations towards the use of data and the execution of processes in a wide range of industries [1]. The increased use of IoT is due to its capability to provide the digital world with real-time information on the physical environment that can be used to improve decision-making and efficiency of operations. To ensure coherence of enterprise design the possibilities and the roles of the IoT components should be addressed early in the business design. Hence, enterprise modelling has become more complex, challenged by the need to integrate physical objects such as actuators and sensors into the digital systems [2]. To model such complex systems, Enterprise Architecture (EA) modelling is necessary for organizations to be able to align their business goals and processes to information technology [3].

J. P. A. Almeida et al. (Eds.): PoEM 2023, LNBIP 497, pp. 57–73, 2024.
https://doi.org/10.1007/978-3-031-48583-1_4

To support EA, different modelling languages have been proposed, ArchiMate being a de facto standard. ArchiMate has already been used in literature to model IoT systems in different domains. However, its usage for such systems is not straightforward and as such it is typically used in an inconsistent manner. In addition, a few authors report limitations and propose extensions to the language in order to offer the necessary modelling capabilities for certain domains, c.f., for example, [4–7]. Considering the current state of the art, more research is needed towards a common ground and to enable the consistent application of a standard EA language for modelling. To this end, the goal of this paper is to propose a set of guidelines to use ArchiMate for modelling IoT systems. The guidelines are defined based on the most common practices reported in the literature in combination with the ArchiMate definitions of the modelling constructs. The guidelines are then evaluated using a case-study based evaluation where four industry cases from different domains are modelled and evaluated by experts in ArchiMate and/or IoT. The evaluation allows us to assess the suitability of the guidelines as well as the strengths and limitations of ArchiMate.

The contributions of this paper are, (i) a literature study on the usage of ArchiMate for IoT systems; (ii) a set of guidelines modelling with ArchiMate, and (iii) the identification of strengths and limitations of ArchiMate when modelling IoT components.

The rest of the paper is organized as follows. Section 2 presents an overview of the state of the art in the use and evaluation of ArchiMate for modelling IoT systems. Based on this literature study, Sect. 3 presents the set of modelling guidelines. Section 3 explains the case-study based evaluation. In Sect. 4, discusses the research findings providing recommendations for future research. Finally, Sect. 5 concludes the paper.

2   Related Work on the Use of ArchiMate for IoT Systems

There are a number of sources reporting on endeavors, both research and practice, that have used or evaluated ArchiMate to describe a specific IoT system.

In the domain of smart cities, ArchiMate has been used in four studies for modeling IoT systems. Smart cities coordinate physical devices, software systems and analytics to offer more efficient services to citizens [8]. Berkel et al. [8], Anthony & Petersen [9], Bastidas et al. [5], and Anthony et al. [10] respectively concentrate on security aspects, electric Mobility as a Service (eMaaS), integrating city goals and objectives into an EA metamodel, and big data energy prosumption services. Bastidas et al. propose extensions to the language to describe performance characteristics like security and availability. However, Berkel et al. [8], Anthony & Petersen [9], and Anthony et al. [10] argue for the use of ArchiMate as is due to its extensive usage in EA modeling.

In the domain of Industry 4.0, several studies concluded ArchiMate to be insufficient, leading them to propose domain-specific extensions. Horstkemper et al. [6] focus on using ArchiMate to model production systems. Their evaluation reveals that existing ArchiMate definitions and elements do not adequately meet the criteria required for Industry 4.0 elements. Similarly, Lara et al. [7] highlight the increasing importance of integrating Operational Technology (OT) with IT in EA in the oil and gas sector, but also argue that ArchiMate's physical layer and newly introduced elements are insufficient for accurately modeling an entire OT architecture. In contrast, Ilin et al. [11] successfully used ArchiMate to create a meta-model for an enterprise implementing Industry 4.0 technologies, showcasing the benefits of EA in analyzing various aspects of company operations.

ArchiMate has been applied in the transportation sector. Ellerm & Morales-Trujillo [3] explore ArchiMate to model security aspects in micromobility. They highlight the similarities between micromobility devices and IoT devices due to embedded systems and connectivity, therefore concluding that micromobility suffers from the same security concerns that IoT faces. Their study reveals that ArchiMate currently lacks the ability to effectively model security, despite the introduction of the Risk and Security Overlay (RSO) extension in 2015. Pittl and Bork [12] focus on the automotive industry and report that ArchiMate's expressiveness is limited when it comes to capturing the specific functionalities of devices, highlighting its high level of abstraction and limitations when used without descriptive labels.

ArchiMate has been used in the agriculture sector, where the IoT technologies have been widely adopted [13]. Chaabouni et al. [14] review ArchiMate for designing an IoT platform for data collection and processing in the agriculture, fishery, and forestry domains. Their evaluation concludes that ArchiMate diagrams were useful to provide adequate documentation, but a balance between the number of models and their complexity was difficult to find.

Another sector in which ArchiMate has been applied is the engineering and infrastructure sector. Antunes et al. [15] derived a proposal based on ontology engineering techniques to specify and integrate the different domains and reasoning and querying as means to analyze the models. This resulted in the conclusion that the core meta-model of ArchiMate lacks expressiveness for capturing the needed information.

Furthermore, two studies focused on analyzing EAs in the aviation industry. Uysal & Sogut [16] use EAs to improve energy efficiency and reduce environmental impact in airports. They created an EA for Energy Management Information Systems (EMIS) which includes IoT devices using ArchiMate. After performing three case studies, they concluded that ArchiMate could represent EA in sustainable airports at a degree of abstraction. Mijuskovic et al. [17] created an EA to understand the organizational impact of combining the usage cloud, fog, and edge computing for an airfield lightning management system (ALMS). Experts evaluated the ArchiMate model positive in supporting researchers and practitioners focusing on exploring approaches and methods to improve sustainability in smart airport solutions.

The previous studies show the importance of ArchiMate in the modelling of IoT systems, however, all the studies surveyed focused on evaluating ArchiMate for a particular application domain but they do not focus on providing guidelines that can be used for the consistent application of ArchiMate for IoT modelling.

3 Modelling Guidelines

ArchiMate is widely adopted in practice and in this regard, it provides a solid foundation for modelling IoT systems. While some authors have proposed domain-specific extensions to capture the intricacies of a particular context, extensions to the standard may increase its complexity, risks for misunderstandings, and tool incompatibility. We focus on evaluating the expressiveness of the standard without any extensions.

The IoT case studies modelled in ArchiMate are analyzed to identify: 1) the IoT elements depicted in such EA and 2) the ArchiMate constructs used to describe such elements. Besides the cases reported in the literature, four models created within the course of "ICT Strategy and Architecture" at KU Leuven for specifying innovative IoT systems for grocery stores were analyzed. Within this course, students learn ArchiMate as described in its specification [18]; these models provide a view on the usage of ArchiMate by novice modelers. After extracting the IoT specific elements used in all the studied models, we completed them by comparing these with the IoT requirements stated in [1, 19, 20]. For example, four student models contained an ArchiMate construct for modelling an IoT device. As such, an IoT device was deemed as an essential part in modelling an IoT system. If then [1, 19, 20] also considered the IoT device as a crucial IoT requirement, it was incorporated as a guideline. Following this process, guidelines 2, 4 and 5 were created. Differently, the IoT requirements mentioned in guidelines 3 and 6 were not used in the case studies, but highlighted as very important by [1, 19, 20]; therefore, we included them in the guidelines as well. Based on the ArchiMate specification by the Open Group, and the usage of ArchiMate in the studied case studies, we defined six guidelines (see Tables 1, 2, 3, 4, 5, and 6) on the use of ArchiMate for modelling the identified IoT elements.

The first element identified is an IoT device, which can be considered as any device connected to the internet that can interconnect the physical world with the digital world. IoT devices differentiate from other regular devices because of their capabilities of monitoring, sensing, and actuating, but also routing, switching, and data processing [19, 21]. Typical IoT devices are sensors or actuators, but also devices that contain those, such as mobile phones, smart fridges, etc. [20].

The following ArchiMate constructs are used to model sensors in the analyzed case studies: equipment, material, device, and node (see Table 1). The Open Group [18], Anthony et al. [10], and Ilin et al. [11] use the equipment construct to model other kind of IoT devices. To further specify which kind of devices, the generalization relationship is used with other equipment elements such as a fitness tracker, home alarm system, etc. Considering that there is no strong majority, the initial guideline will keep the equipment, device, and node elements to describe IoT devices for further evaluation.

In IoT applications, thousands of devices may interact spontaneously and continuously with each other in an ultra-large-scale network [19]. Therefore, it is important to capture the communication channels through which the devices communicate or interact. All the cases modelling this concept used the communication network construct to capture wireless networks. See guidelines in Table 2 for details.

IoT devices communicate in a lot of different ways, therefore the communication protocol must be specified. Protocols are described in [6, 14, 16] with the path element. See guidelines for modeling communication protocols in Table 3.

As the large device and network heterogeneity makes use of and creates an enormous amount of data, these components must be modelled [19]. The passive structure elements in ArchiMate provide specific data objects and artifacts to show the data generated, read, and updated [22]. These elements are used in [8, 16, 17] to show the created data files and databases. The study presented in [9], took a different path and created a data space layer as the domain of e-mobility which uses a lot of online and real-time data. Since these data sources include physical devices, sensors, energy meters, etc., they are modelled as nodes. However, preference is given to the use of artifacts or data objects [18] to model data, while other constructs can be used to model where it is stored or how it is managed. See guidelines in Table 4 for details.

Table 1. Guideline 1 for modelling IoT devices

Guideline 1: IoT devices	
ArchiMate concepts to consider:	Recommendations for modeling:
Equipment represents one or more physical machines, tools, or instruments that can create, use, store, move, or transform materials. [5,7,8,9,10,11] two student cases (2022)	IoT devices describe physical resources connected to the internet that can send and receive data. Typical IoT devices are sensors and actuators, but also resources that contain any combination of those such as smart refrigerators, fitness trackers, mobile phones. A sensor can measure and send data about the physical environment, e.g., temperature, pressure sensor.
Material represents tangible physical matter or energy. [6]	An actuator can change the physical environment, e.g., a switch, a light dimmer, a window blinds motor.
Device represents a physical IT resource upon which system software and artifacts may be stored or deployed for execution. [12, 17] one student case (2022)	The main difference between the types of IoT devices will be their relation to data. While sensors read and send data, actuators modify/write data. When an IoT device needs to be modelled, one of the following constructs should be used:
Node represents a computational or physical resource that hosts, manipulates, or interacts with other computational or physical resources. [15, 16], one student case (2022)	

Since IoT devices generate massive amounts of data, the communication between the sensing devices and the network domain must be managed properly [23]. Therefore, an IoT gateway is one of the most important components of the application using IoTs as it has the functionality of pre-processing data before sending it to the network environment. The studies presented in [9, 11], one group of the students' assignment as well as The Open Group [22] model a gateway with the construct of node. Following the ArchiMate specification, a node should be used for modelling a gateway, see guideline in Table 5.

Table 2. Guideline 2 for modelling communication channels

Guideline 2: Communication channels	
ArchiMate concepts to consider:	Recommendations for modeling:
Communication network *represents a set of structures that connects devices or system software for transmission, routing, and reception of data.* [6,11,12,16,17], all student cases (2022)	The communication channel refers to the link through which data is transmitted between IoT devices or nodes. Communication network Examples: wireless network, internet, local area network

Table 3. Guideline 3 for modelling communication protocols

Guideline 3: Communication protocol	
ArchiMate concepts to consider:	Recommendations for modeling:
Path *Path can be used to represent logical communication relations between two nodes.* [6, 8, 16]	A communication protocol refers to the rules and standards that govern the communication between different devices or systems within an IoT network. Path Examples: IP/ITP, Zigbee, MQTT, XMPP, WIFI, Bluetooth, 5G

Razzaque et al. [19] highlight the importance of location and spatial information about the connected 'things'. When an IoT device is situated in a specific place within a company's facility, this will be modelled as a facility element with an aggregation relationship to the IoT device as The Open Group [22] describes it. The studies presented in [11] and [17] also use the facility construct to indicate the sensors' location. However, when it is on a specific geographical location, the location construct will be used such as in [11] where this construct is used for indicating the environmental location where the technological and production architecture are located. See guideline for modeling locations in Table 6.

Table 4. Guidelines for modelling IoT elements with ArchiMate

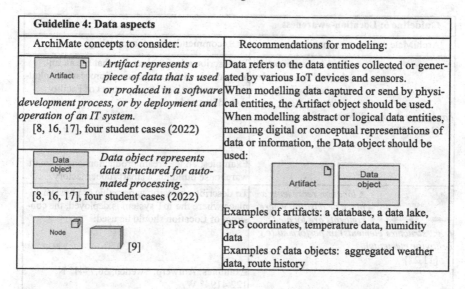

Table 5. Guideline 5 for modelling gateways

Guideline 5: Gateway	
ArchiMate concepts to consider:	Recommendations for modeling:
Node	A gateway refers to a device or software component that acts as a bridge or intermediary between the IoT devices and a central network or the internet.
[9,11], One student case (2022)	Node
	Examples: data acquisition gateway, distributed ledger technology gateway

4   Case-Study Evaluation

A case study-based evaluation is used to validate the presented guidelines following the research methodology practices provided by Runeson et al. [24].

4.1   Design

Four real-world cases of using IoTs from different domains, namely, agriculture, smart buildings, Industry 4.0, and public transportation, are selected to be modelled using ArchiMate. This sufficient variation where four cases investigate the same type of problem. The modelling will assess the feasibility of using the provided guidelines to model the cases and, specifically, their IoT elements. The cases will then be evaluated by both

Table 6. Guidelines for modelling location awareness with ArchiMate

Guideline 6: Location-awareness	
ArchiMate concepts to consider:	Recommendations for modeling:
Facility (diagram) *Facility represents a physical resource that has the capability of facilitating (e.g., housing or locating) the use of equipment.* [11,17,22]	To describe a logical location that has an important role in the execution of processes exploiting IoT technology, the construct of Facility should be used. *Facility* (diagram) Examples: an ice cream production lane, a smart warehouse building, a smart rubber factory.
Location (diagram) *A location represents a place or position where concepts are located (e.g., structure elements) or performed (e.g., behavior elements).* [11,22]	To describe a specific geographic or physical place where the IoT system is deployed, the construct of Location should be used: *Location* (diagram) Examples: Antwerp, Sweden, 36.7741° N; 122.4194° W.

domain experts, who provided the cases but do not necessarily know ArchiMate, and by ArchiMate experts with no prior knowledge of the cases. This limits the effects of using only one interpretation of one single data source [24]. By considering different viewpoints of different roles, or creating several case studies of the same characteristics, it permits us to come to stronger conclusions.

The data collection was in the form of semi-structured interviews with experts. The interviews were divided into several phases [24]. After explaining the objective of the interview, some introductory questions were asked to get insight into background, organization, and knowledge of the respondents. Then the main interview questions were asked. For the domain experts, the questions only applied to their specific case. For the ArchiMate experts the questions applied to all cases. The questions were based on the study of Maes and Poels [25] who developed a model for evaluating the quality of conceptual modelling scripts based on user perceptions based on the following metrics:

- Perceived Ease of Understanding (PEOU): it measures how easy it is to read information and interpret it correctly. We first evaluated the PEOU without giving any information on the language and after explaining the guidelines. We evaluated if the experts could understand these guidelines and if they are sufficient to ensure the consistent modelling of IoT systems.
- Perceived Semantic Quality (PSQ): it measures correctness, completeness, and consistency, and evaluates the quality of the model perceived by the experts.
- Perceived Usefulness (PU) determines whether the model brings improvements to the users' job performance and facilitates communication.
- User Satisfaction (US): it measures how satisfied the experts are on the use of ArchiMate models to represent the information that it needs to capture.

To round up, two concluding questions were asked about the strengths and limitations of ArchiMate for modelling specific IoT cases.

4.2 Results

Five case-owners and three ArchiMate experts were interviewed individually, resulting in eight interviews. Their profiles are summarized in Table 7.

As a representative example, Fig. 1 shows a model of the Belgian train system. When a station visitor enters the station a Bluetooth signal is sent out by a beacon. This is a small IoT device that transmits a signal constantly through Bluetooth which can be seen by other devices such as smartphones or smartwatches. When this signal is noticed by the backend application, the client receives a welcome message when entering the station. As the beacon sends out its signal every 0.5 s, it checks if the message is already sent and if so, the process is not repeated. For a passenger to receive the message, s/he must be logged in to the Wi-Fi network of the station. As the use of the personal location of customers is a very delicate topic regarding privacy issues, the data storage must be modelled properly. The location data is therefore only used for a small amount of time and then deleted.

Table 7. Overview of the participants

Participant	Sector	Function	Knowledge ArchiMate (years)	Knowledge IoT (years)
Expert 1	Industrial environment	Managing Partner	✔ (2)	✔ (7)
Expert 2	Smart building	Chief Technical Officer	✘	✔ (14)
Expert 3	Industry 4.0	Managing Partner - IT	✘	✔ (4)
Expert 4	Industry 4.0	Managing Partner - OT	✘	✔ (3)
Expert 5	Public transportation	Innovation Officer	✘	✔ (8)
Expert A	Integration architecture	Integration architect	✔ (9)	✔
Expert B	Graphical Information System	IT Service Manager	✔ (8)	✔
Expert C	Enterprise architecture	Solution Architect	✔ (12)	✔

As a representative example, Fig. 1 shows a model of the Belgian train system. When a station visitor enters the station a Bluetooth signal is sent out by a beacon. This is a small IoT device that transmits a signal constantly through Bluetooth which can be seen by other devices such as smartphones or smartwatches. When this signal is noticed by the backend application, the client receives a welcome message when entering the station. As the beacon sends out its signal every 0.5 s, it checks if the message is already sent and if so, the process is not repeated. For a passenger to receive the message, s/he must be logged in to the Wi-Fi network of the station. As the use of the personal location of customers is a very delicate topic regarding privacy issues, the data storage must be modelled properly. The location data is therefore only used for a small amount of time and then deleted.

Additionally, the same signal of the beacon is also captured by the smartwatch of train's conductor, which sends the location to the backend application so that the backend knows the train's location. When, consequently, the train's conductor indicates that the situation is safe to leave (i.e., it is the right time, no passengers causing danger, etc.),

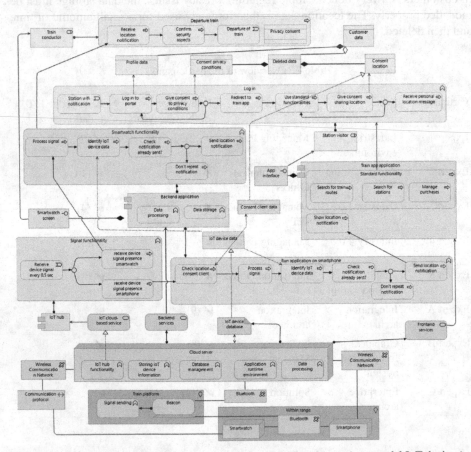

Fig. 1. ArchiMate model for Belgian train system with IoT (using node to model IoT devices).

the train can be cleared to depart. Since the privacy measures in this case are covered through the employer-employee relationship, it is less important for the model.

Perceived Ease of Use (PEOU) – Understandability. The domain experts were not familiar with ArchiMate and therefore did not know what exactly each construct meant, but nevertheless they could understand the models without the need to explain the guidelines. Even though they needed some explanation on the colors used, the domain-experts argued that the fact that they know the case makes it easier to understand the system modelled. However, not having a clear start or end point was perceived as more challenging. In contrast, some domain-experts stated that thanks to the nature of IoT, it is clearer to know where to start. E.g., Expert 1 said: *"We are lucky in the case of IoT platforms because we have a clearer start being the sensors and the end being the dashboard. So, you know where to start and then following the business flow is easier"*.

After the guidelines were introduced, it was clear that both domain-experts and ArchiMate-experts were in favor of the use of such guidelines. Most domain-experts now better understood the ArchiMate constructs used. Besides, they also argued that the use of such guidelines facilitates the use and creation of the models. For the ArchiMate experts (including Expert 1), the guidelines did not change much as they already understood the constructs used and therefore no further explanation was needed. However, all experts agreed that such guidelines were necessary to formulate rules for model understanding and creation so no discussion or misinterpretation can arise. Additionally, a remark supported by all of the experts was that the proposed guidelines captured all relevant elements for modelling IoT systems. With this Expert 3 said: *"I don't immediately see possibilities that are missing. I think with those guidelines you can form everything you need for an IoT architecture."*.

While the name given to a specific ArchiMate construct was considered sufficient for understanding what it modelled, the specific construct used for modelling IoT devices was a discussion point. This inconsistency was already observed in the literature, and again no consensus was reached on how to model this among all experts. However, the distinction between modelling an IoT device that contains other devices; e.g., Expert 5 says: *"It is important to differentiate between a sensor and a device. Because a sensor is going to measure things, while an IoT device is effectively the hardware that is equipped with different sensors, but also configures data."*. The rest of guidelines were considered clear and complete.

Perceived Semantic Quality (PSQ) - Correctness, Completeness, Consistency. Almost all experts were pleased with the level of detail the models provided. Most experts agreed that the models were appropriate for a conceptual description, e.g., to communicate the overall architecture and data flow to business users at the beginning of a project; e.g., Expert 1 said: *"If I take these models and I go to a business user with this and I start going through the flow myself and I do the explanation of what's happening, then he is going to be able to follow it, because he has a nice diagram where he can go through. So, I think there's a very big advantage in that."* Or Expert 4: *"To give a presentation and outline how the data flows through the system, I think the set-up of an overall architecture or data architecture can be very useful."*. However, even though most of them saw the advantages on a bigger level, some things that were relevant in modelling an IoT system were too general. Starting with the communication protocol, it was the aspect which was most criticized. As Expert 3 stated: *"What is particular to an IoT architecture is the difference in communication protocols. If you start putting an abstract layer over that, you do miss a crucial part of the IoT architecture."* Expert C even strongly emphasized that when one wants to model network-specific functionalities (e.g., communication networks or communication protocols) then ArchiMate is not suitable. On the contrary, the interviewees that focused on the conceptual advantages, did not see essential to specify further the specific communication protocol. A similar criticism was stated for the gateways, which were also considered too general by Experts A and C as confusion raised about what kind of a gateway was modelled (e.g., API gateways). However, the inclusion of gateways was considered relevant.

Additionally, ArchiMate lacked in modelling time-based communication such as real-time actions according to Experts 1 and 5 or (a)synchronous communication according to Expert C. Because IoT is sometimes characterized by delivering real-time information, it would be beneficial to include this in the model [24]. In the domain of public transportation, Expert 5 argued that the frequency of events influences the accuracy of data and is therefore very important in this domain: *"A measurement in the morning is different from a measurement in the afternoon"*. Besides, it also impacts the infrastructure of the cloud servers in terms of processing capacity. Expert 1 also addressed the lack of not showing the real-time communication aspect as it has a significant impact on how the flows are executed, but nuances that it does not really matter for a conceptual level model. Based on the ArchiMate-expert's opinion, it would be better to be able to show the (a)synchronous communication in terms of IoT systems. However, they also added that this would only be needed at a level with more technical details, as this would cause an increase in relationships and arrows, and consequently, an increase in the complexity of the models.

Another drawback of ArchiMate arose in the case of industrial IoT whereas the importance of modelling redundancy was addressed by Expert 3: *"the architecture must show that once a failure in a node is detected, another will become operational, so no information or data losses occur."*. However, he did emphasize that this drawback might be specific to industrial IoTs and could be handled at a more technical level.

Even though there were some distinct opinions among the abstraction level towards specific IoT characteristics, ArchiMate experts agreed that different viewpoints could be used. To this end, the modeler can go into more detail on specific aspects of the architecture and only show the relevant parts for those who need specific information. As Expert C explains it: *"You start from a helicopter view which is the overview, and then you go deeper into specific parts. This way, you give the person context, and they can follow depending on the type of person they are"*.

Perceived Usefulness (PU) – Usability. Most experts agreed that the use of ArchiMate and the guidelines described were useful to describe their cases. They said it improved the understanding of the cases and provided a significant improvement to textual descriptions. They also indicated that the guidelines were helpful for modelling and understanding the business cases in a consistent manner.

Some experts indicated that different modelling languages could be used to complement ArchiMate for adding details on some aspects. In this regard, BPMN was the most used for modelling functional flows by business analysts which included modelling different states and actions and thus flowcharts (Experts 1, A and C). Whereas the UML was more suitable for modelling more technical aspects such as an ERD for developers or generating code directly (Experts 1, 3 and C).

User Satisfaction (US) – Effectiveness. Most experts expressed that the ArchiMate models fulfilled their expectations and delivered a lot of possibilities toward communicating with clients, creating an overall view, and the possibility of integrating all different layers of an enterprise into one model.

Table 8 summarizes the results of the interview according to the measured metrics.

Table 8. Interview outcomes

	Expert 1	Expert 2	Expert 3	Expert 4	Expert 5	Expert A	ExExpert B	Expert C
Perceived Ease Of Use (PEOU) - Understandability								
Understandability before explaining guidelines								
General flow	✔	✗	✔	✔	✔	✔	✔	✔
Used elements	✗	✗	✗	✗	✗	✔	✔	✔
Use of colors	✔	✗	✗	✗	✗	✔	✔	✔
Starting point	✔	–	✗	✗	✗	✔	✔	✔
Names used	✔	✔	✔	✔	✔	✔	✔	✔
Guidelines explanation								
Covers all relevant IoT concepts	✔	✔	✔	✔	✔	✔	✔	✔
In favor of guidelines	✔	✗	✔	✔	✔	✔	✔	✔
IoT device options								
Equipment	✔	✔		✔		✔	✔	
Device	✔		✔		✔			
Node	✔							
Perceived Semantic Quality (PSQ) - Correctness, completeness & consistency								
Abstraction level								
General	CL	✗	TL	CL	CL	CL	CL	CL
Communication protocol	✔	✗	✗	✔	✔	✔	✔	✗

(continued)

Table 8. (*continued*)

	Expert 1	Expert 2	Expert 3	Expert 4	Expert 5	Expert A	ExExpert B	Expert C
Time-based communication	✘	–	–	–	✘	–	–	✘
Redundancy	–	–	✘	–	–	–	–	–
Perceived Usefulness (PU) - Usability								
Improves performance?	✔	✘	✔	✔	✔	–	✔	–
Better than textual description?	✔	✘	✔	✔	✔	–	✔	–
Complementarity with other languages?	✔	–	✔	✔	✔	✔	✔	✔
User satisfaction (US) - Effectiveness								
Effective?	✔	✘	✔ With limitations	✔	✔ With limitations	✔	✔	✔

Legend: ✔: Yes, ✘: No, - not relevant // CL: Conceptual Level, TL: Technical Level

5 Discussion

Overall, most domain-experts were pleased with the models created and the proposed guidelines. They saw opportunities in using ArchiMate for modelling their IoT systems at conceptual level. In addition, ArchiMate experts highlighted the possibility to exploit ArchiMate viewpoints as a strength of the language that would allow exploring more details for certain aspects of the design. This could positively contribute to the use of ArchiMate in explaining the business cases and the system design to different audiences. The models created can be used for communication even with domain experts who are not trained in ArchiMate. This is often done so in practice when there is no time or need to train stakeholders in the method used, and the models are primarily used to communicate design options on a conceptual level.

Most experts highlighted the utility of the guidelines to avoid misunderstandings in the use of ArchiMate and to have a common shared understanding of the models. All guidelines for which there was a unique modelling choice were considered appropriate. For Guideline 1, on how to model IoT devices, no agreement was reached by the experts. According to the ArchiMate specification, Equipment, although used frequently, may not be correct as an IoT device does not process materials. A possible source for the confusion might be the Equipment symbol, which could also be understood as data processing, or because IoT devices may be considered to process signals. Our assumption motivating the guideline is that data transfer and processing are the main function of IoT devices with regard to a digital system, and as such, we argue that Node or Device are the most suitable constructs to be used. We recommend using Node when the resource contains different physical devices (e.g., a weather station), or it is important to represent in the architecture the software (system software) or behavior for which the Node is responsible. Otherwise, if representing the physical resource is enough, then we recommend using Device for simplification. For example, a weather station would be modelled as a node, containing different devices, each representing one of the sensors installed in the weather station, such as humidity or temperature sensor.

Based on the abstraction level of ArchiMate, contradictory answers were given by both domain experts and ArchiMate experts on communication protocols and gateways, considered crucial parts of an IoT system. Expert C declared that ArchiMate is not suitable for modelling these network functionalities, however, others were pleased with the level of detail given (Experts 1, 4, 5, A, and B). If more details are desired in a conceptual model, we suggest addressing this by using detailed and appropriate names containing the name of the protocol or the type of gateway. Even though this can be domain specific (e.g., Industry 4.0, public transportation), commonalities between sectors are present, and therefore the way to address these ArchiMate constructs must also follow the proposed guidelines to eliminate inconsistencies.

If more details are necessary at a conceptual level, other complementary languages such as UML or BPMN could be used. However, in specific domains such as Industry 4.0, where the modelling of technical aspects of OT are of high importance to IT, the conceptual design and technical design converge in many ways. In such cases, ArchiMate would be less useful in discussing implementation or technical choices and alternative modelling languages should be used. Additionally, other IoT characteristics, such as time-based communication or data redundancy were considered to be too technical to show in an ArchiMate model but are considered important by a few experts for a more technical view.

6 Conclusions and Future Work

This paper has proposed a set of guidelines for systematically using ArchiMate to model IoT systems. The case studies showed that these guidelines were sufficient and were considered essential for creating an enterprise architecture that used IoT.

The strengths of using ArchiMate to model IoT systems included its ability to provide an overall view of an enterprise architecture, to facilitate communication among stakeholders, and to show the operation of the system at conceptual level. The level of abstraction in ArchiMate was found to be suitable for high-level models of IoT systems but insufficient for deeper levels of detail. The use of domain-specific modeling languages for capturing IoT characteristics was suggested as a potential solution to address these limitations.

In conclusion, ArchiMate was deemed suitable for modeling IoT systems at conceptual level and the guidelines provided a consistent approach for this purpose. Nevertheless, specific extensions might be required if more technical details need to be modelled, like how real-time communication is addressed or the use of backup devices for redundancy.

Future research could involve evaluating ArchiMate with a larger number of experts, comparing the proposed guidelines with other solutions in an empirical setting, and investigating complementarity of using ArchiMate and the proposed guidelines together with other modeling approaches. More specifically, the latter would address the gap existing in in some of the current approaches that aim to support context dependance of enterprise designs. For example, [26] presents a proposal of capability-based configuration of digital twins based on context data coming mostly from IoTs. In similar fashion, [27] presents a context-based ontology for monitoring IoTs. Both approaches consider context data coming from IoTs but they do not go into details of the solution architecture and hence they would benefit from a complementary use of the proposed guidelines.

Acknowledgments. This work was supported by the Flemish Fund for Scientific Research (FWO), Belgium with grant number G0B6922N.

References

1. Compagnucci, I., Corradini, F., Fornari, F., Polini, A., Re, B., Tiezzi, F.: Modelling notations for IoT-aware business processes: a systematic literature review. In: Del Río Ortega, A., Leopold, H., Santoro, F.M. (eds.) BPM 2020. LNBIP, vol. 397, pp. 108–121. Springer, Cham (2020). https://doi.org/10.1007/978-3-030-66498-5_9
2. Meyer, S., Ruppen, A., Magerkurth, C.: Internet of things-aware process modeling: integrating IoT devices as business process resources. In: Salinesi, C., Norrie, M.C., Pastor, Ó. (eds.) CAiSE. LNCS, vol. 7908, pp. 84–98. Springer, Heidelberg (2013). https://doi.org/10.1007/978-3-642-38709-8_6
3. Ellerm, A., Morales-Trujillo, M.E.: Modelling security aspects with ArchiMate: a systematic mapping study. In: SEAA, pp. 577–584 (2020)
4. Anwar, J.M., Gill, Q.A.: A review of the seven modelling approaches for digital ecosystem architecture. In: CBI, pp. 94–103 (2019)
5. Bastidas, V., Reychac, I., Ofir, A., Bezbradica, M., Helfert, M.: Concepts for modeling smart cities: an archiMate extension. Bus. Inf. Syst. Eng. **64**, 359–373 (2021)
6. Horstkemper, D., Stahmann, P., Hellingrath, B.: Assessing the suitability of ArchiMate to model Industry 4.0 production systems. In: IIAI-AAI, pp. 827–832 (2019)
7. Lara, P., Sánchez, M., Villalobos, J.: OT modeling: the enterprise beyond IT. Bus. Inf. Syst. Eng. **61**, 399–411 (2019)
8. Berkel, A.R.R., Singh, P.M., van Sinderen, M.J.: An information security architecture for smart cities. In: BMSD, pp. 167–184 (2018)
9. Anthony, B., Petersen, S.A.: A practice based exploration on electric mobility as a service in smart cities. In: Themistocleous, M., Papadaki, M. (eds.) EMCIS 2019. LNBIP, vol. 381, pp. 3–17. Springer, Cham (2020). https://doi.org/10.1007/978-3-030-44322-1_1
10. Anthony, B.J., Petersen, S.A., Ahlers, D., Krogstie, J., Livik, K.: Big data-oriented energy prosumption service in smart community districts: a multi-case study perspective. Energy Inform. **2**, 36 (2019)
11. Ilin, I., Levina, A., Borremans, A., Kalyazina, S.: Enterprsie architecture modeling in digital transformation era. In: EMMFT 2019, pp. 124–142 (2020)
12. Pittl, B., Bork, D.: Modeling digital enterprise ecosystems with ArchiMate: a mobility provision case study. In: Hara, Y., Karagiannis, D. (eds.) Serviceology for Services. ICServ 2017. LNCS, vol. 10371, pp. 178–189. Springer, Cham (2017). https://doi.org/10.1007/978-3-319-61240-9_17
13. Ruan, J., et al.: Agriculture IoT: emerging trends, cooperation networks, and outlook. IEEE Wirel. Commun. **26**(6), 56–63 (2019)

14. Chaabouni, K., Bagnato, A., Garcia-Dominguez, A.: Monitoring ArchiMate models for DataBio project. In: Franch, X., Männistö, T., Martínez-Fernández, S. (eds.) PROFES 2019. LNCS, vol. 11915, pp. 583–589. Springer, Cham (2019). https://doi.org/10.1007/978-3-030-35333-9_42

15. Antunes, G., Bakhshandeh, M., Mayer, R., Borbinha, J., Caetano, A.: Using ontologies for enterprise architecture integration and analysis. CSIMQ 1, 1–23 (2014)

16. Uysal, M.P., Sogut, M.Z.: An integrated research for architecture-based energy management in sustainable airports. Energy 140(2), 1387–1397 (2017)

17. Mijuskovic, A., Bemthuis, R., Aldea, A., Havinga, P.: An enterprise architecture based on cloud, fog and edge computing for an airfield lightning management system. In: EDOCW (2020)

18. The Open Group: ArchiMate 3.2 Specification (s.d.). https://pubs.opengroup.org/architecture/archimate32-doc/#_Ref209337956. Accessed 16 Mar 2023

19. Razzaque, M.A., Milojevic-Jevric, M., Palade, A., Siobhan, P.: Middelware for Internet of Things. IEEE Internet Things J. 3(1), 70–95 (2016)

20. Torres, V., Serral, E., Valderas, P., Pelechano, V., Grefen, P.: Modeling of IoT devices in business processes: a systematic mapping study. In: CBI, vol. 1, pp. 221–230 (2020)

21. Meyer, S., Sperner, K., Magerkurth, C., & Pasquier, J.: Towards modeling real-world aware business processes. In: ACM Digital Library, no. 8, pp. 1–6 (2011)

22. The Open Group: ArchiMate 3.0 in Practice (Part 4 The Internet of Things). [Youtube], 27 June 2016. Retrieved on 16th of March 2023 from, ArchiMate® 3.0 in Practice (Part 4 The Internet of Things)

23. Chen, H., Jia, H., Li, H.: A brief introduction to IoT gateway. In: ICCTA 2011, pp. 610–613 (2011)

24. Runeson, P., Höst, M., Rainer, A., Regnell, B.: Case Study Research in Software Engineering. Wiley Publications, Hoboken (2012)

25. Maes, A., Poels, G.: Evaluating quality of conceptual models based on user perceptions. In: Embley, D.W., Olivé, A., Ram, S. (eds.) Conceptual Modeling - ER 2006. LNCS, vol. 4215, pp. 54–67. Springer, Heidelberg (2006). https://doi.org/10.1007/11901181_6

26. Sandkuhl, K., Stirna, J.: Supporting early phases of digital twin development with enterprise modeling and capability management: requirements from two industrial cases. In: Nurcan, S., Reinhartz-Berger, I., Soffer, P., Zdravkovic, J. (eds.) BPMDS/EMMSAD -2020. LNBIP, vol. 387, pp. 284–299. Springer, Cham (2020). https://doi.org/10.1007/978-3-030-49418-6_19

27. Vila, M., Sancho, MR., Teniente, E.: Modeling context-aware events and responses in an IoT environment. In: Indulska, M., Reinhartz-Berger, I., Cetina, C., Pastor, O. (eds.) Advanced Information Systems Engineering - CAiSE 2023. LNCS, vol. 13901, pp. 71–87. Springer, Cham (2023). https://doi.org/10.1007/978-3-031-34560-9_5

A Domain-Specific e³value Extension for Analyzing Blockchain-Based Value Networks

Simon Curty[✉][iD] and Hans-Georg Fill[iD]

University of Fribourg, Digitalization and Information Systems Group, Bd de Pérolles
90, 1700 Fribourg, Switzerland
{simon.curty,hans-georg.fill}@unifr.ch
https://www.unifr.ch/inf/digits/en/

Abstract. Adopting blockchain technologies in organizations has multiple implications for business models. To make adoption successful, both the business as well as the technical perspectives must be carefully aligned. However, understanding the impact of the technological changes on business models is a challenge due to the technological complexity, the lack of knowledge in the organization, and regulatory requirements. Further, domain-specific modeling methods that inherently deal with blockchain concepts in business models are currently missing. To address this gap, we present an extension of the *e³value* modeling method to depict blockchain-specific aspects in value networks, including the automatic inference of transparency based on blockchain usage and configuration. The extended modeling method was implemented on the ADOxx metamodeling platform and applied to three exemplary use cases for a first evaluation.

Keywords: Blockchain · Business model · Enterprise modeling · e³value · Value network

1 Introduction

In recent years, major advances have been made in distributed ledger technologies (DLT), commonly known as blockchains. Improvements, e.g., in transaction volumes and energy efficiency give rise to a potential wider adoption [8,30]. The intrinsic qualities of this novel family of technologies, such as decentralized and tamper-proof storage [11], promise opportunities for the digital transformation of businesses and enable new business cases. However, the successful adoption and integration of blockchain technology in an enterprise in real-world scenarios remains challenging. This is on one hand due to: a. the complexity and the comparatively low maturity of the technological ecosystem [13], as is evident by the few standards that have been established so far, and b. by raising concerns, e.g.,

This research was partially funded by the Swiss National Science Foundation [196889].

J. P. A. Almeida et al. (Eds.): PoEM 2023, LNBIP 497, pp. 74–90, 2024.
https://doi.org/10.1007/978-3-031-48583-1_5

regarding interoperability with existing IT systems or cross-blockchain operations. On the other hand, organizational barriers such as the involvement of regulatory requirements, the availability of financial and human resources, and insufficient knowledge about the technology in the organization requiring the development of new skills and competencies may prevent adoption in practice [2]. A major challenge in designing and realizing a business model that reverts to some blockchain-based system is to deal with the complexity in aligning institutional, market, and technology factors [24]. This includes for example leveraging the unique properties in the business model, the positioning on the market, and the implementation and engineering challenges specific to this technology [26].

Techniques and methods incorporating concepts dedicated to blockchains help to address these business challenges. However, such approaches have not been explored extensively. Modeling support for the design and analysis of blockchain business models is comparatively sparse [6]. For this reason, we propose a domain-specific extension of the e³value method for supporting the design of blockchain-based business models. Thereby, an emphasis lies on the increased transparency of blockchain-based applications and the analysis of its propagation through value networks. We consider the transparency of records as one of the most desirable properties of blockchains from a business perspective. On a more general level, transparency is an economic measure to alleviate the information asymmetry between parties, ensuring that no side may have a potentially unfair advantage due to the availability of information [22]. For example, transparency of information may be offered as value proposition to customers and partners (e.g., [3]) or to facilitate trust between parties enabling collaborative efforts (e.g., [21]). For reducing undesirable effects of asymmetric information, blockchains have been proposed previously, e.g., in the context of bank credits [36], and commodity markets [28].

The remainder of this paper is structured as follows. In Sect. 2 we will introduce foundations on blockchains and blockchain-based systems, and related work regarding business models and the design of blockchain-based business models in particular. In Sect. 3 we will present a domain-specific extension of the e³value modeling method to support the design of blockchain-based business models, which will be applied to exemplary use cases in Sect. 4. The paper will conclude with a discussion of the approach in Sect. 5 and an outlook to further research in Sect. 6.

2   Foundations and Related Work

In the following we present brief foundations on blockchain technologies that are necessary for our approach, the representation of business models, and outline prior work on domain-specific languages for blockchain-based business models.

2.1   Blockchain

Blockchain-based applications rely on distributed ledger technologies (DLT), which store transactions between authorized parties in a decentralized, distributed, immutable and trustful way [12]. This is achieved through so-called consensus algorithms that guarantee the validity of transactions. Further, so-called *smart contracts* may be added to transactions in some blockchains for the decentralized execution of algorithms [1]. The access to the ledger may either be restricted to certain parties (*permissioned blockchain*) or it may be openly accessible (*public blockchain*).

According to the recent ISO standard 23635 on Blockchain Governance, blockchain-based applications should follow several principles for ensuring the effective, efficient, and acceptable use of DLT systems [23]. These include for example the support of *openness and transparency* so that stakeholders can observe and audit the dynamics of the system, the *alignment of incentive mechanisms* with the used consensus algorithms and the application's objectives, the provision of *security mechanisms* and the consideration of *privacy impacts and compliance obligations*, or requirements regarding the *interoperability* with other DLT or non-DLT systems.

2.2 Representation of Business Models

The concept of a business model is today commonly regarded as an integrated view on the organization of an enterprise for contributing to the successful management in the decision-making process [38]. It includes information about the interplay of an organization's strategy, resources, customers, market offerings, and revenues, as well as underlying processes and services. For dealing with the complexity of these aspects, various approaches have been proposed. These include formal and semi-formal representations as found in enterprise modeling methods such as 4EM [34], MEMO [15], ArchiMate [20], or SOM [9] as well as specialized approaches such as e^{3}value [18] or the business model canvas (BMC) [31], which is a popular but only graphical way of representing and analyzing these aspects that can however be transitioned to a semi-formal representation as well [37]. Whereas enterprise modeling approaches take a holistic perspective on business and IT aspects, e^{3}value or the BMC focus on the exchange of value between actors. Thereby, e^{3}value is a language and set of techniques for representing and analyzing value networks, i.e., who exchanges what kind of value with whom and what expenses and revenues are created for each actor [18].

2.3 Languages for Blockchain-Based Business Models

Although domain-specific languages and extensions of existing languages for the modeling of blockchain-based business models is a sparsely researched topic [6], several business ontologies and modeling methods have been proposed. In the following we present a selection of these works focusing on organizational and enterprise modeling, and the representation of business models. For a comprehensive overview of modeling methods in the context of DLT, we refer readers to a recent literature survey [6].

An approach to overcome the challenges of integration and adoption of DLT on the organizational level is to revert to enterprise and business ontologies. The Resource-Event-Agent model [29] describes a general business ontology about the relationships of economic concepts. In combination with DEMO, a methodology for enterprise modeling, de Kruijff et al. described a domain ontology for blockchains as a common terminology for business and technical actors alike [7]. Another ontological approach has been presented by Kim et al., where the Toronto Virtual Enterprise Ontology was extended with concepts for provenance tracking in supply chains [27]. Such ontologies may then for example be used as foundation for the design of smart contracts.

Further approaches can be found in the field of Enterprise Architecture for depicting the integration of DLT into the IT architecture or for representing views on the organization in relation to DLT concepts. Jiang and Ræder used a combination of ArchiMate strategy and motivation models for modeling value chains built on blockchain technology [25]. Another approach based on ArchiMate includes a holistic top-down methodology for the design of blockchain-based applications that reverts to ArchiMate's core layers (*business, application, technology*) [3]. Thereby, business models are first explored by drafting a business model canvas [31] and process models. The business model is then reflected on the business layer of the integrated ArchiMate model created subsequently. The alignment of a blockchain business model and the underlying software and IT infrastructure was discussed in [5], where an NFT use case was modeled with ArchiMate.

In the context of blockchain, e³value concepts have been mapped to Solidity code constructs with the aim to generate blueprints for services [16]. In contrast, Poels et al. [33] apply e³value to analyze the viability of DLT business cases. They propose a model pattern to identify business cases where the implementation of DLT could be beneficial. An extension of e³value for blockchain business models was described by [32]. In particular, this work introduces decentralized autonomous organizations as model element and various DLT-related attributes to existing elements. Interactive analysis and the visualization of blockchain value networks regarding transparency and privacy are not considered. Our work is based on the implementation of this extension. However, the design goals and conceptualizations differ substantially.

In summary, the representation of blockchain-based business models is not a well-explored topic. Graphical modeling languages and tools for modeling support are in need as to facilitate the understanding of DLT on organizations. In particular, methods for interactive analysis of transparency, data privacy issues, and system interactions in blockchain-based business models are amiss. Rather than creating a standalone domain-specific language to address these issues, we propose a domain-specific extension to the well-known e³value method.

3   Extending e³value for Blockchain-Based Applications

E³value is a modeling methodology for representing and analyzing electronic business models based on an ontology for supporting the development of ecommerce systems [17]. A business model is seen as a set of actors exchanging value to increase their economic utility, thereby forming a so-called *value network*. In the following, the core concepts of e³value are briefly summarized [18]. Figure 1 shows the basic graphical notation of the modeling elements.

Actors are independent entities that hold the responsibility to ensure their own survival, well-being, and success—the definition of which varies for individual actors.

Value objects are things of value, that is, something valuable to at least one actor. Such an object can be of any nature, e.g., a physical product, a service, currencies, an experience, etc.

Market segments present groups of actors who individually have the same notion on the value of a value object.

Partnerships (or composite actors) are collaborations in which actors cooperate with the goal to offer some value to other actors or market segments.

Value activities are performed by actors to increase utility, generate profit, or advance their mission.

Value ports represent the intent to offer or accept a value object. Value ports are either incoming or outgoing.

Value interfaces group together ports to define atomic value exchanges. Actors, market segments, and value activities may have value interfaces, indicating willingness to exchange the specified value objects. A value interface has at least one outgoing and one incoming port.

Value transfers (or value exchanges) connect an outgoing value port to an incoming one, representing transfers of value objects between the two ports.

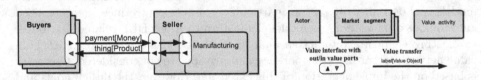

Fig. 1. Standard graphical notation of e³value showing a sample model on the left and the graphical notation on the right.

For the development of a domain-specific extension of e³value to support the design of blockchain-based applications we revert to the *macro process* by Frank [14]. This process consists of seven cyclic phases (*micro processes*), providing guidelines for designing a domain-specific modeling language as summarized in the following:

1. *Clarification of scope and purpose*: extension of the e³value method to support the design and analysis of value networks involving blockchain-based software components.

2. *Analysis of generic requirements*, i.e., requirements that apply to every DSML. We consider the generic requirements of the catalog outlined by Frank [14]. Since our contribution is an extension of an existing modeling language, and for the sake of brevity we omit a discussion on the generic requirements.
3. *Analysis of specific requirements*, i.e., requirements that apply to the artifact in particular. We will present these in Sect. 3.1.
4. *Language specification*, in particular specification of the metamodel and constraints: The metamodel and related inference mechanisms will be presented in Sect. 3.2.
5. *Design and documentation of graphical notation*: The graphical notation of the extensions will be shown in Sect. 3.3.
6. *Development of modeling tool*: The implementation is discussed in Sect. 3.4.
7. *Evaluation and refinement*: The extensions were evaluated and continuously refined throughout the development against the requirements. In Sect. 4 we show the feasibility of the extension for modeling blockchain value networks by means of three exemplary use cases.

3.1 Requirements

At first, we derived seven specific requirements ($\mathbf{SR}_{1-7}$) for the extension on the basis of use scenarios. This includes tasks for which the method should be applicable, as well as descriptions of use cases that the models should capture. The fundamental use case is based on the intended application of e^3value, namely the modeling of value networks as part of a business model. We extend this with analysis tasks regarding blockchain specific properties and their impact on the value network. More specifically, we were interested in depicting the *diffusion of transparency of transactions* in a blockchain network. To refine and analyze collected requirements, mock diagrams were created. This allows for example to clarify visualization and usability concerns. The specific requirements were:

- $\mathbf{SR}_1$: The core semantics of e^3value elements should not be altered fundamentally. Users familiar with e^3value should find the extension to be straightforward in its use of core elements.
- $\mathbf{SR}_2$: A central benefit of e^3value is the comparatively low number of elements. Thus, only a minimal set of elements and attributes should be added.
  $\mathbf{SR}_3$. The modeling concepts should be technology-agnostic, i.e., the domain-specific extensions should be applicable to various blockchain technologies.
- $\mathbf{SR}_4$: Concepts should be provided for specific distributed ledger constructs such as smart contracts, oracles, and decentralized autonomous organizations (DAO) as most DLT use cases involve some of these constructs.
- $\mathbf{SR}_5$: Concepts for blockchain networks, sub-networks, and access control should be provided as access restrictions on the network level determine who can inspect or modify the ledger (public/permissioned ledgers). Networks may be segmented to allow for more fine-grained access control, e.g., to form complex consortia in permissioned blockchains.

- **SR$_6$**: The user should be provided with mechanisms to analyze what value transfers are transparent to which parties through an automatic inference of transparency across the value network – see the aforementioned ISO standard [23]. That is, a value transfer is transparent to a party (actor, market segment, partnership) when information on the occurrence of the transfer is visible to a party upon inspection.
- **SR$_7$**: Transparent transfers on a blockchain involving some sensitive information render a business model non-viable without the necessary precautions as also mentioned in ISO 23635 [23]. Thus, modeling support should be provided for detecting the exchange of sensitive information in a blockchain-based business model.

3.2   Metamodel

The collected requirements formed the basis for the specification of the language metamodel. For this, we reverted to the original e^{3}value metamodel as published in the user guide [18] and extended it with DLT-specific concepts as follows (see Fig. 2):

- **MM$_1$**: The concepts *smart contract, oracle* and *DAO* are represented as types of the *Actor* class (**SR$_4$**). This design choice prevented the change of the e^{3}value actor concept and rather extended it to preserve its original semantics (**SR$_1$**). Further, this allows to form partnerships of DLT actors, and subsequently capture the structure of DAOs in detail.
- **MM$_2$**: A class dedicated to representing the concept of a blockchain network is introduced. Further, we defined two access modes, *public*, for networks without any access restrictions, and *permissioned*, for networks where such restrictions are in place in some form (**SR$_5$**).
- **MM$_3$**: Two super-classes have been added to allow for elements to be aware of partaking networks. Notably, aggregations are introduced for grouping elements, e.g., a network groups actors.
- **MM$_4$**: The relation *part of* specifies the participation of an element in some network. Similarly, the *carrier* relation denotes that a value transfer is carried out over the related network (**SR$_6$**).
- **MM$_5$**: Value transfers have been extended with three additional attributes: The attribute *Sensitive* denotes that the transfer involves information that should not be disclosed to some or all parties (**SR$_7$**). *Off-chain* explicitly denotes that the transfer is not carried out over a network, whether or not the source and target would suggest otherwise. Finally, *Override Network* allows to manually specify the carrier network. This is of use in complex modeling scenarios, or when the automatic selection of a carrier network is ambiguous due to modeling restrictions.

Deciding on the carrier network is the main concern for analyzing the transparency of value transfers (**SR$_6$**), as this property directly depends on the access mode of the network. Actors with access to a network can inspect the ledger and all recorded blockchain transactions. The ledger of a public network is accessible to everyone, whether or not the actor directly participates in the network, e.g., by operating a node. Participation in a network is expressed with the *part of* relation. Consuming a business service hosted by a public network does not require participation. Consequently, value transfers carried out by a public network are transparent, but this property does not propagate beyond the first value interface of an actor or market segment outside of a network.

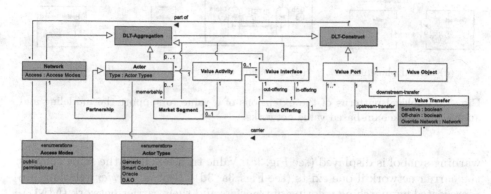

Fig. 2. Extensions of the simplified metamodel of e³value. The colored classes and attributes have been added. Attributes of e³value are omitted.

In a permissioned network, the ledger is accessible only to authorized parties. As such, a transparent value transfer requires the outgoing and receiving value interfaces to be in the same (permissioned) network. Propagating the transparency property beyond the network boundary is impossible in this case. In case multiple networks qualify as carrier, the network lowest in the hierarchy is selected, e.g., a sub-network.

3.3 Graphical Extensions and Modeling Patterns

Of all concepts introduced by the proposed extension, only the *Network* class requires a new dedicated modeling element ($SR_{2,5}$). A network is thereby simply represented as a rectangle, aggregating contained elements. A network's access mode is signified by a variation of the rectangle's border style. Figure 3a illustrates the basic transfer patterns between actors (MM_2). The notation of existing elements corresponds to the examples shown in the e³value user guide [18]. Each participation of an actor in some (sub-)network is expressed by a circular badge in the same color as the related network (MM_4). An icon is displayed that corresponds to the actor's type (see 3b). The individual actor types are depicted in Fig. 3b, where a DAO is a partnership of a smart contract and an oracle (MM_1). The color of the icon relates to the main network, e.g., the network in which a smart contract is deployed. It is impossible for DLT entities to exist outside of a network. To make modelers aware of such an invalid placement, a

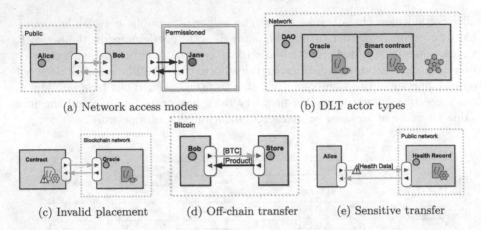

(a) Network access modes   (b) DLT actor types

(c) Invalid placement   (d) Off-chain transfer   (e) Sensitive transfer

Fig. 3. Graphical patterns of the extensions of e^3value to support the modeling and analysis of blockchain-based value networks.

warning symbol is displayed (see Fig. 3c). Value transfers have the same color as the carrier network if one exists (see Figs. 3a, 3d). That is, *carrier* relations are represented by matching coloring of transfers and their carrier network (MM_4). Value transfers that are *off-chain* ignore this coloring rule (see Fig. 3d). If a value transfer is *sensitive* and transparent to all (SR_7), i.e., carried out over a public network, the transfer is decorated with a warning symbol (see Fig. 3c). Thereby, the transfer patterns shown in Figs. 3d and 3e correspond to the metamodel extension (MM_5). Combining these features results in the five basic graphical patterns of the transfer properties and actor types, shown in Fig. 3. These patterns commonly occur in blockchain-based business models. That is, models are a combination of these basic patterns.

3.4 Implementation

The e^3value language with the extension has been prototypically implemented using the ADOxx metamodeling platform [10]. ADOxx was chosen for its maturity, acceptance in academia and industry, and suitability for prototyping modeling methods. Further, the implementation is based on an existing e^3value library for modeling blockchain-inspired businesses [32]. Elements containing others are realized as ADOxx aggregations, notably actors, networks and market segments. Thereby, a binary *is inside* relation is automatically derived for visually contained elements. As such, the *part of* relation (see Sect. 3.2) needs no special implementation. The *carrier* relation between a value transfer and a network is established by an ADOxx expression attribute on the value transfer relation, which computes at run-time the information required for the display of the graphical patterns. Actor types, access modes and some visual parameters, e.g., the color of networks, are implemented as user modifiable attributes on their respective elements. The modeling library for ADOxx is openly available [4].

4   Exemplary Use Cases

In accordance with the *macro process*, the extension was continuously evaluated. Among other measures, the continuous analysis of use cases contributed to refining the method. By means of three fictitious use cases that are inspired by previous, informal discussions with industry experts, we present the application of the extension for designing and analyzing blockchain-based business models.

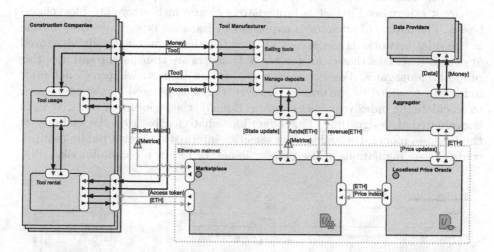

Fig. 4. Value network of a tool rental service realized as decentralized marketplace. The tool supplier operates the marketplace as a smart contract on the public blockchain of the Ethereum mainnet. The pricing model is supported by an oracle service that provides up-to-date regional pricing data.

4.1   Decentralized Marketplace for Tool Rental

A supplier of construction tools explores options for a tool rental marketplace for professionals. This use case is inspired by existing tools-on-demand programs[1]. In the scenario shown in Fig. 4, the marketplace is realized by a smart contract on the public Ethereum mainnet[2] blockchain, thereby leveraging an existing, highly available and durable infrastructure. The marketplace contract contains a registry of all tools for rental. Construction companies may acquire a personal token for retrieving a tool by paying some amount of Ether (ETH), which is the cryptocurrency of Ethereum. The contract supports regionally adjusted pricing. This is achieved by fetching a regional price index for this product category through an oracle. The tool may then be fetched with the access token from a

---

[1] See for example the one by Hilti: https://www.hilti.com/content/hilti/W1/US/en/business/business/equipment/fleet/tools-on-demand.html.

[2] https://ethereum.org.

deposit operated in the region of the manufacturer. Further, the tools function as smart devices, i.e., collecting data and metrics. These are used for analysis purposes, e.g., for development or predictive maintenance. In this scenario, the metrics are collected through the smart contract so that no central server must be operated. Apart from technical issues, this is problematic as the metrics contain personal information of the customer. As such, the related value transfers have been marked as sensitive and a warning sign is shown.

In this modeling scenario, the extension offers insights that would not be apparent otherwise: First, it is immediately clear which actors are blockchain-based. The nature of an actor is expressed by its actor type, indicating its role in the value network. Transparency of value transfers is automatically visualized at design time. It is thus clear, for whom transfers are transparent and how this property propagates. For example, everyone can inspect, what regional price index was provided by the oracle. However, the data set used by the aggregator to calculate the index remains unknown. Equally, the exposure of sensitive data is evaluated at design time. This offers immediate feedback on the viability of the business model: transmission of sensitive information over a public network could violate regulations, cause privacy issues, or result in economic risks.

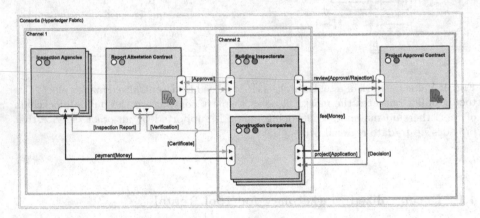

Fig. 5. Value network of a consortium for the construction project proposals and management of inspection reports using two channels.

4.2   Building Inspectorate Consortium

The building inspectorate, a government agency, wishes to modernize their IT systems for approving construction project proposals and submitting building inspection reports. This use case is inspired by a real-world application of blockchain in construction planning [35]. Regulations demand that these systems be kept separate. Construction companies, external inspection agencies and the building inspectorate form a consortium connected through a permissioned blockchain using the Hyperledger Fabric platform as shown in Fig. 5. The two services are operated as smart contracts in dedicated sub-networks, i.e., so-called channels in Hyperledger, which only authorized consortium members can access. As such, information in one sub-network is not exposed to another one. This scenario does not require any kind of cryptocurrency. Instead, payments are made traditionally, off-chain.

Here, the concept of *networks and sub-networks* as additional modeling element allows to separate parts of the value network. Hierarchies of (sub-)networks enable the modeling of complex value networks where actors may participate in several networks, visually indicated by colored badges. This, together with the automatic inference of the carrier network for each value transfer, clarifies value network partitions and actor interactions at first glance. The coloring of value transfers eases the distinction between on-chain and off-chain value transfers.

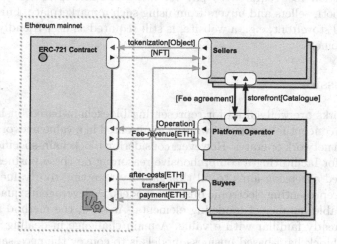

Fig. 6. Value network of a consortium for the construction project proposals and management of inspection reports.

4.3 Non-fungible Token Marketplace

So called non-fungible tokens (NFT) are unique cryptographically verifiable representations of an underlying asset. The asset can be physical, e.g., a property, or digital, e.g., an image. The NFT then encapsulates some type of rights transfer of the associated asset, e.g., for digital art and photography [5]. Here, we regard a derivation of the business model of existing marketplaces[3].

Oftentimes, NFTs may be traded on decentralized marketplaces, whereby sales and transfers of funds and tokens are handled by smart contracts. Such a

---

[3] https://opensea.io/.

scenario is shown in Fig. 6. The marketplace contract is based on ERC721[4], a token standard for the implementation of NFTs for Ethereum. It handles the creation, the so-called *minting*, and transfer of tokens. Additionally, it serves as payment channel. The platform operator offers an off-chain web-based storefront for advertising tokens available for sale. Usage of the marketplace and storefront requires payment of a fee. When a sale closes, the token, and thereby the ownership of the associated digital art, is transferred by the contract to the buyer upon receipt of sufficient payment in cryptocurrency. After deducting the platform fees, funds are transferred to the seller. In summary, the business model of the platform operator involves operation of the marketplace as a service.

Most value transfers in this scenario are carried out over the blockchain. The e^3value extension makes this immediately apparent by automatically coloring the value transfers. Thus, one can derive implications for the viability of the business model: blockchain transactions in public networks generally incur costs in form of a transaction fee, required to pay for infrastructure operation. This could discourage both sellers and buyers from using such a marketplace. Furthermore, a traditional storefront, e.g., a website, is still required as user-friendly interface for the customers.

5   Discussion

Value networks are well-suited for representing blockchain-based business models. There is conceptual overlap of what is represented in a value network and how a blockchain network operates. However, considering blockchain-specific concepts is required for facilitating a comprehensive reasoning on these business models. The proposed extension aims to fill this gap. By reverting to e^3value, a known method for representing electronic business models, we leverage its qualities, e.g., the manageable number of modeling elements. As such, the method is suitable for users already familiar with e^3value. A main challenge in dealing with complexities of blockchain-based business models is to convey the necessary domain knowledge so it can be communicated among non-experts. Our method supports this by inferring and visualizing the propagation of trust—one of the main benefits organizations hope to reap by adopting DLT [2]. The modeling process can be further simplified by reverting to basic modeling patterns, combining them as needed to represent the business model. Through exploring various modeling scenarios, we have found that these patterns are general and applicable in many business cases.

The presented approach originates from the idea of increasing the transparency of information through blockchain networks. The motivation behind relies on the theory of asymmetric information [22] and the problem of incomplete contracts [19]. On the other hand, information transparency is a value proposition in a business model, given its benefit for customers or partners. While transparency of information via public records is one of the major properties of blockchain technology, only vague claims can be made regarding resulting

---

[4] https://eips.ethereum.org/EIPS/eip-721.

benefits for a particular business model without considering the network boundaries of blockchains. Thereby, a network boundary is defined by the hierarchical network structure and access policies. One could argue that the former is a matter of architecture and the latter is a configuration issue, and therefore has no bearing on the business perspective. However, designing viable blockchain-based business models presents a significant challenge due to the interdependent effects of business and apparently exclusive technical decisions, such as network access policies. This further complicates aligning business and technical factors [24]. We argue that the presented solution considers technical concepts to a degree that results in an effectual trade-off that significantly enriches the expressiveness of blockchain-based value networks.

This work is not without limitations: dependency paths of e³value are currently not supported in the prototype, as these are not essential for analyzing transparency of value transfers. However, for simulating blockchain value networks, these would be required to relate value interfaces and coordinate their firing. Further, value transfers do not translate into blockchain transactions. This would be an oversimplification, as not every interaction, resulting in some value with a blockchain incurs a transaction. That is, an *occurrence* of a value transfer may represent an instance of a blockchain transaction in the network. A risk lies in users potentially assuming blockchain transactions and value transfers to be the same. We consider this however a training issue that we plan to investigate in user workshops for further evaluating the method.

6   Conclusion and Outlook

In this paper we proposed a domain-specific extension of the e³value method for supporting the design and analysis of blockchain value networks. Thereby, an emphasis is placed on transparency as property of blockchain networks and how this can be conceptually represented in value networks. For this, an inference mechanism visualizes the transparency of value transfers based on the carrier network and network access configuration. Based on the extended graphical notation, we drafted five basic modeling patterns for blockchain-based business models.

In future work, we plan to further evaluate the method together with domain experts in a user study and add extensions for simulating the value transfers in blockchain value networks as well as for supporting e³value's dependency paths.

References

1. Antonopoulos, A.M., Wood, G.: Mastering Ethereum: Building Smart Contracts and dAPPs. O'reilly Media, Sebastopol (2018)
2. Clohessy, T., Acton, T., Rogers, N.: Blockchain adoption: technological, organisational and environmental considerations. In: Treiblmaier, H., Beck, R. (eds.) Business Transformation through Blockchain, pp. 47–76. Springer, Cham (2019). https://doi.org/10.1007/978-3-319-98911-2_2

3. Curty, S., Fill, H.G.: Exploring the systematic design of blockchain-based applications using integrated modeling standards. In: Proceedings of the PoEM 2022 Workshops. CEUR, vol. 3298. CEUR-WS.org (2022)
4. Curty, S., Fill, H.G.: BLEVEX - Blockchain e3value extension - ADOxx library (2023). https://doi.org/10.5281/zenodo.8380715
5. Curty, S., Härer, F., Fill, H.G.: Towards the comparison of blockchain-based applications using enterprise modeling. In: Proceedings of the ER Demos and Posters 2021. CEUR, vol. 2958, pp. 31–36. CEUR-WS.org (2021)
6. Curty, S., Härer, F., Fill, H.G.: Design of blockchain-based applications using model-driven engineering and low-code/no-code platforms: a structured literature review. Softw. Syst. Model. (2023). https://doi.org/10.1007/s10270-023-01109-1
7. de Kruijff, J., Weigand, H.: Understanding the blockchain using enterprise ontology. In: Dubois, E., Pohl, K. (eds.) CAiSE 2017. LNCS, vol. 10253, pp. 29–43. Springer, Cham (2017). https://doi.org/10.1007/978-3-319-59536-8_3
8. Fernando, Y., Saravannan, R.: Blockchain technology: energy efficiency and ethical compliance. J. Gov. Integrity 4(2), 88–95 (2021). https://doi.org/10.15282/jgi.4.2.2021.5872
9. Ferstl, O.K., Sinz, E.J.: Modeling of business systems using SOM. In: Bernus, P., Mertins, K., Schmidt, G. (eds.) Handbook on Architectures of Information Systems. International Handbooks on Information Systems, pp. 347–367. Springer, Berlin (2006). https://doi.org/10.1007/3-540-26661-5_15
10. Fill, H.G., Karagiannis, D.: On the conceptualisation of modelling methods using the ADOxx meta modelling platform. Enterp. Model. Inf. Syst. Architect. (EMISAJ) 8(1), 4–25 (2013). https://doi.org/10.18417/emisa.8.1.1
11. Fill, H.-G., Meier, A. (eds.): Blockchain. EH, Springer, Wiesbaden (2020). https://doi.org/10.1007/978-3-658-28006-2
12. Fill, H.-G., Meier, A.: Blockchain kompakt. I, Springer, Wiesbaden (2020). https://doi.org/10.1007/978-3-658-27461-0
13. Flovik, S., Moudnib, R.A., Vassilakopoulou, P.: Determinants of blockchain technology introduction in organizations: an empirical study among experienced practitioners. Procedia Comput. Sci. 181, 664–670 (2021)
14. Frank, U.: Domain-specific modeling languages: requirements analysis and design guidelines. In: Reinhartz-Berger, I., Sturm, A., Clark, T., Cohen, S., Bettin, J. (eds.) Domain Engineering, pp. 133–157. Springer, Berlin (2013). https://doi.org/10.1007/978-3-642-36654-3_6
15. Frank, U.: Multi-perspective enterprise modeling: foundational concepts, prospects and future research challenges. Softw. Syst. Model. 13, 941–962 (2014)
16. Gómez, C., Pérez Blanco, F.J., Vara, J.M., De Castro, V., Marcos, E.: Design and development of smart contracts for e-government through value and business process modeling. In: HICSS (2021). https://doi.org/10.24251/HICSS.2021.254
17. Gordijn, J., Akkermans, H., Van Vliet, H.: What's in an electronic business model? In: Dieng, R., Corby, O. (eds.) EKAW 2000. LNCS (LNAI), vol. 1937, pp. 257–273. Springer, Heidelberg (2000). https://doi.org/10.1007/3-540-39967-4_19
18. Gordijn, J., Wieringa, R.: E3value User Guide, 1st edn. The Value Engineers B.V., Soest, NL (2021)
19. Grossman, S.J., Hart, O.D.: The costs and benefits of ownership: a theory of vertical and lateral integration. J. Political Econ. 94(4), 691–719 (1986). https://doi.org/10.1086/261404
20. Group, T.O.: ArchiMate® 3.1 specification (2019). https://pubs.opengroup.org/architecture/archimate3-doc/. Accessed 21 June 2023

21. Härer, F.: Process modeling in decentralized organizations utilizing blockchain consensus. Enterp. Model. Inf. Syst. Architect. (EMISAJ) Int. J. Concept. Model. **15**, 1–17 (2020). https://doi.org/10.18417/emisa.15.13
22. Hillier, B.: The Economics of Asymmetric Information. Macmillan Education, London (1997). https://doi.org/10.1007/978-1-349-25485-9
23. ISO/TC 307 Technical Committee: ISO/TS 23635:2022: Blockchain and distributed ledger technologies - Guidelines for governance. Standard, International Organization for Standardization, Geneva, CH (2022)
24. Janssen, M., Weerakkody, V., Ismagilova, E., Sivarajah, U., Irani, Z.: A framework for analysing blockchain technology adoption: integrating institutional, market and technical factors. Int. J. Inf. Manage. **50**, 302–309 (2020). https://doi.org/10.1016/j.ijinfomgt.2019.08.012
25. Jiang, S., Ræder, T.B.: Experience on using ArchiMate models for modelling blockchain-enhanced value chains. In: EASE 2022 Conference, pp. 375–382. ACM (2022). https://doi.org/10.1145/3530019.3531346
26. Kannengiesser, N., Lins, S., Sander, C., Winter, K., Frey, H., Sunyaev, A.: Challenges and common solutions in smart contract development. IEEE Trans. Software Eng. (2021). https://doi.org/10.1109/TSE.2021.3116808
27. Kim, H.M., Laskowski, M.: Toward an ontology-driven blockchain design for supply-chain provenance. Intell. Syst. Account. Finance Manag. **25**(1), 18–27 (2018). https://doi.org/10.1002/isaf.1424
28. Lakkakula, P., Bullock, D.W., Wilson, W.W.: Asymmetric information and blockchains in soybean commodity markets. Appl. Econ. Perspect. Policy **44**(1), 273–298 (2022). https://doi.org/10.1002/aepp.13159
29. McCarthy, W.E.: The REA accounting model: a generalized framework for accounting systems in a shared data environment. Account. Rev. **57**(3), 554 578 (1982)
30. Nguyen, C.T., Hoang, D.T., Nguyen, D.N., Niyato, D., Nguyen, H.T., Dutkiewicz, E.: Proof-of-stake consensus mechanisms for future blockchain networks: fundamentals. Appl. Opportunit. IEEE Access **7**, 85727–85745 (2019). https://doi.org/10.1109/ACCESS.2019.2925010
31. Osterwalder, A., Pigneur, Y.: Business Model Generation: A Handbook for Visionaries, Game Changers, and Challengers. John Wiley and Sons, Hoboken (2010)
32. Perrelet, S., Fill, H.G., Dibbern, J.: A modeling approach for blockchain-inspired business models: an extension of the e3 -value method. In: HICSS (2022). https://doi.org/10.24251/HICSS.2022.558
33. Poels, G., Kaya, F., Verdonck, M., Gordijn, J.: Early identification of potential distributed ledger technology business cases using e³value models. In: Guizzardi, G., Gailly, F., Suzana Pitangueira Maciel, R. (eds.) ER 2019. LNCS, vol. 11787, pp. 70–80. Springer, Cham (2019). https://doi.org/10.1007/978-3-030 34146-6_7
34. Sandkuhl, K., Stirna, J., Persson, A., Wißotzki, M.: Enterprise Modeling. TEES, Springer, Heidelberg (2014). https://doi.org/10.1007/978-3-662-43725-4
35. Sigrist, N.: Innovation in the construction planning phase - how to prevent building models from being subsequently modified (2023). https://www.swisscom.ch/en/business/blockchain/news/innovation-in-der-bauplanung.html
36. Wang, R., Lin, Z., Luo, H.: Blockchain, bank credit and SME financing. Qual. Quant. **53**(3), 1127–1140 (2019). https://doi.org/10.1007/s11135-018-0806-6

37. Wieland, M., Fill, H.: A domain-specific modeling method for supporting the generation of business plans. In: Modellierung 2020, 19–21. February 2020, Wien, Österreich. LNI, vol. P-302, pp. 45–60. Gesellschaft für Informatik e.V. (2020). https://dl.gi.de/20.500.12116/31846
38. Wirtz, B.W., Pistoia, A., Ullrich, S., Göttel, V.: Business models: origin, development and future research perspectives. Long Range Plan. **49**(1), 36–54 (2016). https://doi.org/10.1016/j.lrp.2015.04.001

Building a New Information Technology Operating Model to Support Digital Transformation: A Case Study in Oil and Gas Sector

Muhammad Suleman[1,2] , Jolita Ralyté[2(✉)] , Samuli Pekkola[1,3] ,
and Tuomas Ahola[1]

[1] Faculty of Management and Business, Tampere University, Tampere, Finland
{muhammad.suleman,tuomas.ahola}@tuni.fi, samuli.j.pekkola@jyu.fi
[2] Institute of Information Service Science, University of Geneva, CUI, Carouge, Switzerland
jolita.ralyte@unige.ch
[3] Faculty of Information Technology, University of Jyväskylä, Jyväskylä, Finland

Abstract. Multinational corporations are facing increasing demands on their IT function due to digital innovation and transformation. However, a traditional IT function often lacks capabilities required for successful digital transformation. This necessitates a comprehensive change in its IT operating model (ITOM), encompassing people, processes, technology, governance, agility, outsourcing, and more. This article presents a case study of a large European oil and gas company's IT function, exploring the design and implementation process of a new ITOM. Qualitative interviews with IT executives and digital leads, along with data analysis, shed light on the involvement of external consulting firms during the design phase, while the implementation phase is driven by internal IT teams. The process is labor-intensive and spans several years, highlighting the complexity of ITOM implementation within a multimodal IT function structure. Key findings stress the need for close alignment among strategic IT leaders and strong business executive ownership. Scaling an agile approach requires an agile mindset achieved through continuous training and clearly defining the role of the product owner. The study has significant implications for IT function transformation through the adoption of a new ITOM, making it relevant for practitioners, researchers, and CIOs alike.

Keywords: IT Operating Model · IT Transformation · Design and Implementation · IT Function · Digital Transformation

© IFIP International Federation for Information Processing 2024
Published by Springer Nature Switzerland AG 2024
J. P. A. Almeida et al. (Eds.): PoEM 2023, LNBIP 497, pp. 91–106, 2024.
https://doi.org/10.1007/978-3-031-48583-1_6

1 Introduction

For decades, researchers and practitioners have debated the role of the information technology (IT) function[1] and its role in achieving strategic organizational goals [1, 2]. Recent rapid emergence of digital technologies and digital transformation have put even more demands on the IT function such as innovation in products and services, customer analytics, data exploitation, cost reduction and agility in response to market demands [3]. However, with growing demands from the business, the IT function cannot sustainably deliver value using outdated IT operating model (ITOM) that was designed years ago to support or enable the previous business model. The concept of ITOM has gained prominence in recent practitioner literature as a key approach for transforming the IT function. The ITOM is defined as a blueprint of the IT function. It includes components like organization design, IT capabilities, people, processes, technology, sourcing, governance, architecture that all together deliver value to the organization [4]. ITOM is also referred as a bridge between the organizational strategy and its execution [5]. Stackpole [6] argues that the current ITOMs within organizations are no longer sufficient and suitable, and are overdue for a redesign. The organization's evolving IT and digital transformation needs require an updated ITOM that can effectively meet these new requirements. Another argument comes from pre-digital organizations (PDOs)[2] which have different maturity levels and lack innovation capabilities due to outdated ITOMs, i.e., legacy information systems (IS), multiple IS running in parallel that needs upgrade or decommissioning, complex IT architecture, missing internal capability for software development [7].

Previous research on IT function transformation has primarily focused on scholarly debates regarding individual ITOM components, such as enterprise technology implementation [8], IT leadership roles [9], IT function profiles [10], IT capabilities and resources [11], organization design of the IT function [12], and IT agility and ambidexterity [2]. Contributions for a holistic view of the ITOM design and implementation remain scarce [13], even though a need for an end-to-end ITOM design and implementation approach have been identified [14]. In particular, ITOM implementation in PDOs has received less attention [15].

In this study, we aim to better understand the process of the design and implementation of an ITOM and to evaluate its impact on the success of the IT function transformation. Thus, we empirically investigate the following research question:

How a multinational organization build an IT operating model in practice?

To answer this question, we conducted a case study where we analyzed the IT function of a big Nordic-based PDO active in oil and gas (O&G) industry and producing non-digital products. In the rest of the paper, we call this company Oil-one (pseudonym). Oil-one is a multinational firm with global presence, over 20 000 employees, established more than 50 years before. Its IT function had passed the ITOM design phase and was going through the implementation phase during our data collection. Drawing on 15

[1] IT function refers to IT department of a multinational company. IT function/IT department would mean the same thing throughout this article.
[2] PDOs are defined as organizations born or established pre industry 4.0 revolution.

semi-structured interviews, we analyzed the ITOM development and implementation process.

The rest of the paper is organized as follows: in Sect. 2 we provide a theoretical background by discussing the literature on ITOM and IT transformation in O&G companies. Section 3 describes the research method and introduces the case study, while Sect. 4 presents the research findings. In Sect. 5 we further discuss the findings and their implication. Finally, Sect. 6 concludes the paper.

2 Foundation and Related Works

We discuss the related literature in three stages. First, we review literature on IT operating model for IT function transformation. Second, we discuss IT function transformation in O&G sector. Third, we look into digital transformation in O&G sector.

2.1 ITOM for IT Function Transformation

In any organization, the IT function is responsible for providing and managing software applications, digital services, and hardware solutions to the entire organization so that the employees can do their job [12, 13]. The chief information officer (CIO) is usually the head of the IT function. The ITOM represents how the IT function operates and delivers value to the business. Academics and practitioners argue that there are different ITOMs to enable and support the business to adopt a new organizational strategy, although these models have not been specifically called ITOMs. The dominant model is referred as Plan, Build, Run (PBR) [16]. In PBR ITOM, 'plan' includes IT strategy alignment, relationship management, and demand management, 'build' focuses on developing and deploying applications and services and product engineering, and 'run' deals with smooth operation of IT systems [17]. This model worked well for a while, but it introduced working in silos and a lack of cooperation between 'build' and 'run', i.e., application development and IT support [18]. In 2013, many firms started to change their perception of the IT function, moving from IT support to IT-enabled business transformation [19]. This brought new challenges to the CIOs to design and implement a new ITOM for digital [5]. Bimodal IT, introduced by the practitioner firm Gartner [20], emerged as a new form of ITOM. It was proposed as a transitional ITOM until the IT function becomes fully digital [2]. However, [21] concluded that designing an ITOM as bimodal IT was not a sustainable solution, as it could introduce two different cultures, two class systems, which creates more conflicts than solutions.

2.2 IT Function Transformation in Oil and Gas Sector

The IT function is complex also in O&G. The O&G value chain is divided in three business streams: (1) upstream dealing with the exploration and production of O&G from onshore and offshore platforms, (2) midstream including the storage and transportation activities, intermediate processing, etc., and (3) downstream performing the refinement, sales and supply [22]. Although all three streams have different requirements from the IT function, a common information system, such as enterprise resource planning (ERP) system, can connect them and assure efficient workflows. The implementation of an ERP software across all streams is highly complex, which makes the work truly difficult for the IT function [23].

According to Edmundson [24], O&G firms are consistently using technology in oil production. They are heavily dependent on their IT function. In the absence of open standards for O&G business processes and information flows and the lack of third-party applications in drilling and seismic processing, the O&G IT function has internally developed routines and software applications for the business [25, 26].

The cost cutting focus has forced the business leaders to initiate corporate transformation and IT function transformation programs [27]. For example, British Petroleum advanced the IT function transformation in three dimensions: purpose, IT roles, and process [28]. Furthermore, in most companies and industries, including O&G, one of the dominant changes within the scope of IT transformation has been the change in the design in the IT organization [29], with a more strategic approach in planning technology investments and emphasizing the value of the IT function to the business [30].

2.3 Digital Transformation in Oil and Gas Sector

The world economic forum [31] stressed that digital transformation is affecting all three streams of the O&G business. The most significant changes relate to digital asset life cycle management (big data analytics, automation, connected field workers, Internet of Things, predictive maintenance, robotics drilling systems) and circular collaborative ecosystems (blockchain, additive manufacturing). While the end-product of the O&G sector is not digital, the exploration, production and transportation of their products are achieved by digital means. This has challenged the current ITOM in O&G. Existing IT functions and their capabilities, and the current ITOM cannot implement and/or support these modern technologies once they are deployed and operational. For example, there is a great amount of data generated by different ERP modules, such as drilling data, well performance management and production data, IoT on oil platforms data, but the IT function is not designed for data management, governance, and exploitation [32].

Generally, PDOs and their enterprise information systems and ITOMs are not designed for digital transformation [33]. O&G has been an asset industry, with a focus on hardware technology. However, digitalization has increased demands in the technology portfolio for software projects rather than hardware projects. This requires significant efforts from the CIOs to scale the ITOM in line with the company's digital ambition and technology opportunities while taking into consideration the lack of talent [34].

3   Research Methods and Settings

We conducted an interpretive case study to answer our research question, *How a multinational organization build an IT operating model in practice?* A case study approach offers the possibility to capture richness of the situation under empirical investigation and to generate insights in various organizational settings [35]. Moreover, Yin [36] argues that a case study is "an empirical inquiry that investigates a contemporary phenomenon within its real-life context, especially when the boundaries between phenomenon and context are not clearly evident". In this paper, we investigate the IT operating model design and implementation in its practical setting. Our aim is to understand how multinational companies design and implement their ITOM. Our case is an IT function/department in a multinational oil and gas company, named Oil-one (pseudonym), headquartered in a Nordic country and geographically present in all continents. We study the ITOM design and implementation process in Oil-one. Oil-one was seen as a forerunner of digital transformation, so its experiences were closely followed by other O&G operator/services companies in the region.

We collected empirical research data from January to August 2021. We conducted 15 semi-structured interviews (see Table 1) from Oil-one, two of whom were interviewed twice. The initial interview was conducted with the CIO of Oil-one, who helped in identifying other members from the IT function involved in the ITOM implementation. The main interview topic for all interviewees was the IT transformation within Oil-one, with particular emphasis on design and implementation of ITOM. Additionally, the CIO and the lead of digital transformation were questioned about the value of IT within Oil-one.

Table 1. The people interviewed at Oil-one.

Position	Interactions	Experience (years)	Type	Duration
Corporate CIO	2	>25	Video Call	58 min
Vice President IT Global Business Service	1	>25	Video Call	65 min
Head of Transformation Program	1	>15	Video Call	70 min
Manager IT Strategy and Transformation	2	>15	Video Call	55 min
Digital Centre of Excellence Lead	1	>15	In person	65 min
Agile Centre of Excellence Lead	1	>20	Video Call	58 min
Senior Advisor IT Projects	1	>20	Video Call	55 min
IT Product Owner	1	>10	In person	50 min
IT Portfolio Lead (1)	1	>15	In person	60 min
IT Portfolio Lead (2)	1	>10	Video Call	45 min
Agile Coach (1)	1	>10	Video Call	62 min
Agile Coach (2)	1	>5	In person	55 min
Enterprise Architect Lead (1)	1	>10	Video Call	60 min

(continued)

Table 1. (*continued*)

Position	Interactions	Experience (years)	Type	Duration
Enterprise Architect Lead (2)	1	>10	Video Call	52 min
Director IT Application Development	1	>10	In person	60 min

All interviews were scheduled for 60 min and conducted both in person and remotely by using Microsoft Teams' software. The actual duration for some interviews lasted for more than 60 min. Most remote interviews were video recorded with the consent of the interviewee. We transcribed the interviews manually. For data analysis, we used NVivo 12[3] qualitative data analysis tool and coded the transcribed data. To protect the privacy of the participants, we have not used their name in the article.

We used Braun and Clark six steps for thematic analysis [37]. Table 2 illustrates the coding process, showing how different categories have been identified from transcribed data. Using the interview transcripts as the primary data source (column 1), we first extracted the key ideas (e.g., Inviting external consultants to use their expert knowledge) that we then coded (e.g., External consultant) and classified into categories (e.g., Building ITOM). The coding was performed on 15 + 2 (two people interviewed twice) interview transcripts. In total 155 open codes were generated and clustered into 17 categories. These codes and categories were again refined and clustered several times. The coding

Table 2. An illustration of the coding process.

Raw data	Key idea	Code	Category	Theme
"So, we started to look into this, and we decided to get some help from an external company. We had contracted with a consulting firm to help Oil-one, and they conducted quite a thorough interviews with business leaders from different departments"	Inviting external consultants to use their expert knowledge	External Consultant	Facilitate CIO for assessment and design	Building ITOM

---

[3] NVivo software https://lumivero.com/products/nvivo/

process ended up with the classification of finding in three major themes that we present in the next section.

4   Findings from the Case Study

We structure our findings into three themes that correspond to the ITOM building phases: (1) analysis of the situation and business requirements elicitation, (2) analysis and design, and (3) implementation.

4.1   Analysis of the Situation and Business Requirements Elicitation

The first set of findings concerns the situation of the IT function at Oil-one before the implementation of the new ITOM and the motivation for building this ITOM.

Fragmented Organizational Setup of the IT Function. The organizational structure of the IT function at Oil-one is multimodal[4]. It is composed of (1) Corporate IT, (2) Global Delivery IT, (3) Business Area IT and (4) Digital unit, each of these units having its own manager. Therefore, the IT setup was very complex in terms of the distribution of responsibilities and reporting structure. Corporate IT was headed by the corporate CIO and responsible for IT directives, IT strategy and IT governance. Global Delivery IT, led by the Vice President, was part of the unit of multifunctional integrated shared business services, and responsible for infrastructure and delivery to the rest of Oil-one business segments. Business Area IT was led by the Vice President and was responsible for applications services for different business segments. Digital unit was newly established unit in 2017 aimed at leveraging industry 4.0 and led by the Chief Digital Officer (CDO). The reporting structure of all 4 units explained by the Vice President: *"There is a corporate IT, setting the guidance, the governance, and the direction for IT in Oil-One. There is business area IT, and then there is a delivery organization for business services"*.

Separate IT Transformation Projects in IT Units. Multimodal IT organizational structure in Oil-one created many issues for the four IT units, in particular weak collaboration between them and unclear division of responsibilities. The overall journey of transforming the IT function at Oil-One has been a multi-year journey started in 2014 in different IT units. Corporate IT and Global Delivery IT had launched many separate projects to align IT units with the business. Prior to 2014, most IT services were outsourced to an external IT vendor.

Reasons for Renewing the ITOM at Oil-One. The reasons for renewing the ITOM included: (1) With global climate change, Oil-one's vision shifted from oil and gas production to renewable energy. The new business strategy focused on leveraging digital technology and creating renewables business unit. Oil-one's change in business strategy required a change in IT strategy. (2) Concerns have arisen about the creation of the Digital unit and the role of CDO in accountability and decision making. The CDO took

---

[4] Multimodal IT function refers to more than 2 separate IT functions in an organization, led by separate IT managers.

the lead from the CIO for overseeing the technology venturing at Oil-one, aiming to test modern digital technologies and their application in oil and gas sector. However, the ownership for the new technology adoption was not transferred to the CDO. Instead, the responsibility for making further decisions remained with the corporate IT function. This lack of accountability and decision-making authority for technology adoption created uncertainty and questioned the relevance and of the CDO role and the existence of the Digital unit. The main reason is that the role of the Digital unit has not been fully understood by the business. This is illustrated by the reluctance expressed by the Corporate CIO: "*CDOs have tried to move into the technology area. They [Digital unit] want to play with the technology like Artificial Intelligence and then don't take responsibility for it*". (3) The business has given a negative assessment of IT performance in all four IT units, e.g., IT service delivery is very slow, cost for providing the service is very high, and IT function is not ready for digital transformation.

Preliminary Business Requirements for ITOM Renewal. Given the current situation of the IT function (including the four IT units), Corporate CIO held a meeting with the business stakeholders and agreed on a business case for renewing ITOM. The main business requirements for ITOM renewal were identified as: IT function should enable the new business model of Oil-one, IT function becomes a business partner, modernize the legacy system and responds faster to business needs.

4.2 Analysis and Design of the New ITOM

The 'Reshape IT' project was initiated by the CIO with the aim of designing a new ITOM for Oil-one's IT function. The project spanned from September 2017 to December 2018 and had two primary objectives: first, to assess the current state of the IT function, encompassing all its units, and second to design a new ITOM. Previously, IT transformation projects were solely led by internal IT teams, without external consulting assistance. Given the existence of many issues concerning the perception of the IT function both within the business and among its internal units, the CIO faced a challenge in relying solely on the internal IT team for conducting a comprehensive assessment of the IT function. To address this challenge and gain an unbiased perspective and an outsider view, the CIO decided to contract an external consulting firm to perform the assessment. This offered fresh insights and impartial analysis. The scope of the 'Reshape IT' project was extensive, focusing on conducting a holistic analysis of both IT and business units (including exploration, drilling, production, subsurface, transportation etc.). The main project activities and their outcomes are explained next.

Involvement of an External Consulting Firm and Identification of Pain Points. The consulting firm interviewed various business stakeholders and identified several points of pain within the IT function. This served as the basis for designing a new ITOM. According to the feedback, the IT function was failing to meet the business expectations in everyday IT service delivery and future digital transformation needs. The points of pain encompassed various issues, such as instability in the IT infrastructure, concerns about information security and business continuity, and an overall low quality of service delivery hindering the efficiency of daily operations. The current ITOM was far from enabling Oil-one's digital ambition, including digital drilling, digital well optimization, and digital twin applications. There was a lack of focus on delivering end-to-end business value from the IT side. The report concluded that to address these challenges, all IT units should prioritize and align their efforts with the business objectives.

Reintroducing Agile/DevOps. When the Global Delivery IT unit embarked on agile transformation journey, agile/DevOps practices were not adequately scaled to meet the business requirements. Quoting the enterprise architect, "agile and DevOps deployment started, but due to significant capability and build gaps, has not kept up with strategy". This results from several issues, such as: lack of cross functional organization of IT teams, unclear ownership of agile/DevOps tools and process, unbalanced ratio between product owners (POs) and IT teams with more POs than IT teams, lack of proper training of POs on the business side, potentially impeding their ability to effectively collaborate with the IT teams, absence of scrum master observed in daily stand-up meetings, lack of autonomy of Agile/DevOps teams in making decisions, and unprioritized product backlog leading to delays in delivering outcomes to the business. The issues highlight significant gaps and deviations in agile and DevOps practices across the business. To address them, the Oil-one IT function must redefine its 'agile and DevOps delivery model'.

Capability Building. The analysis of Oil-one's digital ambition and of the current capabilities of its IT function revealed a significant gap. The existing capabilities within the IT function were insufficient to fully support and deliver on Oil-one's digital strategy. This indicates a need for digital talent both within IT and across the business units. However, the recruitment process was not progressing quickly enough to bring the necessary expertise. Moreover, earlier an agile approach for on-demand IT service delivery was chosen but its service management capability turned out to be unclearly defined. To address these issues, 'Capability building' needed further attention to align with Oil-one's IT strategy.

Legacy Enterprise Architecture (EA) and Cloud Migration. According to the EA head, *"Corporate IT has defined cloud strategy, but we're not going to the cloud because I see legacy architecture will slow us down"*. Indeed, from a technical perspective, several issues were identified within Oil-one's EA and IT infrastructure. Legacy information systems suffered from complex and poor integration. They also accumulated technical debt, coupled with code complexity and the absence of code refactoring. The absence of standard EA framework hindered the organization's ability to become a data-driven organization. Development teams were developing applications without considering the broader technology ecosystem. There was no clear roadmap for migrating to cloud and building a data platform. Oil-one's offshore oil and gas platforms raised cybersecurity concerns regarding the migration of their IS, operational technologies, and IoT to cloud platforms. The lack of a proper standard agile architecture for legacy systems slowed down the migration process to cloud. To address these challenges and enable a smoother migration to the cloud, the recommendation was to prioritize the implementation of 'enterprise architecture and digital infrastructure'.

Design of New ITOM by a Consulting Firm. Based on the business requirements and the points of pain, the consultant proposed a design solution for the new Oil-one's ITOM.

As shown in Fig. 1, it consists of three domains, namely *D1 – Business Requirements and Alignment of Priorities*, *D2 – Core ITOM Components*, and *D3 – Enterprise Architecture and Digital Infrastructure*. D1 defines strategic business requirements (digitalization readiness, cybersecurity, etc.) that the new ITOM should address. D2 introduces new ITOM components (*Product-Centric IT Organizational Design*, *Capability Building* and *DevOps/Agile Delivery Model*) in addition to the exiting components requiring improvement (*IT Governance*, V*endor Management* etc.). D3 is considered as an enabler for D1 and foundation for D2 by addressing the challenges of modernization, agility, data management and migration to cloud. While the three domains are part of the new ITOM, their changes were split into separate but interdependent projects. Due to high-cost factor, the consulting firm left the project and left the implementation work to the internal IT team.

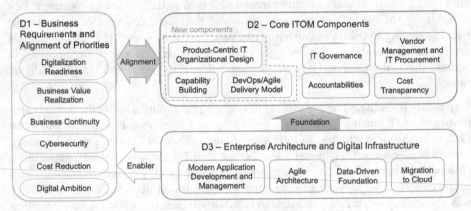

Fig. 1. Design proposal for the new ITOM of Oil-one.

4.3   Implementation of the New ITOM

The 'Transform IT' project (May 2019 – Aug 2020) aimed to implement the new ITOM, designed during the 'Reshape IT' project. Implementing the initiatives in the three ITOM domains (Fig. 1) was split among the different IT function's units i.e., Corporate IT, Global Delivery IT and Business Area IT. To successfully implement new ITOM components and transform the existing ones, it was essential to foster tight collaboration among the IT units. Rather than relying on external consultants, the decision was made to use internal IT teams for the implementation. This approach encouraged early adoption and acceptance of the changes within the organization. The main implementation activities and their outcomes are explained next.

Alignment of Business Priorities: Establishing IT Hubs. To alleviate the point of pain that the IT function is unable to meet the current and future business needs, IT hubs were created to capture business demand and to react to changes faster. As a pilot initiative, an IT hub was established within the exploration department. Its ownership and sponsorship were entrusted to the respective department, with its Senior Vice President (SVP) taking the lead. Experts from the IT function and the exploration department had bi-weekly meetings to discuss ongoing IT issues and new projects where IT help was needed. After the successful outcome and positive feedback on the exploration department's IT hub, more IT hubs were created, one per main business department (e.g., production, subsurface, drilling etc.). Dedicated IT advisors from the Global Delivery IT unit were assigned to all hubs to provide expertise on modern digital technologies relevant for the corresponding department.

Accountabilities and IT Governance. With the new ITOM, the end-to-end account-ability for the customer specific IT delivery was assigned to the local department, while the corporate IT unit was held accountable for enterprise-wide IT delivery. IT delivery at Oil-one was strategically aligned with process area (PA) and functional areas (FA). New roles, such as PA owner and FA owner, were created. These roles were made responsible for connecting with stakeholders, gathering their needs, creating, and prioritizing the requirements backlog. In addition, they were responsible for aligning any dependencies arising from cross IT hubs/departments. To gain business buy-in for digital projects, prioritization was anchored with PA/FA owners. To ensure proper governance of invest-ment in technology (e.g., in-house development, developing with a partner, buying off the shelf), an explicit process was defined. It set that the investments must be justified by data-based evidence, measurement of benefits, accountability, and appropriate reporting.

Agile/DevOps Ways of Working. Although agile transformation was initiated by the Global Delivery IT unit with two agile delivery modes, it did not scale well with the business. To give a rebirth to agile transformation in the IT function, long discussions between the business department SVPs and the heads of IT units concluded that their starting point for an agile journey would be based on 'Transform IT mindset'. An Agile Coach explained this mindset as follows: "*… we set up some principles that were based on Lean and Agile Principles, so it was not a pure agile manifesto, but we created our own manifesto. And then we started with training leaders. We had a [company] from [country] coming over to have two days training for all leaders*". Therefore, the 'Transform IT mindset' was basically an agile manifesto developed for Oil-one. It is based on 5 values: business value over cost, supporting teams over managing deliveries, empowering teams over assigning people to task, technical improvement over IT failure, and product owner support the business capability over supporting one system. As a first step of its implementation, the Global Delivery IT started to train leaders from other departments on agile and lean thinking. The training was provided by an external advisory firm well known for its agile leadership training portfolio. The next step of agile transformation was to form a long-term team using DevOps methodology. The adoption of DevOps aimed to have teams able to take full responsibility for the product lifecycle.

Resource Allocation. With the emphasis on developing digital solutions and allocat-ing resources for projects, the Global Delivery IT unit established an IT competence center. The center was organized in several resource pools, each of them including cross functional teams up to 50 people. A resource manager was assigned to each resource pool. Each Oil-one's business department was entitled to request for IT resources from a resource pool. For each request, the resource manager would form a long-term cross functional team. The idea of long-term team relates to agile product development where a team is formed for a product or a functional area. The teams are self-organization, determination, and high productivity-driven focus on business outcomes.

Capabilities Talent. O&G industry is an asset intensive industry, requiring experts in drilling, well construction, etc. The increasing digitalization activities require skills in new digital technologies. To meet the competing demand for talent, the competence strategy and career development was redefined at Oil-one. It was decided to upskill talent internally on digital tools and technologies and hire the most demanding talent externally to keep a good balance. Developing in-house skills was seen to increase the employees' ability to work and think differently and to apply digital technologies to different Oil-one activities they already knew. For external hires, the idea was to attract top talent with knowledge from different industries and a vision to foster innovation. To retain talent, the Oil-one career path was defined and promoted internally.

Enterprise Architecture and Digital Infrastructure. At Oil-one, the cloud strategy and cloud migration program were managed by the Global Delivery IT. The multi-year program is still ongoing. As Oil-one has several on-site ERP implementations, used as single data sources for numerous business flows, it was not possible to completely migrate to the cloud immediately. Many applications were developed and optimized for the on-premises infrastructure, and moving them to the cloud was impossible. Consequently, a cloud platform was built with an idea that new applications will be developed as cloud-native applications. In four years, cloud migration had advanced very slowly due to legacy applications – even the IT team had sorted out their technical debt, performed refactoring, and simplified complex integrations. To make the integrations between internal and external applications and services, an application programming interface was launched.

5 Discussion and Lessons Learned

Figure 2 presents an overview of the ITOM building process at Oil-one. The figure is reconstructed by the case study. It highlights the main actors and their activities during the design and implementation phases of the new ITOM, leading to the transformation of the IT function itself.

Actors and their Expertise. Although both design and implementation phases are critical for the success of ITOM renewal projects, the design phase was considered particularly demanding in terms of dedicated expertise. To deal with the risk of a bad design possibly hampering the implementation process, hiring an external expert consulting firm to carry out the analysis and design of the ITOM seems like a good decision. In Oil-one, the design of the ITOM was owned and led by the corporate CIO unit involving key business leaders and facilitated by a consulting firm. Based on the case study and [38], we identify the main reasons for hiring an expert firm to support the design phase: (1) availability of expert talent having an extended knowledge from proven case studies in various industries, (2) well defined process models and techniques for data gathering, analysis and design, and (3) availability of advanced soft skills and trained facilitators for group activities fostering collective intelligence.

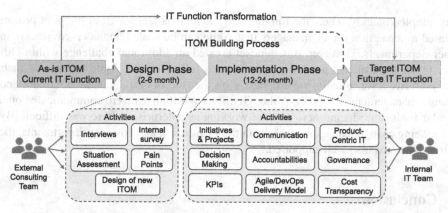

Fig. 2. Overview of the ITOM building process: Design and Implementation.

Analysis and Design Approach. While various data gathering and requirements elicitation tools and techniques exist, the case study at Oil-one indicates that the most popular remains the one-to-one interview. Indeed, the only techniques used at Oil-one for assessing the 'As-is' situation of the IT function were one-to-one interviews with strategic business leaders, followed by an internal survey. Group techniques, such as brainstorming, exploratory workshops or focus groups were not exploited. The issues and the points of pain were discovered by the consultancy firm and were used to constitute the basis for the ITOM renewal. The design of ITOM in three domains (Fig. 1) addresses the challenges faced by the IT function in the former ITOM. Introducing new ITOM components like 'Product-Centric IT', changes the mindset on how technology should be built and owned in the future. We conclude from the design phase that these domains (D1, D2 and D3) were correctly positioned to meet the requirements of the business for the new ITOM.

Responsibility for Implementation. From our findings, we conclude that the ITOM implementation phase is much longer journey than the design phase (see Fig. 2). It requires commitment, ownership and tight governance from business and IT leaders. It is the most critical phase in building a new ITOM for the IT function as the value realization depends on its success [39]. This phase should be mainly run by internal IT teams, that are led by executives from business and IT units with less input from external experts. The reason of such project governance is that eventually the new ITOM will be run and managed by the internal IT teams, and it is best to let them take control of the activities.

Implementation Approach. The new ITOM implementation phase started with the initiatives and projects identified in the three ITOM domains (see Fig. 1) during the design phase. Each had a detailed implementation roadmap with defined KPIs to measure the outcomes and a product owner assigned by the corresponding business department. As the IT function agile transformation was in focus of new ITOM, several people from different business departments were trained on product owner role. They were assumed to take the product owner role immediately in their department. As the pilot project using an agile method was quite successful in the exploration department, the agile approach was adopted quickly. Thus, the training and the lessons learned from the pilot project created a perception for IT managers that Agile can be scaled and adopted quickly in other departments. However, this mindset created an additional challenge within Oil-one. Other departments needed extra efforts to fully embrace Agile because of their low maturity level. Finally, we emphasize on the role of communication, culture and change management (c.f. [40]). Although different initiatives were communicated on a regular basis, introducing new ways of working as enterprise culture was difficult. By introducing change management skills in the IT function and business departments, the culture part was also well supported.

6 Conclusion

In this paper, we report our finding from a case study at a big O&G company aiming to renew its IT Operation Model. While the case study allows us to identify many digital transformation issues, our focus is on the process of building an ITOM. Our investigation is based on 15 interviews with various strategic and executive leaders of the company. Due to the space limit, in this paper we could present only a superficial presentation of issues. However, in short, we found that the process of building a new ITOM is particularly complex and requires extensive expertise in the domain, particularly in the design phase. Implementing ITOM in a multimodal IT setup also needs a strong governance architecture and contribution from all departments. Lack of ownership for activities both in design and implementation phase may lead to unsuccessful ITOM. New ways of working, like Agile/DevOps, require a good change management approach. Otherwise, the organizational culture may impede their adoption.

Our study has limitations insofar as it is a single case study. Therefore, the findings are only generalizable to similar contexts [37]. However, this work lays the foundation to further investigation and exploration of ITOM implementation. We have already conducted and plan to conduct other similar case studies in different industrial sectors to complete the understanding of ITOM building and its practical implications.

References

1. Guillemette, M.G., Paré, G.: Transformation of the information technology function in organizations: a case study in the manufacturing sector. Can. J. Adm. Sci. **29**, 177–190 (2012). https://doi.org/10.1002/CJAS.224
2. Leonhardt, D., Haffke, I., Kranz, J., Benlian, A.: Reinventing the IT function: the role of IT agility and IT ambidexterity in supporting digital business transformation. In: Proceedings of ECIS 2017, pp. 968–984 (2017). https://aisel.aisnet.org/ecis2017_rp/63
3. Vial, G.: Understanding digital transformation: a review and a research agenda. J. Strateg. Inf. Syst. **28**, 118–144 (2019). https://doi.org/10.1016/j.jsis.2019.01.003
4. Bates, S., Brunsman, B., Croier, P.: Market speed - IT operating models in the age of the connected enterprise. In: KPMG Res. (2019)
5. Krigman, E., McKinnon, T.: The new IT operating model for digital. In: IT Q. CEB Res. (2016)
6. Stackpole, B.: Overdue: a new organizing model for IT. Sloan Manage. Rev. (2019)

7. Keller, R., Ollig, P., Rövekamp, P.: Pathways to developing digital capabilities within entrepreneurial initiatives in pre-digital organizations: a single case study. Bus. Inf. Syst. Eng. **64**, 33–46 (2022). https://doi.org/10.1007/s12599-021-00739-3
8. Grant, G.G.: Strategic alignment and enterprise systems implementation: the case of metalco. J. Inf. Technol. **18**, 159–175 (2003)
9. Westerman, G., Weill, P.: What makes an effective CIO? The perspective of non-IT Executives. MIT Sloan CISR Res. Brief. **V**(3C), 1–3 (2005)
10. Guillemette, M.G., Pare, G.: Understanding the transformation of the IT function in organizations. In: Proceedings of AMCIS 2005 (2005). http://aisel.aisnet.org/amcis2005/63
11. Daniel, M., Legner, C., Heck, A.: Understanding IT transformation - an exploratory study. In: Proceedings of ECIS 2011 (2011)
12. Wiedemann, A., Weeger, A.: How to design an IT department? A review and synthesis of key characteristics. In: Proceedings of AMCIS 2016 (2016)
13. Peppard, J.: The metamorphosis of the IT Unit. MIT CISR Res. Brief. **XIX**(7), 1–4 (2019)
14. Mingay, S., Cox, I.: What is an I & T operating model, and how do you accelerate its design process? Gartner (2019)
15. Haffke, I., Kalgovas, B., Benlian, A.: Options for transforming the IT function using bimodal IT. MIS Q. Exec. **16**, 101–120 (2017)
16. Ross, J.W., Beath, C.M., Oncul, B.: The IT unit of the future: new approaches to run and build. MIT CISR Res. Brief. **X**(12), 1–3 (2010)
17. ISG: Plan-Build- Run as an Emerging ADM Model (2013)
18. Agarwal, H., Bommadevara, N., Weinberg, A.: Using a plan-build-run organizational model to drive IT infrastructure objectives. McKinsey Co., 1–6 (2013)
19. Mocker, M., Ross, J.W.: How Royal Philip is moving towards its complexity sweet spot (2014)
20. Scott, D.,,Mingay, S.: Scaling bimodal - fusing IT with the business: a Gartner trend insight report. Gartner (2017)
21. McCarthy, J.C., Leaver, S.: The false promise of bimodal IT: BT provides a customer-led, insights-driven, fast, and connected alternative. Forrester Res. (2016)
22. Colombano, A., Crnkovic, P.: Oil & Gas Company Analysis: Upstream. CreateSpace Independent Publishing Platform, Midstream and Downstream (2015)
23. Mishra, A., Mishra, D.: ERP Project Implementation: Evidence from the Oil and Gas Sector. Acta Polytech. Hungarica. 8, (2011)
24. Edmundson, H.: Ten Technologies From the 1980s and 1990s That Made Today's Oil and Gas Industry. J. Pet. Technol. (2019)
25. Henderson, J.C., Sifons, J.G.: The value of strategic planning: understanding consistency, validity, and IS markets. MIS Q. **12**, 187–200 (1988)
26. Stinchcombe, A.L.: Transforming information systems in organizations: the Norwegian State Oil Company begins operations (1987)
27. Galliers, R.D.: Strategic information systems planning: myths, reality and guidelines for successful implementation. Eur. J. Inf. Syst. **1**, 55–64 (1991)
28. Cross, J., Earl, M.J., Sampler, J.L.: Transformation of the IT function at British petroleum. MIS Q. **21**, 401–420 (1997). https://doi.org/10.2307/249721
29. Boar, B.H.: Redesigning the IT organization for the information age. Inf. Syst. Manag. **15**, 23–30 (1998). https://doi.org/10.1201/1078/43185.15.3.19980601/31131.4
30. Ward, J., Peppard, J.: Strategic Planning for Information Systems. 3rd edn. Wiley & Sons (2002)
31. WEF: Digital Transformation Initiative: Oil and Gas Industry In collaboration with Accenture. World Econ. Forum vol. 32 (2017)
32. Oussov, A., Sorensen, K., Mata, J.: The future of IT: oil & gas industry insights. KPMG Res. (2019). https://doi.org/10.1201/b11953-8

33. Mcmullen, L., Dave, A., Lownedahl, J., Lehong, H., Hill, J.: Follow 7 principles to redesign your operating model before it fails (2020)
34. Cushing, S., McAvey, R.: Why IT operating models are under strain and how oil and gas CIOs should respond. Gart. Res. (2018)
35. Eisenhardt, K.M.: Building theories from case study research. Acad. Manag. Rev. **14**, 532–550 (1989)
36. Yin, R.K.: Case Study Research: Design and Methods. SAGE Publications, Thousand Oaks (2013)
37. Braun, V., Clarke, V.: Successful Qualitative Research: A Practical Guide for Beginners. SAGE Publications, London (2013)
38. Bates, S., Jones, T.: Creating a future-ready IT function - today. KPMG Res., 1–8 (2019)
39. Jöhnk, J., Röglinger, M., Thimmel, M., Urbach, N.: How to implement agile it setups : that the design and implementation of ITOM. In: Proceedings of ECIS (2017)
40. Paasivaara, M., Behm, B., Lassenius, C., Hallikainen, M.: Large-scale agile transformation at Ericsson: a case study. Empir. Softw. Eng. Softw. Eng. **23**, 2550–2596 (2018)

Modeling Tools and Approaches

A Vision for Flexible GLSP-Based Web Modeling Tools

Dominik Bork[1]([✉])[ID], Philip Langer[2], and Tobias Ortmayr[2]

[1] Business Informatics Group, TU Wien, Vienna, Austria
dominik.bork@tuwien.ac.at
[2] EclipseSource, Vienna, Austria
{planger,tortmayr}@eclipsesource.com

Abstract. In the past decade, the modeling community has produced many
feature-rich modeling editors and tool prototypes not only for modeling standards but particularly also for many domain-specific languages. More recently,
however, web-based modeling tools have started to become increasingly popular
in the industry for visualizing and editing models adhering to such languages.
This new generation of modeling tools is built with web technologies and offers
much more flexibility when it comes to their user experience, accessibility, reuse,
and deployment options. One of the technologies behind this new generation of
tools is the Graphical Language Server Platform (GLSP), an open-source client-
server framework hosted under the Eclipse foundation, which allows tool developers to build modern diagram editors for modeling tools that run in the browser
or can be easily integrated into IDEs such as Eclipse, VS Code, or Theia. In this
paper, we describe our vision for more flexible modeling tools which is based
on our experiences from developing several traditional and web-based modeling
tools in an industrial and academic context. With that, we aim at sparking a new
line of research and innovation in the modeling community for modeling tool
development practices and to explore opportunities, advantages, and limitations
of web-based modeling tools, as well as bridge the gap between scientific tool
prototypes and industrial tools being used in practice.

Keywords: Web modeling · Modeling tool · GLSP · LSP · Language Server
Protocol · Flexibility · Deployment · Tool development

1 Introduction

Efficient techniques and platforms for the development of modeling languages and
tools, such as language workbenches and meta-modeling frameworks, have been a
research endeavor in the modeling community since decades [21,22,41]. This is not surprising, because many of the innovative contributions of this community, such as new
domain-specific languages or algorithms to process or transform models, only 'come
to life' with appropriate tool support. This tool support is not only essential for properly evaluating the feasibility and characteristics of the proposed approaches, but also
for sparking new research initiatives around this topic, allowing others to build upon
existing work. This is why, for instance, the premier outlets for cutting-edge modeling

© IFIP International Federation for Information Processing 2024
Published by Springer Nature Switzerland AG 2024
J. P. A. Almeida et al. (Eds.): PoEM 2023, LNBIP 497, pp. 109–124, 2024.
https://doi.org/10.1007/978-3-031-48583-1_7

research (i.e., the BPM, ER, and MODELS conferences) offer dedicated tool tracks to encourage researchers in sharing their modeling tools alongside their theoretical and conceptual contributions. Historically, tool development workshops date back to even 2010 [31].

In recent years, there has been a trend towards migrating software development tools (IDEs) to web-based applications and making them available as a cloud service. Prominent examples of this are Github Codespaces and the transition from Visual Studio to VS Code. This move to the cloud was only recently transferred to the development of modeling tools. While the strengths of web and cloud-based modeling tools are undisputed compared to the traditionally heavy-weight desktop modeling tools [35, 36], research into their development, deployment, and operation is still in its infancy. With Eclipse GLSP and emf.cloud, the Eclipse Foundation has provided the first important technologies for the development of cloud-based modeling tools from scratch and made them available as open-source libraries. With this vision paper, we aim to spark a new line of research that explores and utilizes the many flexibility options enabled by this new breed of GLSP-based web modeling tools.

The remainder of this paper is organized as follows. Section 2 provides background information on how GLSP uses the concepts of the Language Server Protocol (LSP) [4] to support the editing of graphical diagrams (i.e., models). The need for flexible web modeling tools is discussed in Sect. 3. Section 4 then elaborates on the many flexibility options offered by GLSP-based web modeling tools. Our vision toward flexible modeling tools is summarized in Sect. 5 before we conclude this vision paper in Sect. 6.

2 Background

In the following, we will briefly establish the relevant foundations necessary to understand the workings of GLSP.

2.1 Language Server Protocol

In industry, tool providers are striving for making tool development increasingly efficient. A modern and popular example of such an endeavor is the Language Server Protocol (LSP) [4], which evolved to be the de-facto standard for developing language editing support in modern Integrated Development Environments (IDEs) since it was originally introduced by Microsoft, RedHat, and Codeenvy in 2016 [5].

The core idea behind LSP is to split the traditionally rather monolithic language implementations of IDEs into a language client, which is a user-facing generic editor, and a language server, which encapsulates the implementation of the language smarts of a language, such as parsing, indexing, and refactoring support, in an IDE-independent backend component. The protocol of LSP itself standardizes the communication between these two components so that the client only needs to be able to interpret and understand the protocol instead of the specific programming language, whereas the server can focus on the language support but does not need to consider the specifics of the respective IDE. This reduces the complexity of realizing language support on different IDEs and opens up the development of language support in an arbitrary programming language, independently of any IDE into which the language shall be integrated. Currently, version 3.17 of the protocol describes 40 different messages between client and server and has an implementation for over 100 different programming languages/technologies [28, 29].

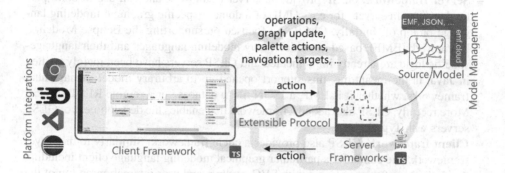

Fig. 1. Overview of GLSP components and their interplay.

2.2 Graphical Language Server Protocol

Initially, LSP has only been defined and used for text-based languages. Still, it was quickly discovered that this concept could also be applied to other areas, one of them being graphical languages by the research community [36] and the open-source modeling community at Eclipse [32]. Soon after, the Eclipse Graphical Language Server Platform (Eclipse GLSP) [12] has been established as an open-source project that uses an LSP-like protocol, as well as generic framework components to enable the development of custom, web-based diagram editors, transferring LSP's client/server architecture for diagrams (see Fig. 1). Thus, the server is responsible for model management, editing logic, validation, and manipulation of the underlying model(s) and communicates via a JSON-RPC (web-)socket to a client, which is responsible for rendering the graphical representation of a model and handling user interactions. Besides a defined set of protocol message types, the communication between the client and the server is centered around a *graphical model*, which is shared between the client and the server and which describes the hierarchical structure and state of a diagram based on an attributed, typed graph on a two-dimensional coordinate system. On the client, this graphical model is rendered as an SVG element inside a browser with the help of Eclipse Sprotty[1]. User interactions on this SVG graph on the client may result in GLSP actions, which are, depending on their type, either handled locally on the client, e.g., for panning, zooming, or visual feedback, or they are transferred back to the server, e.g., to perform a manipulation of the underlying model(s). If an action on the server results in a model change that affects the diagram, the server processes the change in its internal model management and eventually sends a new version of the graphical model to be rendered back to the client to refresh the diagram view.

---

[1] https://github.com/eclipse/sprotty.

GLSP is under active development by the community since 2017, with the next major release v2.0.0 (expected in late 2023). Since its inception, we observe an increasing adoption of GLSP in industry[2] and popularity[3]. In its current version, GLSP provides four types of components for realizing modern web-based modeling tools (see Fig. 1):

- **Server framework.** GLSP provides a server framework one can use to build particular diagram servers for e.g., UML or a domain-specific graphical modeling language on top of. Initially, GLSP was focused on supporting the Eclipse Modeling Framework (EMF), based on which many modeling languages and their language-specific logic are already implemented and GLSP servers have been mainly written in Java. In the meantime, this support opened up to arbitrary model management frameworks, whether it is EMF, a JSON file, a database or a remote REST service. More recently, GLSP also added a framework that enables the development of GLSP servers with TypeScript.
- **Client framework.** GLSP also provides a client framework. Similarly to the server framework, one can build a particular graphical modeling language client including the definition of the rendering with SVG, styling, and user interaction on top of the provided GLSP client framework. As the rendering and user interaction may heavily differ between one graphical modeling language and another, the client framework allows users to take full control over the SVG view implementations for rendering and enable the customization, as well as adding additional editing tools to control user interaction.
- **Protocol.** The messages that can be exchanged between the GLSP clients and servers are specified in a flexible and extensible GLSP protocol which standardizes, at a language-agnostic abstraction level, the communication between arbitrary clients and servers.
- **Platform integration.** GLSP provides platform integrations and reusable components that take an implemented GLSP diagram client and integrate it seamlessly into platforms such as Eclipse RCP, Eclipse Theia, or VS Code. These components provide the clue code necessary to register an editor to a certain file type or some other commands specific to the integrated platform. With that, GLSP aims at enabling the integration of GLSP editors into multiple tool platforms and applications with maximum reuse.

3   On the Need for Flexibility

The idea behind LSP and GLSP is not just driven by the goal of migrating (modeling) tools toward a web-based UI technology stack. It aims also at breaking with monolithic architectures, tight coupling with underlying tool platforms, and fixed deployment architectures (such as a desktop client or a cloud-based deployment). In fact, the tool market in recent years has significantly changed. Instead of a single heavy-weight

---

[2] See https://ecdtools.eclipse.org/adopters for companies that agreed to be publicly listed as adopters alongside several more companies who do not want to be named.

[3] On Github, the GLSP project has about 180 new discussion threads per year and around 1400 weekly downloads on npmjs.com.

monolithic desktop application that needs to support all possible tasks along the software development process, users expect their language-specific tools to be compatible and only lightly integrated with multiple tool platforms or editors such as VS Code, Eclipse Theia, VI, or Emacs. This enables a more flexible combination of the best-in-class components. Also, more development tools need to support both, running as a desktop application operating on a local file system, but also being deployed in the cloud based on ephemeral, task-, or context-specific workspaces. Users expect to click a link, for instance on a pull request, and end up in a prepared and readily configured tool, running in the browser, where the changes of the pull request are already checked out, possibly pre-built, and all runtime components, such as those required for debugging or generating and running code, are available in the cloud container, while still being able to edit the project at hand with full editing support of a powerful IDE running in the browser. Thus the components working on those diverse environments must be agnostic and loosely coupled with the filesystem and their runtime (browser, cloud infrastructure, or desktop). Any change applied by the user in this environment is eventually put into a new commit on that pull request to store the state back into the repository. After a task is completed, the workspace is thrown away and a new one is created for the next task at hand. This trend, which increasingly becomes the state of the art in software engineering, slowly arrives also in the world of modeling tools, too.

Flexibility with respect to the modeling approach itself is not a new topic, see [19,37]. There even have been scientific workshops in the past that were dedicated to flexible tools [31]. Within the modeling community, flexibility is often related to informal vs. formal modeling [3,16,20,43] or the availability of multiple, stakeholder-specific concrete syntaxes (cf. blended modeling [11,18]). Many works focus on mitigating the dichotomy [31,37] between very formal and powerful tools supporting experts in later stages of engineering projects with the informal, flexible, and creativity-fostering tools that can be used by non-experts in the earlier stages [39,42].

There is only very little research that concerns the flexibility of language workbenches or metamodeling platforms. In most of the papers reporting such platforms, the term 'flexible' [2,40] refers to the flexibility of i) supporting arbitrary modeling languages, and ii) realizing domain-specific concrete syntaxes. FlexiSketch [42] is an example of a tool that allows sketching models, i.e., using an informal approach to create early designs which are then later translated into formal models adhering to a formal modeling language. Interesting concepts for a modular composition and customization of metamodels have been presented in [44].

What is lacking so far, and what we propose in this vision paper, is to move the flexibility discussion to the platforms we use to develop modeling tools, and consequently, to the flexibility entailed in the deployed and used tools themselves. In the next section, we will basically take this idea of flexibility and walk through the GLSP architecture and its components (cf. Sect. 2.2), and give some examples of where flexibility is crucial and how it is enabled by GLSP.

4 Flexibility of GLSP-Based Web Modeling Tools

Over the years, the community around GLSP pushed toward making several aspects of GLSP more flexible and versatile across all GLSP components (cf. Fig. 1). This not only involves benefiting from the full power of the web-based UI technology stack (SVG, HTML5, CSS) for implementing modern diagram frontends, but also having more freedom in choosing the programming language for the backend, supporting multiple tool platforms at the same time, deploying logic in the browser or in the backend, and enabling to hook up GLSP servers with arbitrary model management backends, such as EMF, other file formats, databases, remote filesystems or REST APIs. In the remainder of this section, we summarize and reflect on the use cases and flexibility that has been added to GLSP by the community based on industry needs.

4.1   Flexibility via Inversion of Control

One of the main goals of the GLSP initiative is to provide a flexible and reusable framework for building graphical modeling tools that can be easily integrated into any application frame and deployment scenario. Every aspect of the framework might need to be extended or customized. Therefore, following the example of modern web-based tools such as Eclipse Theia and Sprotty, an *Inversion of Control* pattern based on dependency injection is used. Each GLSP component encapsulates implementation logic and services into reusable feature modules. Modules can be extended or customized toward the needs of a specific use case. This facilitates a composable architecture of reusable and interchangeable components. We observe that the flexible, modular approach has become one of the main arguments for adopting GLSP by the industry because adopters can fully tailor the framework to their needs.

4.2   Flexibility on the Client

Recently, language workbenches and frameworks for building modeling tools, such as Eclipse GEF, GMF runtime, GMF tooling, and Sirius, were building an increasing number of abstraction layers hiding the details of the actual user interface implementation. While this arguably makes it very simple to get started, as technical details are hidden away, this also hampers the power of tool developers to carefully design the user experience, often leading to generic and poor usability, as was also reported by adopters of that technologies [1]. With the modern, web-based user interface technology stack, including HTML5, CSS, and SVG, new opportunities for rethinking the dusty usability concepts of traditional modeling tools arise.

With the increasing adoption of Eclipse GLSP in industry, we increasingly observed the force driven by industrial use cases to avoid burying the user interface implementation below layers of abstraction, as was often the case in traditional modeling frameworks, but rather empower tool developers with direct access to the excellent and well-known UI technologies to give them full control over look and feel of their modeling tools. This certainly does not mean having to build everything from scratch. Instead, the reusable user interface concepts are provided as a library of shapes, editing tools, UI components, etc., which can be used as is, but also be customized or even replaced entirely. Consequently, in GLSP, the SVG generation and CSS styles for diagrams are not hidden anymore behind abstract diagram configurations, but are directly exposed in the form of reusable library components, which are open to modification in order to give full flexibility in realizing advanced model representation and the user interaction by means of editing tools (cf. [9] for a taxonomy of advanced features). This decision also enables GLSP-based tool developers to benefit from the rich set of available experience of working with languages like SVG but also to use the availability of excellent debugging tools for these languages. Besides the SVG view implementations, adopters of GLSP can even fully customize the editing tools of the modeling tool to account for the particular needs of a domain-specific user group and introduce features, such as highlighting the valid target elements after the user selected the source element of a newly created edge, etc. The generation of SVG can even be highly dynamic (a gallery of examples is provided online[4]). Recent research showed, how the standardized mapping of a graph model element to an SVG element can be flexibly extended by dynamically adjusting e.g., the rendered i) form, and ii) content of the elements based on the currently visible *zoom level* [8], see Fig. 2 for an illustration of the dynamic adaptation of the rendered model in the GLSP client contingent on the current zoom level[5].

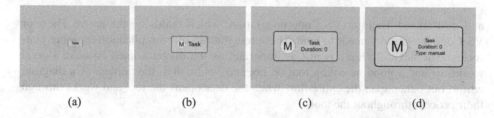

(a)   (b)   (c)   (d)

Fig. 2. Dynamic GLSP-client side rendering.

Lastly, several use cases raised the need for adding additional UI controls, implemented in plain HTML, CSS, and JavaScript, on top of the diagram. This allows adding controls, e.g., for enabling or disabling certain filters or for editing certain aspects of the model with web forms or complex text boxes after, for instance, selecting a diagram element.

4.3 Flexibility on the Integration

Based on our experience, flexibility also matters when thinking of integrating the GLSP-based diagram editors into a tool platform like Eclipse, VS Code, or Eclipse Theia. With GLSP, there is a clear separation of concerns in place where the diagram editor is kept entirely platform independent and only integrated via platform-specific glue code, which in turn interfaces to the platform's native APIs. From this separation of concerns follows that a GLSP tool developer can not only use the diagram editors with maximum reuse across multiple tool platforms but also benefit from the full power of the platform's native APIs to implement a seamless integration between the editor and the tool platform, including populating error markers to the platform's problems view, allowing navigating across views and editors to diagram elements, etc.

The architecture of this separation is schematically illustrated in Fig. 3 for Theia and VS Code. The GLSP diagram client exposes an interface to which an extended

---

[4] https://www.eclipse.org/glsp/gallery/.
[5] Semantic Zoom video: https://www.youtube.com/watch?v=iBs-fGwq15Y.

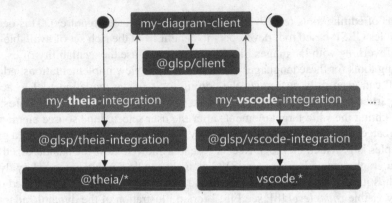

Fig. 3. Flexible platform integration of GLSP diagram editors.

and customized Theia or VS Code integration, which builds on the native Theia or VS Code integration, needs to bind. These integrations allow replication for other platforms. The flexibility here is just as important as the diagram itself because a good workflow and a good modeling tool do not start and end at the borders of a diagram editor, but rather span the entire flow when the user opens the tool and works through their process throughout the tool.

4.4   Flexibility in the Protocol

A core enabler of the flexibility of GLSP-based modeling tools is the protocol that is being used to coordinate the GLSP clients with the GLSP server. This protocol shares the fundamental idea behind the Language Server Protocol (LSP) [4] and is designed to cover the most common actions adhering to graphical diagram editors out of the box. As diagram editors are usually very specific in their interaction and capabilities though, it is worth noting that the protocol is intended to be enhanced with custom actions, which can either be sent from the client to the server to, for instance, execute some model processing on the source model or to notify the server about UI events in custom UI controls. Likewise, the server can define custom actions to send to the client, e.g., to inform the client about validity checks or about additional domain-specific information.

Another flexibility enabled by the protocol is that it abstracts away from the underlying technologies used to implement the GLSP client and GLSP server. This enables the development of further client and server frameworks in different technologies – something we see now with the new TypeScript-based GLSP server framework alongside the existing one for Java. Here is where we see that GLSP further inherits the strengths of the LSP where we recognize an increase of available LSP clients[6], LSP servers[7], and LSP Software Development Kits[8]. It would be surprising to not see similar developments surrounding GLSP in the near future.

---

[6] https://microsoft.github.io/language-server-protocol/implementors/tools/.

[7] https://microsoft.github.io/language-server-protocol/implementors/servers/.

[8] https://microsoft.github.io/language-server-protocol/implementors/sdks/.

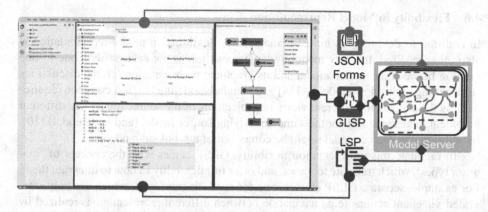

Fig. 4. Flexibility in model management.

4.5 Flexibility in the Model Management

Flexibility in model management was a huge objective with the 1.0 release of GLSP. It is now the developer's choice how to realize model management, i.e., to decide *which format* to use, which *framework* to use, whether it is *local or remote*, and whether it is realized as a *shared service* across users or *isolated*. This flexibility certainly entails additional implementation effort for specific model management frameworks, as model commands, loading, and saving models are inherently specific to the used model management. To mitigate this effort, GLSP with its 1.0 release pulled out the generic implementations into reusable model management modules to simplify writing GLSP servers that interact with EMF, JSON, and emf.cloud[9]. This flexibility not only supports the migration of existing tools into GLSP but also prevents a lock-in in the future.

Eventually, this also enables model management reuse across multiple deployments and in different platform integrations. For example, a local tool can interact with the local file system while when integrated into a web application, the same tool, with just a replaced model management module, can use a shared model management or a shared model server where several people can have read/write access.

GLSP comes now with the emf.cloud model server component which enables multiple widgets in the modeling tool to interact with the same underlying model. The emf.cloud model server essentially provides a component that loads and manages these runtime states of the model so that they can be then interacted with from different widgets with different services like GLSP editors, JSON forms, and LSP editors (see Fig. 4). They all manipulate overlapping parts of the same underlying model and the model server encapsulates these model states and ensures consistent collaborative modeling using multiple forms/widgets.

---

[9] https://github.com/eclipse-emfcloud/emfcloud-modelserver.

4.6   Flexibility in Model Representation

In addition to flexibility in model management, flexibility in model representation is also often required. In many modeling languages there is not necessarily a one-to-one relation between the source model and its graphical representation (cf. the discussions surrounding multi-view modeling [34] and blended modeling [11]). A common requirement is the support for different views or projections of the source model i.e., different graphical representations for the same underlying source model (and metamodel) [10]. In addition, the source model might be composed of a set of submodels.

To facilitate this representation flexibility, GLSP comes with the concept of 'diagram types', which translate to views, and offer full flexibility in how to integrate them. For example, separate GLSP editors, one for each diagram type, which are only integrated via client actions (e.g., navigation between different representations realized by the individual editors). Alternatively, one GLSP server can support two (or more) diagram types with one shared data or with multiple source models.

4.7   Flexibility on the Server

Due to the clear protocol-based separation between the client and the server, tool developers can choose to write their GLSP servers in any programming language as long as they adhere to the defined protocol. However, writing servers from scratch entails quite some effort. GLSP, therefore, provides server frameworks that already cover all generic features and also provides supporting libraries to implement the diagram-specific functionality.

At its inception, GLSP only provided a Java-based server framework. With GLSP 1.0, however, a framework for TypeScript has been added, which gives tool developers the flexibility to choose what is the best fit for their project without the penalty of having to implement a server from scratch. The TypeScript-based server framework has significant advantages for use cases where one is targeting a VS Code or non-cloud-based Theia platform, as these already come with the nodejs runtime and, thus, don't entail any additional runtime requirements, such as a Java Virtual Machine, on the user's machine. Moreover, a TypeScript-based GLSP server leads to a more homogenous development stack alongside the TypeScript-based client.

4.8   Flexibility in Deployment

The GLSP architecture and the flexibilities discussed at the outset, especially on the server and the model management, enable high flexibility with respect to the deployment of GLSP-based modeling tools. Figure 5 illustrates common deployment options observed in the industry. Note that this illustration is not aimed to be comprehensive and further options are likely possible. The deployment options are clustered along three decisions: i) which tool integration to use?; ii) which GLSP server framework to use?; and iii) which model management framework to use?

From a runtime perspective, one can further decide whether the components run in their own, separate processes, in one single process, or even in separate containers, which is particularly valuable in a cloud infrastructure scenario. While in Eclipse it

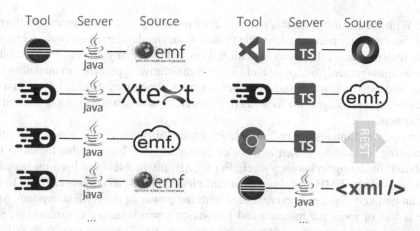

Fig. 5. Flexibility in deploying GLSP-based modeling tools.

makes sense to have everything running in one process if your server is Java-based, in VS Code, extensions typically run a separate nodejs process. In a Theia cloud deployment, one can deploy a separate Docker container and even go as far as extracting the model management into its own potentially shared container. Eventually, having a TypeScript-based server even enables lightweight deployment scenarios, in which no separate process and no cloud infrastructure is required at all and the entire GLSP editor, including the client and the server, is running in the browser only.

5   The Vision for Flexible Web Modeling Tools

This vision paper aims to spark attention to the possibilities offered by highly flexible platforms like Eclipse's Graphical Language Server Platform (GLSP) and the web modeling tools built with them. The modeling community has a long tradition of developing modeling tools. However, often these innovative tools remain on a scientific prototypical level [33] and only a few of them, e.g., Papyrus [24], reach a maturity level that qualifies for wide-spread educational and industrial application. Based on our experience, we believe one aspect that results in this situation is the fact that traditional metamodeling platforms do not rely on standardized, extensible, and open technologies and protocols—or, if so, they hide them behind some layers of abstraction to ease the development for tool developers with less software engineering experience. Moreover, often they do not naturally adopt a modular approach, once the development is concluded, a packaged final product is compiled which hampers extension and interoperability. This lack of flexibility in traditional tools is what often causes the lack of maturity and widespread use. In the context of web development and web-based modeling tools, however, such flexibility is invariant for longevity. This is why we believe platforms such as GLSP will have a prosperous future—with flexibility and modularity built in.

We believe with the uptake of platforms like GLSP it is now time to move forward as a community and bridge the gap between academic prototypes and modern industrial tools. With the flexibility of this new breed of modeling tool development platforms, researchers and engineers are now able to start from standardized base (web) technologies to realize state-of-the-art tools, with full control over many aspects, from usability to model management, to explore and facilitate innovative approaches to modeling languages and tools. The use of standard open-source technologies should also account for sustainability and mitigate the lock-in effect which is particularly harmful in a scientific environment.

An open and interesting endeavor toward the realization of this vision is to bring the existing tools and the vast amount of powerful EMF-based technologies to this web-based modeling technology stack. For GLSP, this problem has been mitigated in so far, as with the EMF model server in emf.cloud, there is a component ready to use that can be likely equipped and extended with the power of the EMF ecosystem. Still, there is lots of room for research and innovation towards easing the transition, providing modern and responsive front-ends to existing EMF technologies, such as EMF Compare, model query and transformation approaches, model refactoring, and many great achievements of the modeling community. For all those approaches, we would be thrilled to see not only a one-to-one migration but also a re-evaluation of how the usability and flexibility of those approaches can be enhanced based on the power of this new web-based technology stack.

To learn from existing solutions and to not re-do the same mistakes from the past, it would be also essential to establish a broader open knowledge base of best practices and successful tool developments with GLSP [26]. With the further maturing of the technologies and the increasing attention by the community, we expect this is just a matter of time. Given that GLSP has this clear separation of concerns, such a knowledge base or a source code repository would greatly foster reuse across modeling tools. Therefore, existing high-quality solutions can be easily injected and reused for common requirements while unique features of a specific modeling tool can still be customized to the highest extent.

The open and flexible architecture of these new breeds of modeling tools also enables the efficient injection of external functionality and features that are also built on base web technologies. For example, existing frameworks for testing the accessibility of web applications can now be adapted to test modeling tools with respect to their accessibility for modelers with disabilities – a topic mostly ignored until now with increasing importance. Moreover, the open technology stack also eases the reuse and injection of AI/ML solutions to support downstream conceptual modeling tasks like model pattern discovery [15], domain classification [25,38], model completion [7], refactoring [23], repair [14], and model transformation [6]. All this should ease the realization of smart modeling assistants [13,30].

To realize this vision, it is essential, that the modeling community further strengthens the links to industry and open-source communities, such as the Eclipse GLSP community. By increasing collaborations, researchers can gain access to the needs of the industry while the platform vendors can learn from the innovative approaches developed in academia and support translating them into common platform features.

6   Conclusion

In this paper, we envisioned the future of much more flexible web modeling tools. Using the Graphical Language Server Protocol (GLSP) platform as the currently most promising modeling tool development platform, we elaborated in detail on the many facets of flexibility that are enabled by this new breed of tool development platforms. Obviously, our presentation is focused on the concrete flexibility enabled by GLSP. However, as GLSP heavily utilizes standardized web technologies and communication protocols, and architecturally aligns with state-of-the-art approaches for textual language engineering (LSP) [17], we believe many of the presented flexibilities can be translated to other, future web modeling tool development platforms we are not aware of today. By moving from proprietary technologies toward standardized open-source web technologies, the tools developed by the modeling community can eventually bridge the current gap between academic prototypes and modeling tools used in industry. This may also foster collaborations between the modeling research community and practice [27].

References

1. Abrahão, S., et al.: User experience for model-driven engineering: challenges and future directions. In: 2017 ACM/IEEE 20th International Conference on Model Driven Engineering Languages and Systems (MODELS), pp. 229–236 (2017). https://doi.org/10.1109/MODELS.2017.5
2. Atkinson, C., Gerbig, R.: Flexible deep modeling with melanee. In: Betz, S., Reimer, U. (eds.) Modellierung 2016, 2.-4. März 2016, Karlsruhe - Workshopband LNI, vol. P-255, pp. 117–122. GI (2016). https://dl.gi.de/20.500.12116/843
3. Bork, D., Alter, S.: Satisfying four requirements for more flexible modeling methods: theory and test case. Enterp. Model. Inf. Syst. Archit. Int. J. Concept. Model. 15, 3:1–3:25 (2020). https://doi.org/10.18417/emisa.15.3
4. Bork, D., Langer, P.: Language server protocol - an introduction to the protocol, its use, and adoption for web modeling tools. Enterp. Model. Inf. Syst. Arch. Int. J. Concept. Model. 18(9), 1–16 (2023). https://doi.org/10.18417/emisa.18.9
5. Bünder, H.: Decoupling language and editor-the impact of the language server protocol on textual domain-specific languages. In: MODELSWARD, pp. 129–140 (2019)
6. Burgueno, L., Cabot, J., Li, S., Gérard, S.: A generic LSTM neural network architecture to infer heterogeneous model transformations. Softw. Syst. Model. 21(1), 139–156 (2022)
7. Burgueño, L., Clarisó, R., Gérard, S., Li, S., Cabot, J.: An NLP-based architecture for the autocompletion of partial domain models. In: La Rosa, M., Sadiq, S., Teniente, E. (eds.) CAiSE 2021. LNCS, vol. 12751, pp. 91–106. Springer, Cham (2021). https://doi.org/10.1007/978-3-030-79382-1_6
8. Carlo, G.D., Langer, P., Bork, D.: Advanced visualization and interaction in glsp-based web modeling: realizing semantic zoom and off-screen elements. In: Syriani, E., Sahraoui, H.A., Bencomo, N., Wimmer, M. (eds.) Proceedings of the 25th International Conference on Model Driven Engineering Languages and Systems, MODELS 2022, Montreal, Quebec, Canada, 2022, pp. 221–231. ACM (2022). https://doi.org/10.1145/3550355.3552412
9. Carlo, G.D., Langer, P., Bork, D.: Rethinking model representation - a taxonomy of advanced information visualization in conceptual modeling. In: Ralyté, J., Chakravarthy, S., Mohania, M.K., Jeusfeld, M.A., Karlapalem, K. (eds.) Conceptual Modeling - 41st International Conference, ER 2022, Hyderabad, India, 2022, Proceedings. Lecture Notes in Computer

Science, vol. 13607, pp. 35–51. Springer, Heidelberg (2022). https://doi.org/10.1007/978-3-031-17995-2_3

10. Cicchetti, A., Ciccozzi, F., Leveque, T.: A hybrid approach for multi-view modeling. Electron. Commun. Eur. Assoc. Softw. Sci. Technol. **50**, 1–13 (2011). https://doi.org/10.14279/tuj.eceasst.50.738

11. David, I., et al.: Blended modeling in commercial and open-source model-driven software engineering tools: A systematic study. Softw. Syst. Model. **22**(1), 415–447 (2023). https://doi.org/10.1007/s10270-022-01010-3

12. Eclipse Foundation: Eclipse graphical language server platform. https://ithub.com/eclipse-glsp/glsp. Accessed 10 June 2023

13. Feltus, C., Ma, Q., Proper, H.A., Kelsen, P.: Towards AI assisted domain modeling. In: Reinhartz-Berger, I., Sadiq, S. (eds.) ER 2021. LNCS, vol. 13012, pp. 75–89. Springer, Cham (2021). https://doi.org/10.1007/978-3-030-88358-4_7

14. Fumagalli, M., Sales, T.P., Guizzardi, G.: Towards automated support for conceptual model diagnosis and repair. In: Advances in Conceptual Modeling: ER 2020 Workshops CMAI, CMLS, CMOMM4FAIR, CoMoNoS, EmpER, Vienna, Austria, 3–6 November 2020, Proceedings, vol. 39, pp. 15–25. Springer, Heidelberg (2020). https://doi.org/10.1007/978-3-030-65847-2_2

15. Fumagalli, M., Sales, T.P., Guizzardi, G.: Pattern discovery in conceptual models using frequent itemset mining. In: Conceptual Modeling: 41st International Conference, ER 2022, Hyderabad, India, 17–20 October 2022, Proceedings, pp. 52–62. Springer, Heidelberg (2022). https://doi.org/10.1007/978-3-031-17995-2_4

16. Gabrysiak, G., Giese, H., Lüders, A., Seibel, A.: How can metamodels be used flexibly. In: Proceedings of ICSE 2011 Workshop on Flexible Modeling Tools, Waikiki/Honolulu, vol. 22 (2011)

17. Giner-Miguelez, J., Gómez, A., Cabot, J.: Describeml: a tool for describing machine learning datasets. In: Kühn, T., Sousa, V. (eds.) Proceedings of the 25th International Conference on Model Driven Engineering Languages and Systems: Companion Proceedings, MODELS 2022, Montreal, Quebec, Canada, 23–28 October 2022, pp. 22–26. ACM (2022). https://doi.org/10.1145/3550356.3559087

18. Glaser, P., Bork, D.: The biger tool - hybrid textual and graphical modeling of entity relationships in VS code. In: 25th International Enterprise Distributed Object Computing Workshop, EDOC Workshop 2021, Gold Coast, Australia, 25–29 October 2021, pp. 337–340. IEEE (2021). https://doi.org/10.1109/EDOCW52865.2021.00066

19. Guerra, E., de Lara, J.: On the quest for flexible modelling. In: Wasowski, A., Paige, R.F., Haugen, Ø. (eds.) Proceedings of the 21st ACM/IEEE International Conference on Model Driven Engineering Languages and Systems, MODELS 2018, Copenhagen, Denmark, 14–19 October 2018, pp. 23–33. ACM (2018). DOI: https://doi.org/10.1145/3239372.3239376

20. Harel, D., Rumpe, B.: Modeling languages: Syntax, semantics and all that stuff - Part I: The Basic Stuff. Technical report, Technical report (2000). http://citeseerx.ist.psu.edu/viewdoc/summary?doi=10.1.1.10.1512

21. Jarke, M., Gallersdörfer, R., Jeusfeld, M.A., Staudt, M.: Conceptbase - a deductive object base for meta data management. J. Intell. Inf. Syst. **4**(2), 167–192 (1995). https://doi.org/10.1007/BF00961873

22. Kelly, S., Lyytinen, K., Rossi, M.: MetaEdit+ a fully configurable multi-user and multi-tool CASE and CAME environment. In: Constantopoulos, P., Mylopoulos, J., Vassiliou, Y. (eds.) CAiSE 1996. LNCS, vol. 1080, pp. 1–21. Springer, Heidelberg (1996). https://doi.org/10.1007/3-540-61292-0_1

23. Lahijany, G.M., Ohrndorf, M., Zenkert, J., Fathi, M., Kelte, U.: Identibug: model-driven visualization of bug reports by extracting class diagram excerpts. In: 2021 IEEE International Conference on Systems, Man, and Cybernetics (SMC), pp. 3317–3323. IEEE (2021)

24. Lanusse, A., et al.: Papyrus uml: an open source toolset for MDA. In: Proceedings of the Fifth European Conference on Model-Driven Architecture Foundations and Applications (ECMDA-FA 2009), pp. 1–4. Citeseer (2009)
25. López, J.A.H., Rubei, R., Cuadrado, J.S., Di Ruscio, D.: Machine learning methods for model classification: a comparative study. In: Proceedings of the 25th International Conference on Model Driven Engineering Languages and Systems, pp. 165–175 (2022)
26. Metin, H., Bork, D.: On developing and operating glsp-based web modeling tools: Lessons learned from bigUML. In: Proceedings of the 26th International Conference on Model Driven Engineering Languages and Systems, MODELS 2023. IEEE (2023). https://model-engineering.info/publications/papers/MODELS23-GLSP-Development-Web.pdf
27. Michael, J., Bork, D., Wimmer, M., Mayr, H.C.: Quo vadis modeling? findings of a community survey, an ad-hoc bibliometric analysis, and expert interviews on data, process, and software modeling. Softw. Syst. Model. (2023). https://doi.org/10.1007/s10270-023-01128-y
28. Microsoft language server protocol implementations. https://microsoft.github.io/language-server-protocol/implementors/servers/. Accessed 13 June 2023
29. Microsoft language server protocol specification. https://microsoft.github.io/language-server-protocol/specifications/specification-current/. Accessed 13 June 2023
30. Mussbacher, G., et al.: Opportunities in intelligent modeling assistance. Softw. Syst. Model. 19(5), 1045–1053 (2020). https://doi.org/10.1007/s10270-020-00814-5
31. Ossher, H., van der Hoek, A., Storey, M.D., Grundy, J., Bellamy, R.K.E.: Flexible modeling tools (flexitools2010). In: Kramer, J., Bishop, J., Devanbu, P.T., Uchitel, S. (eds.) Proceedings of the 32nd ACM/IEEE International Conference on Software Engineering - Volume 2, ICSE 2010, Cape Town, South Africa, 1–8 May 2010, pp. 441–442. ACM (2010). https://doi.org/10.1145/1810295.1810419
32. Langer, P.: Towards a graphical language server protocol for diagrams?, eclipsecon 2018. https://www.youtube.com/watch?v=snh1UTSH3Zw. Accessed 10 June 2023
33. Pourali, P., Atlee, J.M.: An empirical investigation to understand the difficulties and challenges of software modellers when using modelling tools. In: Wasowski, A., Paige, R.F., Haugen, Ø. (eds.) Proceedings of the 21th ACM/IEEE International Conference on Model Driven Engineering Languages and Systems, MODELS 2018, pp. 224–234. ACM (2018). https://doi.org/10.1145/3239372.3239400
34. Reineke, J., Stergiou, C., Tripakis, S.: Basic problems in multi-view modeling. Softw. Syst. Model. 18(3), 1577–1611 (2019). https://doi.org/10.1007/s10270-017-0638-1
35. Rodríguez-Echeverría, R., Izquierdo, J.L.C., Wimmer, M., Cabot, J.: An LSP infrastructure to build EMF language servers for web-deployable model editors. In: Hebig, R., Berger, T. (eds.) Proceedings of MODELS 2018 Workshops. CEUR Workshop Proceedings, vol. 2245, pp. 326–335. CEUR-WS.org (2018)
36. Rodríguez-Echeverría, R., Izquierdo, J.L.C., Wimmer, M., Cabot, J.: Towards a language server protocol infrastructure for graphical modeling. In: Wasowski, A., Paige, R.F., Haugen, Ø. (eds.) Proceedings of the 21th ACM/IEEE International Conference on Model Driven Engineering Languages and Systems, MODELS 2018, Copenhagen, Denmark, 14–19 October 2018, pp. 370–380. ACM (2018). https://doi.org/10.1145/3239372.3239383
37. Rose, L.M., Kolovos, D.S., Paige, R.F.: Eugenia live: a flexible graphical modelling tool. In: Ruscio, D.D., Pierantonio, A., de Lara, J. (eds.) Proceedings of the 2012 Extreme Modeling Workshop, XM 2012, Innsbruck, Austria, 1 October 2012, pp. 15–20. ACM (2012). https://doi.org/10.1145/2467307.2467311
38. Rubei, R., Di Rocco, J., Di Ruscio, D., Nguyen, P.T., Pierantonio, A.: A lightweight approach for the automated classification and clustering of metamodels. In: 2021 ACM/IEEE International Conference on Model Driven Engineering Languages and Systems Companion (MODELS-C), pp. 477–482. IEEE (2021)

39. Sandkuhl, K., et al.: From expert discipline to common practice: a vision and research agenda for extending the reach of enterprise modeling. Bus. Inf. Syst. Eng. **60**(1), 69–80 (2018). https://doi.org/10.1007/s12599-017-0516-y
40. Smolander, K., Lyytinen, K., Tahvanainen, V.-P., Marttiin, P.: MetaEdit—a flexible graphical environment for methodology modelling. In: Andersen, R., Bubenko, J.A., Sølvberg, A. (eds.) CAiSE 1991. LNCS, vol. 498, pp. 168–193. Springer, Heidelberg (1991). https://doi.org/10.1007/3-540-54059-8_85
41. Steinberg, D., Budinsky, F., Merks, E., Paternostro, M.: EMF: Eclipse Modeling Framework. Pearson Education, Boston (2008)
42. Wüest, D., Seyff, N., Glinz, M.: Flexisketch: a lightweight sketching and metamodeling approach for end-users. Softw. Syst. Model. **18**(2), 1513–1541 (2019). https://doi.org/10.1007/s10270-017-0623-8
43. Zarwin, Z., Sottet, J.S., Favre, J.M.: Natural modeling: retrospective and perspectives an anthropological point of view. In: Proceedings of the 2012 Extreme Modeling Workshop, pp. 3–8. ACM (2012)
44. Zivkovic, S.: Metamodel composition in hybrid modelling: a modular approach. Ph.D. thesis, University of Vienna (2016). https://doi.org/10.25365/thesis.41648

Investigating Quality Attributes in Behavior-Driven Development Scenarios: An Evaluation Framework and an Experimental Supporting Tool

Yves Wautelet[1]([⊠]) [iD], Anousheh Khajeh Nassiri[2], and Konstantinos Tsilionis[3] [iD]

[1] KU Leuven, Brussels, Belgium
yves.wautelet@kuleuven.be
[2] UCLouvain, Louvain-la-Neuve, Belgium
anousheh.khajehnassiri@uclouvain.be
[3] Eindhoven University of Technology, Eindhoven, The Netherlands
k.tsilionis@tue.nl

Abstract. Behavior-Driven Development (BDD) refers to an agile development practice to express the fulfillment of a requirement often depicted in a user story. BDD is meant to facilitate the understanding of how to properly execute requirements among role-divergent stakeholders in a software project. In that way, the development team avoids an excessive focus on coding at the early requirements definition stage and can focus on truly capturing the features and behaviors that are expected by the end-users. In BDD, user-driven scenarios are written in structured natural language following a defined template. Notwithstanding, not much attention has been placed in the literature in terms of defining/studying the quality aspects of the written BDD scenarios; therefore, practitioners tend to use the technique in an ad-hoc manner. In this study, we explore the quality attributes assigned to a well-written BDD scenario. We refine an existing framework by establishing formal definitions for each of the scenarios' attributes, study their applicability through real BDD scenarios, and link them to the quality attributes appointed to user stories. We then develop and present an experimental Computer-Aided Software Engineering (CASE) tool that helps practitioners assess the quality of the BDD scenarios through the automated evaluation of a set of conforming quality attributes namely *Uniqueness*, *Essentiality*, *Integrity*, and *Singularity*. We further validate the framework and the tool by collecting two expert opinions.

Keywords: Behavior Driven Development · BDD Quality Attributes · User Story

1 Introduction

Within a typical agile software development process, a product backlog is an ordered list of items or tasks, prioritized in a way that maximizes the value the

© IFIP International Federation for Information Processing 2024
Published by Springer Nature Switzerland AG 2024
J. P. A. Almeida et al. (Eds.): PoEM 2023, LNBIP 497, pp. 125–142, 2024.
https://doi.org/10.1007/978-3-031-48583-1_8

software product delivers [16]. For the sake of coherency, a common way to write the description of a product backlog item is to use user stories [3,15]. These are structured statements (e.g., *As a ⟨type of user⟩, I want ⟨goal⟩, so that ⟨some reason⟩*) that define information about what the user expects from the to-be software (i.e., requirements).

Despite their popularity, user stories do not sufficiently detail how the requirements that they express can be validated, so it is often convenient to complement them with test documentation techniques (see, for example, *Test-Driven Development* [1], and *Acceptance Test-Driven Development* [11]). In Behavior-Driven Development (BDD) [12], one of such testing techniques, a number of test scenarios can be defined for each user story in the project, to provide an additional explanation of the behavior of the feature from the end-user's perspective. Indeed, BDD scenarios constitute a way of 'executing' a requirement; this means that the system under development should effectively support the BDD scenario for the requirement depicted in the corresponding user story to be marked as validated and complete. Only then the requirement can be integrated into the deliverable release conceded to the users at the end of the sprint.

There are some studies that focus on assessing the quality of user stories. We can notably mention the *Quality User Story (QUS)* framework by Lucassen et al. [9,10] which means to assess the quality of user stories based on a collection of attributes studied on a syntactic, semantic, and pragmatic level. We can also mention the *Unified User Story Template* by Wautelet et al. [23,24] meaning to increase the quality of the writing process for user stories by offering a guiding template with specific explications of its incorporating terms. Also, Wautelet et al. [22] evaluate the impact of the user stories quality on the ability to understand and structure software requirement and conclude on a positive impact. However, to the best of our knowledge, there has been limited research on how to write qualitative BDD scenarios or evaluate their quality once they have been written. The present study not only leverages the existing literature to investigate what quality attributes are assigned to a BDD scenario; it is also meant to extend such literary works by studying how quality attributes that enhance the user story format can be applied in the field of BDD. Since both techniques exploit structured natural language but more work has been done on user stories, and given the fact that BDD scenarios are mostly written in conjunction with user stories, it makes sense to evaluate the extent to which the quality attributes of user stories fit the field of BDD scenarios' definition. We aim to build and formalize a consolidated list of quality attributes that practitioners could use when writing BDD scenarios. For this reason, a primary list is being built out of BDD literary works (we mostly rely on the works of Oliveira et al. [13,14]). Then, a comparison is made with a list of quality attributes assigned to user stories as described in the study of Lucassen et al. [9]. Finally, we develop (i.e., code and test) an experimental Computer-Aided Software Engineering (CASE) tool to help a requirements test engineer to assess the BDD scenario qualities and manage the quality flaws in a semi-automated manner; this means that the tool can autonomously identify some quality issues by pointing out the BDD elements that need further evaluation. This way, the quality of BDD scenarios can be improved. For further validation, we interview 2 experts in the field of requirements engineering and ask them to provide feedback on our framework and CASE-tool.

Overall, Sect. 2 shortly describes BDD as well as the state-of-the-art in search of quality when writing BDD scenarios. Section 3 describes the research approach. Section 4 and Sect. 5 present the main contributions: first, we collect BDD quality attributes and accompany them with formal definitions to refine the existing ones found in the literature; we also evaluate them on BDD scenarios from a dataset. Second, we survey the link between the quality attributes of user stories and BDD scenarios. Third, we provision an experimental CASE-tool that implements the automatic evaluation of defined quality criteria and is meant to support BDD practitioners. Lastly, Sect. 6 concludes the paper and discusses limitations and future research directions for this study.

2 Background

2.1 A Generic Overview of BDD as a Testing Practice

To reiterate, BDD can be characterized as a customer-oriented practice of testing the validity of requirements when the latter are usually collected in the form of user stories. Hence, its deliverables (BDD scenarios) should be easily read and understood by non-technical stakeholders participating in a new software project [2]. In other words, BDD is purposed to ensure that the real objectives of stakeholders are met by the delivered software [17]. For that purpose, BDD employs tools like Cucumber[1] or Jbehave[2] that are used to automate acceptance tests or, more precisely, to turn them into executable specifications of the collected requirements [21]. Cucumber employs the Gherkin language format that structures BDD scenarios around 3 concise dimensions, namely the *GIVEN*, *WHEN*, and *THEN*. The overall benefit of the particular language format is that it produces a non-technical and comprehensive syntax. Essentially, these 3 dimensions are meant to communicate that *given* a particular context describing the scenario, *when* an event is triggered by the user or the system, *then* we should be expecting a specific system outcome. Ideally, scenarios are written in conjunction with their corresponding user stories to have an agreement with the user on the requirement and its validation. In Gherkin specifically, requirements and their corresponding scenarios are clustered around a particular feature and grouped into a single text file (i.e., the feature file). In the end, Cucumber verifies whether the software conforms with the described specification and generates a report indicating success or failure for each scenario. Figure 1 visualizes the conventional format for user stories and BDD scenarios.

---

[1] https://cucumber.io/.
[2] https://jbehave.org/.

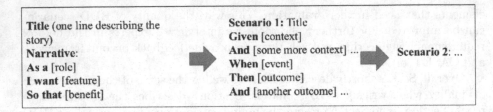

Fig. 1. User Story and BDD Scenario template (from: [17]).

2.2 Related Work on Improving the Overall Quality of the BDD Process

Tsilionis et al. [19,20] furnish a specific ontology that performs a visual association between the dimensions of user stories and their corresponding BDD scenarios. These studies are ultimately providing a unified template that entails a specific set of concepts along with their semantic description that could serve as a guiding aid for agile practitioners to write better BDD scenarios. Although these studies are meant to augment the rigor within the entire BDD scenarios' writing process, quality issues within the scenarios are not explicitly addressed. Similarly, Heng et al. [6] extend the previous studies by linking the BDD-based ontology with the one for user stories depicted in [23,24].

Gupta et al. [5] describe a methodology that starts from BDD scenarios to complement the information provided in user stories. Their work essentially employs Natural Language Processing (NLP) techniques with the ultimate goal of generating conceptual models out of specific BDD scenarios. Similarly, Snoeck et al. [18] use BDD scenarios and user stories as input to (at least partially) generate an (object-oriented) software architecture within the Merode framework. Once again, these researches study the linkage between user stories and BDD scenarios but from a software architecture perspective. In that aspect, quality attributes, as such, are not specifically addressed.

Oliveira et al. [13], in their quest to define a *qualitative* BDD scenario, they used the BABOK framework [8] and the INVEST criteria [21] to come up with an initial list of attributes for BDD scenarios. This list was subsequently refined with the help of 8 novice practitioners, yielding the following attributes to describe a qualitative BDD scenario: (i) *Concise* (being to the point), (ii) *Testable* (having a single goal), (iii) *Understandable* (incorporating a consistent use of business terms and outputs), (iv) *Unambiguous* (validating a single action), and (v) *Valuable* (clearly stating its purpose). The aforementioned quality attributes were further refined in the study of Oliveira et al. [14] as the authors conducted a larger number of semi-structured interviews with 18 BDD practitioners. As a result, the last study considers a BDD scenario as qualitative when it is:

(i) Unique: Testing something fundamentally different to other scenarios;
(ii) Integrous: Respecting the GIVEN, WHEN, THEN dimensions;
(iii) Essential: Avoiding unnecessary steps;

(iv) Singular: Having a single purpose and demonstrating this purpose clearly;
 (v) Complete: On the scenario level, presenting all the information needed to understand and follow the corresponding steps. On the feature level, providing enough coverage for all the scenarios in a feature file to test a specific feature;
 (vi) Clear: Avoiding vague statements, excessive details, and technical jargon;
(vii) Focused: Being declarative rather than being imperative;
(viii) Ubiquitous: Incorporating a consistent use of business terms.

Lastly, Binamungu et al. [2] used the quality attributes of Oliveira et al. [14] as inputs to propose a list of principles for assessing the quality of BDD suites aggregated at the level of the feature-file.

3 Research Objectives and Method

This research follows the paradigm of Design Science [7], which is not meant to find an underlying truth in reality but rather to develop an artifact that is useful in helping solve a problem that has been identified in the real world. Conventionally, Design Science Research (DSR) projects should identify and articulate a distinct number of research cycles. We briefly document how such DSR cycles are presently instantiated.

3.1 Relevance Cycle

The Relevance Cycle initiates the research by addressing a particular domain opportunity (or problem) as well as assessing how the design artifact can improve the environment [7]. With this frame of reference, the identified challenge within the presently-studied field is the lack of adopted rules and consistency in the evaluation of quality for BDD scenarios. Such scenarios are written with various quality levels by practitioners and this jeopardizes the harmonization of communication between various stakeholders while hurting any automation effort for acceptance testing. We are thusly trying to address this problem by providing an evaluation framework to guide the quality attribution within the BDD writing process. The term *'quality'* will be used here in the same manner as defined in the works of Oliveira et al. [13, 14]. Furthermore, a CASE-tool that could identify any conformance of the BDD scenarios to specific quality attributes in a semi-automated manner, or at least provide support in the process, is an identified opportunity. In line with this, the main research question that we aim to address is the following: *How can we write a qualitative BDD scenario as well as assess and improve the quality of an existing scenario in a semi-automated manner?*

3.2 Rigor Cycle

This cycle is meant to elaborate on the appropriate theories and/or methods for constructing the artifacts that are meant to support the augmentation of the domain knowledge [7]. In this light, we take the quality attributes for BDD scenarios by Oliveira et al. [14], as presented in Sect. 2.2, and try to challenge and map those attributes with the ones defined for user stories in the work of Lucassen et al. [9]. We essentially use the aforementioned (and rigorously validated) frameworks as groundwork to build our study. We then investigate how we can adapt the components of the AQUSA tool (this is a CASE-tool presented in the work of Lucassen et al. [9] to evaluate the quality attributes of user stories) in order to make it conformed to BDD scenarios.

3.3 Design Cycle

The Design Cycle is meant to zoom in on the process of constructing and evaluating artifact(s) [7]. Section 4 is meant to partially materialize this cycle; this happens with the elaboration of an evaluation framework that enhances the quality attributes presented in previous studies by (i) accompanying them with rule-based expressions, (ii) confronting them with real BDD examples, and (iii) comparing them with the quality attributes for user stories. Section 5 is meant to complete the materialization of this cycle. This happens with the presentation (and testing) of a CASE-tool that aims to assist with the evaluation of the conformance of rule-based quality criteria for BDD scenarios from a given dataset.

4 Evaluation Framework for BDD Scenarios' Quality Attributes

This section describes the set up for the development of the custom framework for the evaluation of the quality of BDD scenarios. To reiterate, we take the quality attributes presented in Oliveira et al. [14] and further elaborate on how to concretely apply such attributes in real BDD examples. These examples are essentially instances of a dataset[3] meant to test an experimental CASE-tool. In parallel, we try to bring an extra level of rigor in the whole process by trying to map the quality attributes described in the study of Oliveira et al. [14] to the ones defined in Lucassen et al. [9] to evaluate whether (and how) quality attributes from user stories can be applied in the context of BDD scenarios; this process is being exemplified below. Next, we overview how some of these quality attributes can be supported by a CASE-tool (see Sect. 5).

In general, a BDD scenario μ, contains three elements represented as triples $\mu = \langle c, e, o \rangle$, where c denotes the *context*, e the *event*, and o the set of *outcomes*. A set of scenarios in a feature file is denoted by $S = \{\mu_1, \mu_2, .., \mu_n\}$. Ultimately, the aggregation of the feature file with its corresponding user stories define the requirements for a specific feature of a software product. In the remaining of this section, the 8 quality criteria presented in Sect. 2.2, will be more formally defined and checked in terms of their proximity to those quality attributes presented in the QUS framework [9].

---

[3] The build-up of the dataset and the CASE-tool are being concretely described in Sect. 5.

4.1 Uniqueness as Quality Attribute and Correspondence to QUS

Starting from the definition given by Oliveira et al. [14], we describe presently a BDD scenario as *unique* if it lacks any complete duplicate or semantically identical scenario within a specific feature file. The logical negation of this criterion stipulates that, within a feature file, there are 2 scenarios can either be full-duplicates or semantic duplicates. In other words, a BDD scenario μ_1 is considered a full-duplicate of scenario μ_2 when μ_1 and μ_2 are completely identical. Contrastignly, a BDD scenario μ_1 is deemed a semantic duplicate of scenario μ_2 when μ_2 employs a different event e or context c to achieve a similar outcome o as μ_1. In this case, the outcomes $o1$ and $o2$ are either identical or semantically equivalent. To provide some examples from our dataset:

μ_1: GIVEN that I am logged into the system as "user1", WHEN I update my language to "Polish", THEN my default language should be "Polish".

μ_2: GIVEN that I am logged into the system as "user1", WHEN I update my language to "Turkish", THEN my default language should be "Turkish".

μ_3: GIVEN that I am logged into the system as "pdavis", WHEN I update my language to "Italian", THEN my default language should be updated to "Italian".

μ_4: GIVEN that the user is in the settings page, WHEN (s)he updates the language to "Italian", THEN the default language should be updated to "Italian".

Although the aforementioned examples are not full duplicates, they are all used to describe the same feature, namely the ability of a user to change the default language settings in a system. Examples μ_1, μ_2 and μ_3 are semantic duplicates and they should be detected as such since they are showcasing an identical outcome but using different narratives in their *event* dimension. However, μ_4 should not be detected as a duplicate because it incorporates a set of preconditions (which are not present in the other 3 scenarios) that have to hold true to be able to change the systems' language settings.

We instantly record a similarity in the way *uniqueness* is framed above for BDD scenarios and the way it is described in the study of Lucassen et al. [9] for user stories. The latter associates the *uniqueness* attribute with the ability to render 2 user stories *conflict-free*. In the following example, the convoluted *Epic US: As a visitor, I am able to see a list of news items, so that I stay up to date* could be improved in quality by providing specific and *conflict-free* user stories such as *US1: As a visitor, I am able to see breaking news* and *US2: As a Visitor, I am able to see sports news*.

There are methods that can help detect conflict-instigating user stories in a project. For example, Duszkiewicz et al. [4] elaborate on a tool employing a cosine similarity index to evaluate the proximity of 2 or more user stories in a defined backlog. In the context of BDD scenarios, we propose to investigate the satisfaction of the *uniqueness* attribute in two levels: first, we can implement a primary check on the titles of the scenarios in a feature file. In the case that 2 or more titles are full or semantically equal, this is a sign that the uniqueness criterion is not satisfied. Secondly, we can delve into the scenario level to investigate whether 2 written scenarios in a file are semantic or full duplicates. The CASE-tool, as described in Sect. 5, is being built with the aforementioned premises in mind.

4.2 Integrity and Essentiality as Quality Attributes and Correspondence to QUS

Starting from the definition given by Oliveira et al. [14], we describe presently a BDD scenario as *integrous* when containing a *context*, an *event*, and an *outcome*. This means that each tuple of the set $\mu = \langle\ c,\ e,\ o\ \rangle$ must be non-empty. Additionally, we describe a BDD scenario as *essential* when each tuple of the set $\mu = \langle\ c,\ e,\ o\ \rangle$ contains a single-element. To adhere to the latter, additional explanations or details such as comments, references, descriptions of expected behavior, steps, or testing hints must be moved in other sections of the feature file.

In the scenario *'GIVEN that the test server is ready, THEN the server has 0 active connections'*, taken as an example from our dataset, the WHEN dimension is missing; hence, the scenario violates the *integrity* criterion. We also showcase the below scenario from our dataset:

- *GIVEN the user is on the sign-up page;*
- *WHEN the user enters* ⟨firstname⟩ *into the firstname field; WHEN the user enters* ⟨lastname⟩ *into the lastname field; WHEN the user enters* ⟨username⟩ *into the username field; WHEN the user enters* ⟨password⟩ *into the password field; WHEN the user enters* ⟨height⟩ *into the height field; WHEN the user enters* ⟨weight⟩ *into the weight field; WHEN the user enters* ⟨gender⟩ *into the gender field; WHEN the user enters* ⟨age⟩ *into the age field; WHEN the user clicks on the sign-up button;*
- *THEN the title should be* ⟨title⟩*.*

The last scenario satisfies the *integrity* attribute; it is, however, violating the *essentiality* attribute by incorporating a multitude of complex steps for the WHEN dimension. A way of stipulating to both attributes is by proceeding in the separation of all the steps related to the WHEN dimension into distinguishable, individual scenarios.

The *integrity* and *essentiality* quality attributes for BDD scenarios, as framed above, can be considered as the counterparts for 3 user stories' quality attributes. These refer to the *well-form*, *full sentence*, and *minimality* attributes. The first one is described within the QUS framework as the state in which every user story has to contain a *role* (i.e., describing the user requesting a specific functionality) and a *means* (i.e., a description of the functionality itself). If a user story also contains *some ends* (i.e., the benefit stemming from this functionality) then the *full sentence* criterion is also fulfilled. Finally, if a user story contains all the aforementioned elements without the use of any additional notes then the *minimality* criterion is also fulfilled. The AQUSA tool investigates the advocacy of the aforementioned attributes by checking the use of separating punctuation marks such as "()", "{}", "⟨⟩" and, "-" which refer to the use of additional comments and remarks within the user story. We use the same premise for the development of our experimental CASE-tool (see Sect. 5).

4.3 Singularity as Quality Attribute and Correspondence to QUS

"Starting from the definition given by Oliveira et al. [14], we describe presently a BDD scenario μ as *singular* when each element of the tuple $\langle\, c, e, o\, \rangle$ is associated with the same purpose ρ and they are consumed to describe that purpose. In that aspect, consolidating or aggregating scenarios into larger and more complex ones reduces the accuracy of the scenario's intended purpose. We hereby offer an example from our dataset: *GIVEN I am on the home page, WHEN I click on "Create", THEN the customer should be created and the customer details should be displayed, AND WHEN the customer logs on, THEN the Premium Welcome Page should be displayed.*

In the aforementioned example, the scenario should be decomposed in smaller functional chunks that work towards the manifestation of a single purpose. So, another way of writing the above would be: *Scenario 1: GIVEN I am on the home page, WHEN I click on "Create", THEN the customer should be created,* and *Scenario 2: GIVEN I am on the home page, WHEN I click on "Create", THEN customer details should be displayed,* and *Scenario 3: GIVEN I am on the home page, WHEN the customer logs on, THEN the Premium Welcome Page should be displayed.*

We notice that the *singularity* quality attribute in the context of BDD scenarios can be plotted to the *atomic* one described in the QUS framework. For example, let us consider the following user story as provided in [9]: *As a user, I am able to click a particular location from the map and thereby perform a search of landmarks associated with that latitude-longitude combination.* This user story consists of 2 separate requirements, namely the act of clicking on a location and the display of associated landmarks. Therefore, it should be split into 2 separate user stories to comply with the *atomic* criterion. For the development of our CASE-tool, it would be interesting to search for terms, symbols, and notations that signal cases of conjunction within scenarios such as 'AND', '&', and 'OR'.

4.4 Completeness as Quality Attribute and Correspondence to QUS

The definition given by Oliveira et al. [14] leads us to investigate the *completeness* quality attribute in 2 levels. **On the feature level**, let F be the set of features in the application. For each feature f belonging to the set F, we define a set of scenarios $(\mu_1, \mu_2, .., \mu_n)$ as *complete* for a feature f if the 2 following conditions are met: 1) the feature file generated from the scenarios $(\mu_1, \mu_2, .., \mu_n)$ covers all the necessary scenarios required for feature f, and 2) the feature file generated from the scenarios $(\mu_1, \mu_2, .., \mu_n)$ includes all the essential scenarios for the implementation and functionality of feature f. **On the scenario level**, a scenario μ can be defined as *complete* if and only if all the information needed to understand and follow the steps consecutively within μ is available. We hereby offer an example from our dataset: *GIVEN the Address Book is running, WHEN I add a new person, THEN the address book contains '1' person.* On a feature level, the aforementioned scenario cannot be considered as *complete* unless the feature file contains another scenario that specifies that you first need to create an address book, then create a new entry in the address book.

The *completeness* attribute for BDD scenarios is identical to the homonymous *completeness* attribute in the QUS framework [9]. The latter emphasizes the importance of having the necessary user stories to describe in a complete and non-redundant manner a particular functionality in a project.

4.5 Clarity and Focus as Quality Attributes and Correspondence to QUS

Starting from the definition given by Oliveira et al. [14], we define presently a scenario μ as *clear* when it is written in a non-ambiguous manner. We realize that it is difficult to offer a formal rule-based definition for *clarity* since ambiguity is endogenous to every notation that is heavily reliant on structured natural language. In that aspect, we propose to use this attribute in conjunction with the *focus* one. We can define a BDD scenario μ as *clear* and *focused* when it describes *what* the scenario should do and what is the requirement that is trying to validate. The parts related to *how* to solve the problem should be left out of the scenarios since they influence the use of jargon which might be negating the clarity attribute. To offer an example from our dataset: *GIVEN the coffee machine is started, WHEN I switch to the setting mode, THEN the setting should be: "...".* This is a scenario that violates both the *clarity* and *focus* attributes as the expected behavior of the coffee machine is neither clear nor could it be easily corresponded to the requirement it is meant to validate.

These 2 quality attributes can be easily juxtaposed to the *unambiguity* and *problem-orientation* quality attributes as defined in the QUS framework. The latter describes that technical jargon should be avoided when noting down user stories in order to reduce ambiguity, and that user stories should clearly try to address a specific functionality.

4.6 Ubiquity as Quality Attribute and Correspondence to QUS

Ubiquity is defined by Oliveira [14] as a scenario's capacity to be consistent in its use of business terms. During our search, we did not find a comparable quality attribute in the QUS framework for user stories. This attribute was also difficult to formalize and check for violations in the examples offered in our dataset. These indications make us challenge the importance of having this attribute included in the set of BDD quality criteria. However a larger dataset could justify its inclusion. Future work should include a more focused investigation on this quality attribute.

5 Presentation of the CASE-Tool and Some Experimental Results

5.1 Running and Testing the CASE-Tool

This section presents our CASE-tool supporting the quality evaluation process for BDD scenarios. The tool has been developed by one of the researchers with the use of the Python[4] programming language and was evaluated by the rest of the team. The tool has been implemented as an extension of the AQUSA tool. As a reminder, the latter targets the quality evaluation of user stories while our tool in extended to evaluate BDD scenarios.

The lack of a publicly available dataset containing scenarios in a Gherkin format has led us to built our own dataset (which we use as input for the tool) in a bottom-up manner. Explicitly, we used GitHub as our primary source of data collection where we found around 200 repositories that contained acceptance tests for software related projects. We focused on repositories that contained only Gherkin-formatted scenarios written in English. Eventually, we put together 50 different scenarios that were compliant with our criteria and we manually checked whether they fit the quality attributes specified in Sect. 4. This means that we checked whether each scenario is *Unique, Essential, Singular, Integrous, Complete, Clear,* and *Focused.* This investigation and annotation was performed by all the members of the research team individually until a consent has been reached on the quality attribution for each scenario. It is worth mentioning that out of these 7 quality attributes, due to space restrictions, we will be presenting below the process of algorithmically checking the quality support with the use of the CASE-tool for only the first 4 quality attributes.

To establish the accuracy of the tool, we used our dataset where we had already manually identified the quality level of each scenario. Then we submitted the same dataset to our CASE-tool and compared both results. For example, in order to check the validity of the *uniqueness* attribute for each scenario, we used the user interface of the tool to quickly scroll through the titles of the scenarios to check whether they are unique in a feature file or not. If they were equal, they should have been both returned as duplicates. On the scenario level, we checked if 2 written scenarios in a feature were exact duplicates. Once again, if this was the case, the tool should be reporting both of them as duplicates. To offer another example, to investigate the validity for the *essentiality* attribute for each scenario, we used the user interface of the tool to check for separating punctuation marks within the scenarios such as: "()", "{}", "⟨⟩" and, "-" (similarly to the AQUSA tool). We assume that a scenario that contains the aforementioned symbols has a high chance of using them to give an additional explanation for the proper execution of the feature the scenario is trying to validate. Whenever, the tool identified such symbols, we recorded them as a potential breach of *essentiality.* By and large, this approach is prone to generate false positives.

---

[4] The source code and dataset are being provided in the online appendix: https://data.mendeley.com/datasets/4bcd94yh6r/1.

To give an example from our dataset, the symbol ">" which is used to indicate "greater than" is generally misconceived as an additional comment for the written scenario. Therefore, one must be vigilant about the syntax that they use while writing scenarios.

To better understand the logic behind the accuracy testing for our tool, Table 1 displays the output results for the first 4 BDD scenarios included in our dataset. The first column *(GWT: GIVEN, WHEN, THEN)* contains the scenarios in Gherkin format. We used abbreviations for the description for those scenarios in that column due to space restrictions. The full description of those scenarios can be found in the appendix. The columns *Unique, Essential, Integrous,* and *Singular* are the ones that have been manually checked and annotated by the research team as explained above. The word '*Yes*' in these columns means that each one of these 4 scenarios has been cleared by the research team, so they are abiding by the corresponding quality attribute. The columns including the word '*anomaly*' as part of their names are the outcomes produced by the tool. For example, the word '*False*' in the column '*anomaly_duplicate*' means that the tool has checked a particular scenario (in our case one of the 4 scenarios in our dataset) and it has declared that an anomaly has not been found during the check for a particular quality attribute. Conversely, when the word '*True*' is being reported in one of these columns, this means that the tool has detected a particular anomaly during its automated quality attribute investigation. Accordingly, any mismatches between our manually annotated columns and the automated results produced by the tool should be performed by comparing these 2 relevant columns. To make it more clear, the following columns should be compared together: *Essential* with *anomaly_punctuation, Integrous* with *anomaly_full_gwt* and *Singular* with *anomaly_conjunction.* It is worth mentioning that the column *Unique* has to be simultaneously compared with columns *anomaly_duplicate* (this serves as a primary investigation for duplicates in the titles of the scenarios) and *anomaly_duplicate_based_on_a_feature* (this serves as secondary investigation for exact duplicates within the syntax of the written scenarios.

Table 1. Our dataset after running the tool

GWT	Unique	Essential	Integrous	Singular	anomaly_duplicate	anomaly_duplicate_based_on_a_feature	anomaly_full_gwt	anomaly_conjunction	anomaly_punctuation
Given addres book is...when I create...then...is empty.	yes	yes	yes	yes	False	False	False	False	False
Given address book is ...when I ...then ...contains 1 person.	yes	yes	yes	yes	False	False	False	False	False
Given I am on the ...when I do nothing then...see the title.	yes	yes	yes	yes	False	False	False	False	False
Given I select the post when I add ...then...on the blog	yes	yes	yes	yes	False	False	False	True	False

Any mismatches between these columns could either be the result of a False Positive (FP) or a False Negative (FN) in the returned results of the tool. We record a FP in the results when the tool detects a defect which was not recorded as a defect during the manual investigation by the research team. We record a FN in the results when the tool fails to report a defect that was captured during the manual investigation by the research team. Overall, the tool checks each of the four criteria for each of the scenarios. Therefore, there can be scenarios reported by the tool as having more than one defect.

Table 2. Report of the defects of the attributes in our tool

Attributes	Unique	Essential	Integrous	Singular
FP	0	3	0	4
FN	6	3	0	2

Table 2 shows how the tool performs overall in recognizing the quality attributes for all the BDD scenarios within our dataset when juxtaposed with the manually checked quality attributes as performed by the research team. For the *integrity* quality attribute, we observe neither FP nor FN. This means that the tool manages to recognize the quality criteria for the scenarios in the same manner as the manual check. However, for the *uniqueness* quality attribute, we do observe 6 FN with regards to the semantic understanding of the scenarios. In this case, the tool failed to recognize several violations addressing the conformance to the uniqueness criterion. It is interesting to observe the recorded FP and FN concerning the *essentiality* attribute; for that particular attribute, all the discrepancies between the manual and the automated checks are caused by the non-moderated use of punctuation symbols within the scenarios. An easy fix for that would be to inform the BDD practitioners about the suggested use of such symbols well in-advance before the BDD scripting process begins. Similarly, the discrepancies between the manual and the automated checks for the *singularity* attribute seem to be caused by syntactic choices when writing the scenarios. Overall, the percentage of the scenarios with at least one defect correctly detected by the tool approaches 70%.

Finally, the CASE-tool interface can also provide reports on which scenarios might be containing a violation. It does so by highlighting which dimension(s) may be problematic for a particular BDD scenario. An example of such a report[5], concerning the *integrity* attribute for a particular scenario within our dataset, is provided below:

```
GIVEN: [21]  WHEN:[11,37,38]  THEN:[]
```

The report reads as follows: *The BDD scenario in the row 21st of the dataset is missing the GIVEN dimension; the BDD scenarios in rows 11, 37, and 38 of*

---

[5] Due to space restrictions, we provide only a snapshot of the user-interface report.

the dataset are missing the WHEN dimension; there are no scenarios in our dataset that miss the THEN dimension. Such a report can give a quick overview to the practitioner. In our specific example, the BDD practitioner can easily notice that 4 scenarios out of the 50 within the entire dataset might be violating the integrity attribute. Of course, this trait of the tool might seem pedantic for a small dataset; however, it can be valuable for larger dataset containing a couple of hundreds, if not more, scenarios.

5.2   Expert Opinions on the Framework and CASE-Tool

To obtain further validation on the framework and the tool, we conducted 2 interviews with software engineering experts that were retrieved from the professional network of one of the researchers. The background and experience of these experts have been the object of cross-reference among the members of the research team to ensure the attraction of relevant profiles that can infuse a level of pluralism in the provision of their feedback. To be specific, the 1st interviewee is an expert in software development and, in the context of his work, he uses BDD scenarios written by third parties on a daily basis. The 2nd interviewee holds a PhD degree in Information Systems, has extensive knowledge in writing user stories and BDD scenarios, and is currently employed as a business analyst in an organization providing IT Services. The interview protocol was the same for both interviewees; it can be synopsized as such: The entire framework as well as a thorough demonstration of the tool was provided to them. Then a series of questions were asked to evaluate the usefulness and relevance of the framework as well as the understandability and the easiness to use the CASE-tool. The use of a semi-structured interview format allowed us to modify our follow-up questions based on the interviewees' provided answers. Both interviews were recorded, and the feedback was analyzed and compiled by one of the authors of the paper.

Since both interviewees already had experience with the AQUSA tool for user stories, they were able to easily relate the criteria and the use of our experimental tool in the BDD context. One of the main questions guiding our interviews was: *"Can you discuss any benefits, and if yes which ones, that such a tool could offer to a BDD practitioner?"*. Follow-up questions were made on the basis of the elements pointed out. Due to space restrictions, their provided feedback is epitomized below in 2 contextual installments. The first one summarizes their feedback in terms of formally defining the *BDD quality attributes* (see Sect. 4) which are then provided as input for the CASE-tool:

– The *Uniqueness* attribute is being described in an interesting way as there are 2 separate fail-safe mechanism checks that can be made to avoid duplicates when different roles participate in the team as acceptance tests scripters;
– The *Essentiality* attribute is being defined as integrity maximizer of the written BDD scenarios; however, there are times that it might be unavoidable to have extra explanations about the feature(s) that the scenario validates. The most important element that the definition of this attribute brings is the

attention that practitioners need to pay to their syntax and the proper use of symbols.
- The *Integrity* attribute is very interesting as it can be used as the first level of control in terms of checking whether all dimensions are actually included in a scenario. This serves as a control metric to keep scenarios in line with concurred norms;
- The *Singularity* attribute, as defined in the framework, could create some ambivalence; bypassing the singularity attribute could help practitioners to reduce work since BDD scenarios with similar contexts/preconditions can be merged. Such scenarios could be, however, over-complicated and problematic in terms of validation.

The second contextual installment summarizes their feedback on the *CASE-tool*:

- A BDD scenario that successfully passes the quality attributes will be easily and quickly understood by everyone in the team. Therefore, an optimized (meaning fully automated) version of such a tool will save time by reducing the extra overhead of business engagement and will increase collaborations for practitioners;
- The introduction of such a tool will make the software development team to have a clear benchmark or a point of reference during discussions if necessary;
- The tool would report the BDD scenarios that are at times written in an informal natural language which does not follow the exact BDD structure/syntax (this comment refers to the *integrous* quality attribute of BDD scenarios);
- A downside would be that not all anomalies maybe reported well by the tool as some features may be more complex;
- It may be risky to fully rely on a tool, since human judgment and experience are indispensable during the early BDD drafting stages where the definitions of the quality attributes have not yet reached a decent level of maturity.

6   Conclusion, Limitations and Future Work

The present study has followed the DSR precepts to answer the research question *How can we write qualitative BDD scenarios as well as assess and improve the quality of an existing scenario in a semi-automated manner?*. To this end, we searched the literature which presented a list of quality attributes that could be assigned to BDD scenarios. Following, we formally defined these attributes and checked their correspondence with quality attributes assigned to user stories. Next, we have used some of those attributes as input to a newly-built artifact in the form of an experimental CASE-tool. The latter has been tested on a dataset and presented to 2 experts.

Overall, the practice of writing better BDD scenarios that conform to some universally accepted standards can improve the development cycles within agile processes. Having an optimized way of checking (and validating) requirements can be a serious boost to the productivity of the development team that might have an extra tool at hand in its quest to produce software that matches more closely to the requests of its end-users. This is the **operational benefit** that draws roots from the results of our work. In fact, this is in agreement with the experts mentioning that the framework and the tool provide a partial but nonetheless concrete answer to the need for unification and guidance that is required in the BDD field. They specifically mention unification, standardization, and the application of predetermined rules as the main strengths of the framework and tool. They do, however, notice that the ability to add extra information that does not fit into the BDD structure is sometimes needed to deliver the complete specification of a requirement; this remark addresses the way the *essentiality* and *integrity* attributes are formally defined by the framework which gives us some directions for future work. In any case, it appears from the interviewees that writing BDD scenarios is not a momentary event but a continuous process in agile projects so some flexibility should be provided to adhere or not to quality rules at different stages of the project; in fact, any mature supporting CASE-tool should explicitly take this into account. On the other hand, the value of negotiating the optimization of the entire BDD process via the formal description of quality attributes goes beyond the mere facilitation of operational-level software development procedures. In this case we can speak about some **strategic benefits**. For example, the ability to compare scenarios of various quality levels and to study which ones can be meritorious in holistically representing user-driven system functionalities (and how to best validate these functionalities) can moderate some of the scalability issues that are concomitant within the entire feature-driven development process; the latter is, by definition, intended to inspire the design of innovation-encapsulating functionalities that satisfy a variety of stakeholders and play a major role in influencing the attainment of organizational strategic objectives.

We hereby point out some of the limitations encountered during the conduct of this study: *first*, our dataset consisted of 50 instances. However, working with a larger dataset would have allowed us to train our tool on a set of more complex rules. Additionally, we proceeded in a manual, case-by-case, assembly of the dataset which might have influenced a chance of selection bias within the data itself. However the assembly followed a thorough multi-level discussion on the description of the included scenarios based on their attributes.

Second, the definitions we used to frame the quality attributes might suffer from experimenter bias which means that an independent third party with a slightly different dataset might have conceptualized slightly differ formal rules. To give an example, the list of defined punctuation marks could be more extensive in another dataset. Similarly, in the context of scalability, our tool is designed based on the format of our dataset. Thus, further adjustments would be unavoidable for another dataset.

Third, we need to point out that the CASE-tool, as an experimental artifact, is still not at the optimal level of user-friendliness. So more work is necessary to bring it into a 'plug-n-play' mode to accommodate a professional setting.

As future work, we point out the need to gain more maturity in the automatic evaluation of the BDD scenarios' quality. Of course, it would be interesting to make the tool capable of integrating with different management tools such as *Jira, Trello, MS Excel,* or *Google spreadsheets.* The amelioration of the tool would happen in an iterative manner to get constant feedback from the practitioners who use it in real-life projects.

References

1. Beck, K.: Test-Driven Development: By Example. Addison-Wesley Professional (2003)
2. Binamungu, L.P., Embury, S.M., Konstantinou, N.: Characterising the quality of behaviour driven development specifications. In: Proc. of the 21st Int. Conf. on Agile Software Development, XP 2020. LNBIP, vol. 383, pp. 87–102. Springer (2020)
3. Cohn, M.: User Stories Applied: For Agile Software Development. Addison-Wesley Professional (2004)
4. Duszkiewicz, A.G., Sørensen, J.G., Johansen, N., Edison, H., Silva, T.R.: On identifying similar user stories to support agile estimation based on historical data. In: Proceediungs of the First International Workshop on Agile Methods for Information System Engeeniring (Agil-ISE 2022), Leuven, Belgium. CEUR Workshop Proceedings, vol. 3134, pp. 21–26 (2022)
5. Gupta, A., Poels, G., Bera, P.: Generating multiple conceptual models from behavior-driven development scenarios. Data Knowl. Eng. **145**, 102141 (2023)
6. Heng, S., Tsilionis, K., Wautelet, Y.: Building user stories and behavior driven development scenarios with a strict set of concepts: Ontology, benefits and primary validation. In: Proceedings of the 38th ACM/SIGAPP Symposium on Applied Computing, SAC 2023. pp. 1422–1429. ACM (2023)
7. Hevner, A.R., March, S.T., Park, J., Ram, S.: Design science in information systems research. MIS Quart. **28**, 75–105 (2004)
8. IIBA, A.: Guide to the business analysis body of knowledge (babok guide) ver 3.0 (2015)
9. Lucassen, G., Dalpiaz, F., van der Werf, J.M.E.M., Brinkkemper, S.: Improving agile requirements: the quality user story framework and tool. Requir. Eng. **21**(3), 383–403 (2016)
10. Lucassen, G., Dalpiaz, F., Werf, J.M.E.M., Brinkkemper, S.: The use and effectiveness of user stories in practice. In: Daneva, M., Pastor, O. (eds.) REFSQ 2016. LNCS, vol. 9619, pp. 205–222. Springer, Cham (2016) https://doi.org/10.1007/978-3-319-30282-9_14
11. Melnik, G., Maurer, F.: Multiple perspectives on executable acceptance test-driven development. In: Concas, G., Damiani, E., Scotto, M., Succi, G. (eds.) XP 2007. LNCS, vol. 4536, pp. 245–249. Springer, Heidelberg (2007). https://doi.org/10.1007/978-3-540-73101-6_46
12. North, D., et al.: Introducing BDD. Better Softw. **12** (2006)
13. Oliveira, G., Marczak, S.: On the empirical evaluation of BDD scenarios quality: preliminary findings of an empirical study. In: IEEE 25th International Requirements Engineering Conference Workshops, RE 2017 Workshops, Lisbon, Portugal, pp. 299–302. IEEE Computer Society (2017)

14. Oliveira, G., Marczak, S., Moralles, C.: How to evaluate BDD scenarios' quality? In: do Carmo Machado, I., Souza, R., Maciel, R.S.P., Sant'Anna, C. (eds.) Proceedings of the XXXIII Brazilian Symposium on Software Engineering, SBES 2019, Salvador, Brazil, pp. 481–490. ACM (2019)
15. Patton, J., Economy, P.: User Story Mapping: Discover the Whole Story, Build the Right Product. O'Reilly Media, Inc. (2014)
16. Sedano, T., Ralph, P., Péraire, C.: The product backlog. In: Atlee, J.M., Bultan, T., Whittle, J. (eds.) Proceedings of the 41st International Conference on Software Engineering, ICSE 2019, Montreal, QC, Canada, May 25–31, 2019, pp. 200–211. IEEE/ACM (2019)
17. Shafiee, S., Hvam, L., Haug, A., Wautelet, Y.: Behavior-driven development in product configuration systems (short paper). In: Felfernig, A., Tiihonen, J., Hotz, L., Stettinger, M. (eds.) Proceedings of the 20th Configuration Workshop, Graz, Austria, September 27–28, 2018. CEUR Workshop Proceedings, vol. 2220, pp. 49–52. CEUR-WS.org (2018)
18. Snoeck, M., Wautelet, Y.: Agile MERODE: a model-driven software engineering method for user-centric and value-based development. Softw. Syst. Model. **21**(4), 1469–1494 (2022)
19. Tsilionis, K., Wautelet, Y., Faut, C., Heng, S.: Unifying behavior driven development templates. In: 29th IEEE International Requirements Engineering Conference, RE 2021, Notre Dame, IN, USA, 20–24 September 2021, pp. 454–455. IEEE (2021)
20. Tsilionis, K., Wautelet, Y., Heng, S.: Building a unified ontology for behavior driven development scenarios. In: Taibi, D., Kuhrmann, M., Mikkonen, T., Klünder, J., Abrahamsson, P. (eds.) PROFES 2022. LNCS, vol. 13709, pp. 518–524. Springer, Cham (2022). https://doi.org/10.1007/978-3-031-21388-5_36
21. Wake, B.: Invest in good stories, and smart tasks. Retrieved 13 December, 2011 (2003)
22. Wautelet, Y., Gielis, D., Poelmans, S., Heng, S.: Evaluating the impact of user stories quality on the ability to understand and structure requirements. In: Gordijn, J., Guédria, W., Proper, H.A. (eds.) PoEM 2019. LNBIP, vol. 369, pp. 3–19. Springer, Cham (2019). https://doi.org/10.1007/978-3-030-35151-9_1
23. Wautelet, Y., Heng, S., Kiv, S., Kolp, M.: User-story driven development of multi-agent systems: a process fragment for agile methods. Comput. Lang. Syst. Struct. **50**, 159–176 (2017)
24. Wautelet, Y., Heng, S., Kolp, M., Mirbel, I.: Unifying and extending user story models. In: Jarke, M., et al. (eds.) CAiSE 2014. LNCS, vol. 8484, pp. 211–225. Springer, Cham (2014). https://doi.org/10.1007/978-3-319-07881-6_15

Semiautomatic Design of Ontologies

Michael Grüninger[1]([⊠]), Amanda Chow[1], and Janette Wong[2]

[1] University of Toronto, Toronto, Canada
gruninger@mie.utoronto.ca, amanda.chow@mail.utoronto.ca
[2] RBC, Toronto, Canada
janette.wong@rbc.com

Abstract. The design of ontologies is a time-consuming and resource-intensive endeavour. Rather than (manually) design the ontology first and then associate it with data, can we (semiautomatically) design the ontology from the data itself? This paper presents a novel approach to the semi-automated design of ontologies that incorporates axiom generation from data models, semantic parsing, and ontology learning from examples and counterexamples via search through an ontology repository.

Keywords: ontologies · first-order logic · ontology design

1 Introduction

Many tasks within an enterprise require correct and meaningful communication and integration among intelligent agents and information resources. A major barrier to such interoperability is semantic heterogeneity: different applications, databases, and agents may ascribe disparate meanings to the same terms or use distinct terms to convey the same meaning. It has been widely recognized that the development and application of ontologies will play a central role in achieving semantic integration. An ontology is a computer-interpretable specification that is used by an agent, application, or other information resource to declare what terms it uses, and what the terms mean. Ontologies support the semantic integration of software systems within an enterprise through a shared understanding of the terminology in their respective (possibly implicit) ontologies. However, the design of ontologies is a time-consuming and resource-intensive endeavour. Supporting the entire ontology lifecycle requires an ontology designer with extensive expertise in mathematical logic, together with a host of domain experts who provide the semantic requirements and who validate different versions of the ontology throughout its development.

Although ontologies might not be explicitly specified, an enterprise typically has artefacts (such as data models, datasets, enterprise data warehouses, databases, and natural language documentation) which implicitly specify the intended semantics for concepts and relationships. The SEADOO (SEmi-Automated Design Of Ontologies) project explores techniques for extracting

© IFIP International Federation for Information Processing 2024
Published by Springer Nature Switzerland AG 2024
J. P. A. Almeida et al. (Eds.): PoEM 2023, LNBIP 497, pp. 143–158, 2024.
https://doi.org/10.1007/978-3-031-48583-1_9

knowledge from natural language texts and data models, and then finding the best matching ontology from within an ontology repository (see Fig. 1). In this paper, we give an overview of the components of SEADOO – Data Model Transformation, Semantic Parsing, and the Hashemi Procedure. The first two components use techniques similar to other approaches to ontology learning. with an emphasis on the latter The primary novel contribution of this paper is the Hashemi Procedure with its use of an ontology repository to generate axioms for the ontology.

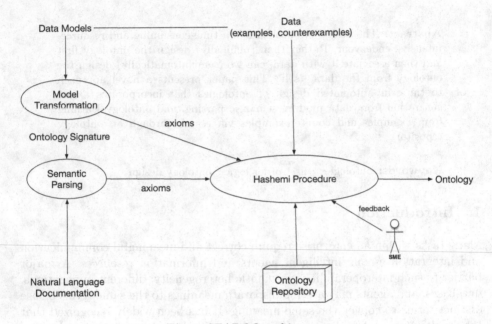

Fig. 1. SEADOO architecture.

2 Ontology Learning

Given the challenges for manually designing ontologies, there has been extensive research done on ontology learning ([2,15]). Teasing out the relationships among the diverse array of techniques can be daunting, but two distinctions are helpful for establishing comparability.

2.1 What is Being Learned?

Given the prevalence of Semantic Web applications, almost all approaches to ontology learning focus on ontologies specified in OWL. As such, techniques for ontology learning can often differ depending on whether they are learning concepts, concept hierarchies, rules, or logical theories. One widely used approach that reflects these distinctions is the Ontology Learning Layer Cake ([16]). At the base of the Layer Cake are terms and their synonyms. Above these are concepts and their subsumption taxonomy via concept descriptions. The top two levels constrain the relations (e.g. domain-range constraints) and introduce rules.

Different techniques focus on different layers. For example, semantic parsing [3] can be used to learn terms and synonyms, Formal Concept Analysis has been used to learn taxonomies [11], and approaches such as [12,18] can learn axioms in the description logic $\mathcal{AE}$.

2.2   What Data Is Being Used?

Ontology learning techniques can also be distinguished by whether they use unstructured, semi-structured, or structured data. Given the widespread availability of information resources such as webpages and documentation, unstructured natural language text is most often the source data for ontology learning ([3,18]). As such semantic parsing (discussed in more detail in Sect. 4) plays a key role in extracting terms, concepts, and relations from phrases and other linguistic constructs in the text. Techniques for semantic parsing identify semantic patterns [8] to match against natural language statements.

Learning from semistructured data typically uses database schemas to generate the ontology's axioms. There are also data mining techniques, such as association rule mining [15] that discover patterns in the relational databases themselves, and not just their schemas.

Learning from structured data uses formal structures (i.e. intended interpretations in some logic) as the basis for specifying examples for learning algorithms ([12,13]), and it is this approach which will be used in the current paper.

3   Data Model Transformation

The first component of SEADOO is the Axiom Generator, which extracts and transforms data models (such as Entity Relationship diagrams and UML class diagrams), and outputs statements in both first-order logic and natural language. In particular, the Axiom Generator is comprised of two interrelated components: a parser script (the Parser) and an assembler script (the Assembler). As the information contained within the metadata models takes the form of an ER diagram, a format unfriendly to data extraction when read in its logical or physical form, it is first exported to a more workable XML output. The first component (the Parser) is designed to extract the aforementioned axiom-relevant data from the XML outputs, collecting them into a dataframe which is exported in CSV format. The second component (the Assembler) runs a script to read the CSV output of the Parser, combining the information of each unique relationship into an axiom in first-order logic. The axiom that is created is determined by identifying the information that is contained within each relationship, and categorizing it to one of a number of prebuilt axiom templates. To improve the intelligibility of the outputs for those not well versed in reading first-order logic, the Assembler also converts the logical phrase of each generated axiom into natural language form.

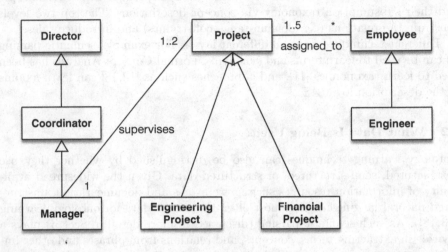

Fig. 2. Data model for use case.

For example, given the UML class diagram in Fig. 2, the Axiom Generator correctly generates the first-order sentences:

$$(\forall x, y)\, supervises(x, y) \supset Manager(x) \wedge Project(y) \tag{1}$$

$$(\forall x)\, Manager(x) \supset (\exists y, z)\, supervises(x, y) \wedge supervises(x, z) \wedge (y \neq z) \tag{2}$$

$$(\forall x)\, Project(x) \supset (\exists y)\, supervises(y, x) \tag{3}$$

$$(\forall x, y, z)\, supervises(x, y) \wedge supervises(z, y) \supset (x = z) \tag{4}$$

$$(\forall x, y, z, u)\, supervises(x, y) \wedge supervises(x, z) \wedge supervises(x, u)$$
$$\supset ((y = z) \vee (y = u) \vee (z = u)) \tag{5}$$

In this way, the Axiom Generator can transform any enterprise model specified as a UML class diagram into a set of first-order sentences that can be incorporated into an ontology. However, there are first-order sentences that cannot be expressed within a class diagram but which are nevertheless required to capture the intended semantics of concepts within the enterprise. For this, we turn to the other two primary modules within SEADOO – semantic parsing and the Hashemi Procedure for ontology matching.

4   Semantic Parsing

Semantic Parsing is the task of converting a natural language sentence into a logical formula [4]. Using a set of generic and financial domain ontologies, the SEADOO has implemented a semantic parser that can generate logical formulae that are equivalent to the intended semantics of a restricted class of natural language statements.

An ontology-based semantic parser typically begins with phrase mapping, in which each class and relation in the signature of an ontology is associated with a set of natural language phrases. Given the association of the ontology signature with phrases in the natural language statement, logical formula construction then generates the first-order sentence for the question [8]. Within existing implementations of semantic parsers, the coupling between these two functionalities is not clear; in particular, it is difficult to determine how a specific ontology determines the logical form, or whether this functionality is in fact independent of the ontology.

An additional challenge is that different senses of a word are associated with different ontologies. For example, the word "in" can be associated with temporal ontologies ("what are the residential mortgages with late payments in September?") or spatial ontologies ("what are the residential mortgages in Toronto"). Furthermore, different people might use different ontologies to axiomatize the intended semantics of concepts that are associated with the same natural language words even in technical contexts. For example, the intended semantics of the phrase "active client" can vary across groups within the same enterprise. In general, any approach requires heuristics for detecting and selecting the correct ontology that axiomatizes the intended semantics of the different senses of words in the natural language sentences.

Several semantic parsers have been developed over the past ten years ([14,17]), although it is not clear whether or not such implementations are reusable across different domains and ontologies. The initial work in the project determined that none of the existing semantic parsers could be reused or extended to support semiautomated ontology design from natural language corpora for arbitrary ontologies. Work to date has developed a prototype semantic parser that can translate restricted natural language sentences into first-order formulae. In particular, the current design and implementation are restricted to stative verbs, i.e. verbs that express a state rather than an action.

Semantic parsing poses two fundamental research questions:

Correctness of Logical Formula Construction: *Given a natural language sentence, is the first-order sentence generated by the semantic parser the correct sentence?*

There are two cases, depending on whether we are using the natural language statement to generate new axioms or whether we are using the natural language statement to generate a logical query. In the first case, the logical sentence is correct if its satisfying interpretation is equivalent to the intended semantics of the ontology. In the second case, the logical sentence is correct iff the answer given by a human to a natural language question is equivalent to the solution returned by the reasoner when given the logical sentence as a query. This research question therefore addresses the problem of ontology validation.

Correctness of Question Answering: *Given the first-order sentence that is the output of the semantic parser, is the answer returned by the reasoner correct?*

This research question is implicitly an evaluation of correctness and completeness of the ontology that is generated by the semantic parser. The correctness of the ontology is demonstrated through ontology verification techniques and the completeness of the ontology is demonstrated through the validation of the ontology with respect to competency questions. These two tasks – ontology verification and ontology validation – are addressed in the third component of SEADOO which explicitly proposes first-order axioms for the ontologies by finding the best matching ontology from within an ontology repository.

5   Ontology Design Through Ontology Matching

5.1   Axiomatizing Intended Models

Ontology verification is concerned with the relationship between the intended models of an ontology and the models[1] of the axiomatization of the ontology [10]. This is done by demonstrating that there is a one-to-one correspondence between the models of the ontology and the models of a mathematical theory which is known to be consistent. An even more difficult challenge is ontology validation – are the intended models of the ontology indeed the correct models of the ontology?

The identification and specification of the intended models of an ontology is inherently a dialogue between the subject matter expert (who implicitly knows the models of the ontology) and the ontology designer (who is attempting to axiomatize the class of intended models). This project will explore techniques for eliciting intended models from the subject matter expert and evaluating these models with respect to expert responses. The primary objective here is the design of a procedure that finds the best match between a theory in the COLORE ontology repository and the set of intended and unintended models as identified by a domain expert. The procedure consists of two parts – elicitation of intended models and the proposal of models for existing ontologies. The first component locates the possible ontologies somewhere in the repository by providing bounds for the ontologies that characterize the intended models. In the second part, models of existing ontologies, coupled with subject matter expert responses, tighten this bound. The result is an ontology that is semi-automatically generated from sets of intended and unintended models.

With ontology verification, we want to characterize the models of an ontology up to isomorphism and determine whether or not these models are equivalent to the intended models of the ontology. Relationships between first-order ontologies within a repository can be used to support ontology verification. The fundamental insight is that we can use the relationships between ontologies to assist us

---

[1] A model of a logical theory is a truth assignment for the relations in the signature of the theory that satisfies all sentences in the theory.

in the characterization of the models of the ontologies. The objective is the construction of the models of one ontology from the models of another ontology by exploiting the relationships between these ontologies and their modules in the repository.

The challenge within this project is that the ontologies that are being designed are new, and do not explicitly exist within any ontology repository. The Hashemi Procedure implemented in this project identifies the mathematical theory whose models best match the examples and counterexamples. This is the same mathematical theory that is the basis for verification of the domain ontology. The Procedure then maps this mathematical theory to the domain ontology via translation definitions. In this way, we do not rely on the prior existence of a domain ontology.

In a sense, the mathematical theories in COLORE serve as ontology patterns from which we axiomatize the desired domain ontology. The central claim is that every ontology is logically synonymous to the combination of mathematical theories that serve as ontology patterns in COLORE [1]: Orderings, Graphs, Geometries, and Magmas (generalizations of groups in algebra).

Even if there is no single theory in the repository that is definably equivalent to the ontology that we want, we can still use the models of mathematical theories already in the repository to construct the ontology for the data. In general, we need to combine existing mathematical theories in order to construct the correct and complete ontology for given datasets, each of which will correspond to a module of the domain ontology. In this way, we get an ontology that is modular by design rather than needing to modularize the ontology afterwards.

5.2 Ontology Repositories

The SEADOO project uses the COLORE ontology repository [9], which is a project that is building an open repository of ontologies specified using Common Logic (ISO 24707). It serves as a testbed for ontology evaluation and integration techniques, and that can support the design, evaluation, and application of ontologies in first-order logic.

The basic organizational principle in COLORE is the notion of a hierarchy, which is a set of ontologies[2] with the same signature.

Definition 1. [9] A <u>hierarchy</u> $\mathbb{H} = \langle \mathcal{H}, \leq \rangle$ is a partially ordered, finite set of theories $\mathcal{H} = T_1, ..., T_n$ such that

1. $\Sigma(T_i) = \Sigma(T_j)$, for all i, j;
2. $T_1 \leq T_2$ iff T_2 is an extension of T_1;
3. $T_1 < T_2$ iff T_2 is a non-conservative extension of T_1.

---

[2] We follow previous work in terminology and notation [9] treating ontologies and their modules as logical theories. We do not distinguish between logically equivalent theories. For every theory T, $\Sigma(T)$ denotes its signature, which includes all the constant, function, and relation symbols used in T, and $\mathcal{L}(T)$ denotes the language of T, which is the set of first-order formulæthat only use the symbols in $\Sigma(T)$.

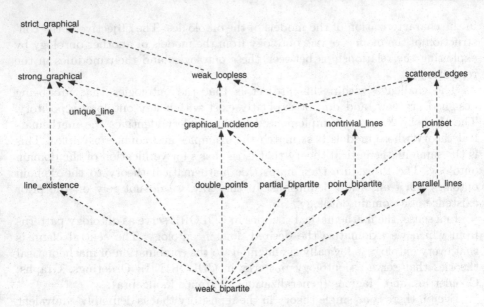

Fig. 3. The Bipartite Incidence Structure Hierarchy from COLORE

An example of a hierarchy is shown in Fig. 3[3]. Shown in this Figure is a set of mathematical theories known as bipartite incidence structures [5], which generalize the concepts familiar from Euclidean geometry. Points and lines are disjoint sets of elements and there is an incidence relation (called **in**) between points and lines.

Most importantly, the ontologies within a hierarchy form a partially ordered set with minimal elements.

Definition 2. A theory T in a hierarchy is a <u>root theory</u> iff it does not non-conservatively extend any other theory in the same hierarchy.

The root theory for the Bipartite Incidence Structure Hierarchy is the theory *weak_bipartite*.

5.3 Examples and Counterexamples

We begin by considering some properties of the ontologies within a hierarchy before applying these properties to the Procedure used to propose axioms for the intended ontology.

As discussed in the Introduction, the intended semantics of concepts within an enterprise are often implicit within the datasets of the enterprise, both those that are considered to be clean as well as those which are known to contain errors. One key insight of SEADOO is that clean datasets without any errors

---

[3] The Common Logic axioms for all theories in this Figure can be found at: https://github.com/gruninger/colore/tree/master/ontologies/bipartite_incidence.

should be considered to be consistent with the ontology, and hence they can be considered to be a specification of intended models for the ontology. On the other hand, datasets with quality problems should be inconsistent with the ontology. They can be considered to be a specification of interpretations that falsify one or more axioms of the ontology. In other words, a clean dataset can be considered to be an intended model of the ontology for that dataset. In this way, clean datasets serve as examples of intended models, while datasets with errors serve as counterexamples of intended models.

In the following, the set of examples will be denoted by

$$\mathfrak{M} = \{\mathcal{M}_1, ..., \mathcal{M}_n\}$$

and the set of counterexamples will be denoted by

$$\mathfrak{F} = \{\mathcal{F}_1, ..., \mathcal{F}_n\}$$

Definition 3. A theory T matches all examples in $\mathfrak{M}$ iff

$$\mathfrak{M} \subseteq Mod(T)$$

A theory T avoids all counterexamples in $\mathfrak{F}$ iff

$$\mathfrak{F} \cap Mod(T) = \emptyset$$

For example, suppose $\mathcal{M}_1$ is the example:

$$\mathbf{point} = \{\langle \mathbf{p_1} \rangle, \langle \mathbf{p_2} \rangle, \langle \mathbf{p_3} \rangle\}$$

$$\mathbf{line} = \{\langle \mathbf{m_1} \rangle, \langle \mathbf{m_2} \rangle, \langle \mathbf{m_3} \rangle\}$$

$$\mathbf{in} = \{\langle \mathbf{p_1}, \mathbf{m_1} \rangle, \langle \mathbf{p_1}, \mathbf{m_2} \rangle, \langle \mathbf{p_2}, \mathbf{m_2} \rangle, \langle \mathbf{p_2}, \mathbf{m_3} \rangle, \langle \mathbf{p_3}, \mathbf{m_3} \rangle, \langle \mathbf{p_3}, \mathbf{m_1} \rangle\}$$

and $\mathcal{F}_1$ is the counterexample:

$$\mathbf{point} = \{\langle \mathbf{p_1} \rangle, \langle \mathbf{p_2} \rangle\}$$

$$\mathbf{line} = \{\langle \mathbf{m_1} \rangle, \langle \mathbf{m_2} \rangle\}$$

$$\mathbf{in} = \{\langle \mathbf{p_1}, \mathbf{m_1} \rangle, \langle \mathbf{p_1}, \mathbf{m_2} \rangle, \langle \mathbf{p_2}, \mathbf{m_2} \rangle\}$$

nontrivial_lines and *double_points* matches $\mathcal{M}_1$ and avoids $\mathcal{F}_1$.

In practice, users present their examples and counterexamples using the signature of their domain For example, given the signature {*Project, Manager, supervises*} an example dataset would be

```
Manager(Alice).
Project(MAT456)
supervises(Alice,MAT456).
```

We use translation definitions to map the domain signature to the signatures of the mathematical theories.

$$(\forall x)\ Project(x) \equiv point(x) \tag{6}$$

$$(\forall x)\ Manager(x) \equiv line(x) \tag{7}$$

$$(\forall x, y)\ supervises(x, y) \equiv in(x, y) \wedge line(x) \wedge point(y) \tag{8}$$

so that the dataset actually used by the Procedure would be

```
line(Alice).
point(MAT456)
in(Alice,MAT456).
```

We can utilize the properties of a hierarchy in COLORE to show the following two results:

Lemma 1. *If T_1 matches all examples in $\mathfrak{M}$ and $T_2 \leq T_1$, then T_2 matches all examples in $\mathfrak{M}$.*

For example, since *point_bipartite* is weaker than *nontrivial_lines*, it also matches $\mathcal{M}_1$.

Lemma 2. *If T_1 avoids all counterexamples in $\mathfrak{F}$ and $T_1 \leq T_2$, then T_2 avoids all counterexamples in $\mathfrak{F}$.*

For example, since *double_points* avoids $\mathcal{F}_1$ and *graphical_incidence* extends *double_points*, we know that *graphical_incidence* also avoids $\mathcal{F}_1$.

The set of best matches for $\mathfrak{M}$ and $\mathfrak{F}$ therefore forms intervals in the hierarchy $\mathbb{H}$ which are suborderings of chains within the partial ordering of theories in $\mathbb{H}$. (A chain in a hierarchy is a linearly ordered set of theories.)

Theorem 1. *If T_1 is the strongest theory that matches $\mathfrak{M}_1$ and T_2 is the strongest theory that matches $\mathfrak{M}_2$, and $\mathfrak{M}_1 \subseteq \mathfrak{M}_2$, then*

$$T_2 \leq T_1$$

Suppose we have a theory T that matches $\mathfrak{M}$. As a result of Theorem 1, if we add more examples $\mathfrak{M}'$ so that

$$\mathfrak{M}' \not\subseteq Mod(T)$$

(i.e. we add new examples that are not matched by T), then we need to weaken T to a new theory T' such that

$$\mathfrak{M}' \subseteq Mod(T')$$

Theorem 2. *If T_1 is the weakest theory that avoids $\mathfrak{F}_1$ and T_2 is the weakest theory that avoids $\mathfrak{F}_2$, and $\mathfrak{F}_1 \subseteq \mathfrak{F}_2$, then*

$$T_1 \leq T_2$$

As a result of Theorem 2, if we add more counterexamples $\mathfrak{F}'$ so that

$$\mathfrak{F}' \cap Mod(T) \neq \emptyset$$

then we need to extend T to a new theory T' such that

$$\mathfrak{F}' \cap Mod(T') = \emptyset$$

Lemma 3. *Given a chain $\mathbb{C}$ in the hierarchy $\mathbb{H}$ and a set of examples $\mathfrak{M}$, there exists a unique theory $T \in \mathbb{C}$ such that*

$$\mathfrak{M} \subseteq Mod(T)$$

$$T < T' \Rightarrow \mathfrak{M} \not\subseteq Mod(T')$$

We will denote this theory by $MAX(\mathbb{C}, \mathfrak{M})$.

Revisiting the earlier examples, there are two different chains to consider; in one chain $\mathbb{C}_1$, we have $line\_existence = MAX(\mathbb{C}_1, \mathfrak{M})$, while in the other chain $\mathbb{C}_2$, we have $graphical\_incidence = MAX(\mathbb{C}_1, \mathfrak{M})$.

Lemma 4. *Given a chain $\mathbb{C}$ in the hierarchy $\mathbb{H}$ and a set of examples $\mathfrak{M}$, there exists a unique theory $T \in \mathbb{C}$ such that*

$$\mathfrak{F} \cap Mod(T) = \emptyset$$

$$T < T' \Rightarrow \mathfrak{F} \cap Mod(T') \neq \emptyset$$

We will denote this theory by $MIN(\mathbb{C}, \mathfrak{F})$.

In the earlier examples, we have $weak\_bipartite = MIN(\mathbb{C}_1, \mathfrak{F})$.

Theorem 3. *Let $\mathbb{C}$ be a chain in the hierarchy $\mathbb{H}$. Let $\mathfrak{M}$ be a set of examples and let $\mathfrak{F}$ be a set of counterexamples.*

T is a theory in $\mathbb{C}$ that matches all examples in $\mathfrak{M}$ and avoids all counterexamples in $\mathfrak{F}$ iff

$$MIN(\mathbb{C}, \mathfrak{F}) \leq T \leq MAX(\mathbb{C}, \mathfrak{M})$$

We will refer to the pair of theories $[MIN(\mathbb{C}, \mathfrak{F}), MAX(\mathbb{C}, \mathfrak{M})]$ as the bracket for the chain $\mathbb{C}$.

In the earlier examples, we have the following two brackets for the two chains in the hierarchy:

$[weak\_bipartite, line\_existence], [weak\_bipartite, graphical\_incidence]$

5.4   The Hashemi Procedure

The idea of using an ontology repository for ontology acquisition is the basis for the Hashemi Procedure, which has two phases – an initial Discovery phase in which we use examples and counterexamples provided by the user, and a subsequent Dialogue phase in which we generate models of candidate theories which the user classifies as either examples and counterexamples. The feedback provided by the user refines the upper and lower bounds of each bracket.

Algorithm 1. Hashemi Procedure

Require: Chain decomposition $\mathcal{C}$ of a hierarchy, set of examples $\mathfrak{M}$, set of counterexamples $\mathfrak{F}$.

Ensure: $\mathcal{B}$ is a set of brackets for each chain in $\mathcal{C}$.

$\quad \mathcal{B} \leftarrow \emptyset$

$\quad Discovery(\mathcal{C}, \mathfrak{M}, \mathfrak{F}, \mathcal{B})$

$\quad Dialogue(\mathcal{B})$

Discovery. Given the examples $\mathfrak{M}$, we start with the maximal theory in each chain $\mathbb{C}_i$ in $\mathbb{H}$, and find the strongest theory T_i^s that matches $\mathfrak{M}$ (which exists by Lemma 3). Given the counterexamples $\mathfrak{F}$, start with the minimal theory in each chain $\mathbb{C}_i$ in $\mathbb{H}$, and find the weakest theory T_i^w that avoids $\mathfrak{F}$ (which exists by Lemma 4). Within each chain $\mathbb{C}_i$ in the hierarchy $\mathbb{H}$, the pair $[T_i^w, T_i^s]$ forms a bracket. By Theorem 3, any theory between the bounds of the bracket is a candidate since it matches all examples and avoids all counterexamples.

Algorithm 2. Discovery

Require: Chain decomposition $\mathcal{C}$ of a hierarchy, set of examples $\mathfrak{M}$, set of counterexamples $\mathfrak{F}$.

Ensure: $\mathcal{B}$ is a set of brackets for each chain in $\mathcal{C}$.

$\quad$ **for all** $\mathbb{C}_i \in \mathcal{C}$ **do**

$\quad\quad T_i^s \leftarrow MAX(\mathbb{C}, \mathfrak{M})$

$\quad\quad T_i^w \leftarrow MIN(\mathbb{C}, \mathfrak{F})$

$\quad\quad$ **if** $MIN(\mathbb{C}, \mathfrak{F}) \leq MAX(\mathbb{C})$ **then**

5: $\quad\quad\quad \mathcal{B} \leftarrow \mathcal{B} \cup \{[T_i^w, T_i^s]\}$

$\quad\quad$ **end if**

$\quad$ **end for**

Theorem 4. *Suppose we are given a chain decomposition $\mathcal{C}$ of a hierarchy, a set of examples $\mathfrak{M}$, and a set of counterexamples $\mathfrak{F}$. If the Discovery$(\mathcal{C}, \mathfrak{M}, \mathfrak{F}, \mathcal{B})$ Procedure terminates, then $\mathcal{B}$ is a set of brackets for each chain in $\mathcal{C}$.*

Dialogue. As we can see from Algorithm 2, the Discovery Phase provides a set of brackets in each chain; in general, this means that there are multiple possible theories that match all examples and avoid all counterexamples. Without additional examples and counterexamples, we cannot improve on this set. Instead, the Dialogue Phase refines the set of possible theories by generating models and allowing the user to classify them as examples and counterexamples.

Given a bracket $[T_i^w, T_i^s]$ in a chain $\mathbb{C}_i$, we want to determine whether T_i^s is too strong (i.e. omits intended models) and T_i^w is too weak (i.e. allows unintended models). For each chain $\mathbb{C}_i$ with bracket $[T_i^w, T_i^s]$, generate a model $\mathcal{N}$ of $T_i' \cup \neg T_i^s$, where $T_i' \ll T_i^s$ (it is the theory covered by T_i^s in the chain). If $\mathcal{N}$ is an example (i.e. the user classifies $\mathcal{N}$ to be an intended model which is omitted by T_i^s), set the new bracket to be

$$[T_i^w, T_i']$$

In other words, we weaken T_i^s to allow $\mathcal{N}$ to be a model. If $\mathcal{N}$ is a counterexample, no change is made to the bracket.

For each chain $\mathbb{C}_i$ with bracket $[T_i^w, T_i^s]$, generate a model $\mathcal{N}$ of $T_i^w \cup \neg T_i^*$, where $T_i^w \ll T_i^*$ (it is the theory that covers T_i^w in the chain). If $\mathcal{N}$ is a counterexample (i.e. the user classifies $\mathcal{N}$ to be an unintended model), set the new bracket to be

$$[T_i^*, T_i^s]$$

In other words, we extend T_i^w to eliminate $\mathcal{N}$ as a model. If $\mathcal{N}$ is an example, no change is made to the bracket. If the brackets for all chains $\mathbb{C}_i$ are not empty, the bracket for the entire hierarchy is

$$[\bigcup_i T_i^w, \bigcup_i T_i^s]$$

Any combination of these theories is a candidate for the ontology. For example, suppose that one of the models that the system generates in the Dialogue Phase is:

$$\mathbf{point} = \{\langle p_1 \rangle, \langle p_2 \rangle, \langle p_3 \rangle, \langle p_4 \rangle\}$$
$$\mathbf{line} = \{\langle m_1 \rangle, \langle m_2 \rangle, \langle m_3 \rangle, \langle m_4 \rangle\}$$
$$\mathbf{in} = \{\langle p_1, m_1 \rangle, \langle p_1, m_2 \rangle, \langle p_1, m_3 \rangle, \langle p_2, m_3 \rangle, \langle p_2, m_4 \rangle,$$
$$\langle p_3, m_2 \rangle, \langle p_3, m_4 \rangle, \langle p_4, m_1 \rangle, \langle p_4, m_4 \rangle\}$$

which the user classifies as a counterexample. The best matching theory is then *strong_graphical*. Using the translation definitions in formulae (6),(7), and (8), we can generate the set of axioms in the domain signature which are logically synonymous with *graphical_incidence*. In addition to the sentences (1)-(5), we have

$$\forall p_1, p_2, l_1, l_2 \, Project(p_1) \wedge Project(p_2) \wedge Manager(l_1) \wedge Manager(l_2)$$
$$\wedge \, supervises(p_1, l_1) \wedge supervises(p_2, l_2) \wedge supervises(p_2, l_1)$$
$$\wedge \, supervises(p_2, l_2) \supset ((p_1 = p_2) \vee (l_1 = l_2)) \tag{9}$$
$$\forall x, y \, Project(x) \wedge Project(y) \wedge (x \neq y)$$
$$\supset (\exists z \, Manager(z) \wedge supervises(x, z) \wedge supervises(y, z)) \tag{10}$$

If the brackets for all chains $\mathbb{C}_i$ are empty, then the theory does not exist in the hierarchy. Although this might not seem surprising if we are designing new ontologies, remember that the hierarchies that we are using as ontology patterns are mathematical theories. If the ontology that we are designing does not correspond to any theory in the hierarchy, then we have effectively identified a new theory which has never been identified within the mathematical literature i.e. we have uncovered new mathematics.

Algorithm 3. Dialogue

Require: Set of brackets $\mathcal{B}$.
Ensure: $\mathcal{B}$ is a revised set of brackets
    for all $[T_i^w, T_i^s] \in \mathcal{B}$ **do**
        $T_i' \ll T_i^s$
        for all $\Phi_{ij} \in T_i^s \setminus T_i'$ **do**
            if $Mod(T_i' \cup \neg\Phi_{ij}) \neq \emptyset$ **then**
5:             $\mathcal{N}_{ij} \in Mod(T_i' \cup \neg\Phi_{ij})$
                if $\mathcal{N}_{ij}$ is an intended model **then**
                    $T_i^s \leftarrow T_i'$
                end if
            end if
10:    **end for**
        $T_i^w \ll T_i^*$
        for all $\Phi_{ij} \in T_i^* \setminus T_i^w$ **do**
            if $Mod(T_i^w \cup \neg\Phi_{ij}) \neq \emptyset$ **then**
             $\mathcal{N}_{ij} \in Mod(T_i^w \cup \neg\Phi_{ij})$
15:            **if** $\mathcal{N}_{ij}$ is an unintended model **then**
                $T_i^w \leftarrow T_i^*$
            end if
            end if
        end for
20:    **if** $T_i^s < T_i^w$ **then**
        $\mathcal{B} \leftarrow \mathcal{B} \setminus [T_i^w, T_i^s]$
        end if
    end for

---

6   Relationship to Ontology Learning

As we saw earlier, ontology learning in general is an active area of research. One approach discussed earlier was the Ontology Learning Layer Cake ([16]), in which a distinction is made between learning the signature of the ontology and the concepts, hierarchies, relations, and axioms of the ontology. Within SEADOO, the signature is explicitly supplied by the user, either within the data model or within the classes and relations of the datasets. The primary focus of both the Data Model Transformation and the Hashemi Procedure is on the generation of the axioms of the ontology (i.e. the top layer). Moreover, the semantic parser supplements the axioms generated by the rest of SEADOO; we are not learning the ontology directly or solely from natural language text.

The three components of SEADOO each address different kinds of data as the sources for learning. The Semantic Parser focuses on unstructured natural language text, Data Model Transformation uses semistructured data models, and the Hashemi Procedure requires formal structures (i.e. the specification of satisfying and falsifying first-order interpretations).

The approach proposed in this paper has a strong affinity to inductive logic programming ([6,7]). Both have the objective of generating axioms that require the expressiveness of first-order logic rather than OWL, and in both cases, formal structures are used as data. The primary difference is that while inductive logic programming searches through the space of well-formed formulae, the Hashemi Procedure is searching through a repository of existing logical theories that serve as ontology patterns.

7   Summary

The ability to learn first-order ontologies from an enterprise's datasets would reduce many of the barriers towards the creation of an ontology-driven enterprise. Beyond the effort required to manually design ontologies, one drawback of the conventional ontology lifecycle is the need to map an ontology's concepts to the data models and databases within the enterprise. Rather than manually designing the ontology first and then associating it with data, in this paper we have proposed techniques by which we can semiautomatically design the ontology from the data itself.

A key innovation over other approaches to ontology learning (such as inductive logic programming) is to use existing mathematical theories as ontology patterns to search for the ontology that satisfies all examples and falsifies all counterexamples. This approach works because of the methodology of ontology verification, through which any first-order ontology is shown the be logically synonymous with the combination of mathematical theories.

SEADOO has been implemented and demonstrated as a proof-of-concept within RBC. The subject domains used for evaluation have been based on simple data models, and the next step will be to scale up to enterprise-wide data warehouses.

References

1. Aameri, B., Grüninger, M.: Reducible theories and amalgamations of models. ACM Trans. Comput. Logic **24**, 1–24 (2023)
2. Asim, M.N., Wasim, M., Khan, M.U.G., Mahmood, W., Abbasi, H.M.: A survey of ontology learning techniques and applications. Database **2018**, bay101 (2018)

3. de Azevedo, R.R., Freitas, F., Rocha, R., Menezes, J.A.A., Pereira, L.F.A.: An approach for automatic expressive ontology construction from natural language. In: Computational Science and Its Applications–ICCSA 2014: 14th International Conference, Guimarães, Portugal, June 30–July 3, 2014, Proceedings, Part VI 14, pp. 746–759 (2014)

4. Berant, J., Liang, P.: Semantic parsing via paraphrasing. In: Proceedings of the 52nd Annual Meeting of the Association for Computational Linguistics (Volume 1: Long Papers), pp. 1415–1425 (2014)

5. Buekenhout, F.: An introduction to Incidence Geometry. In: Buekenhout, V. (ed.) Handbook of Incidence Geometry, pp. 1–25. North-Holland (1995)

6. Cropper, A., Dumančić, S., Muggleton, S.H.: Turning 30: new ideas in inductive logic programming. arXiv preprint arXiv:2002.11002 (2020)

7. Cropper, A., Hocquette, C.: Learning logic programs by discovering where not to search. In: Proceedings of the AAAI Conference on Artificial Intelligence, vol. 37, pp. 6289–6296 (2023)

8. Dahab, M.Y., Hassan, H.A., Rafea, A.: TextOntoEx: automatic ontology construction from natural English text. Expert Syst. Appl. **34**, 1474–1480 (2008)

9. Gruninger, M., Hahmann, T., Hashemi, A., Ong, D., Ozgovde, A.: Modular first-order ontologies via repositories. Appl. Ontol. **7**, 169–210 (2012)

10. Gruninger, M.: Ontology validation as dialogue (2019). http://ceur-ws.org/Vol-2518/paper-WINKS3.pdf

11. Jia, H., Newman, J., Tianfield, H.: A new formal concept analysis based learning approach to ontology building. In: Sicilia, MA., Lytras, M.D. (eds.) Metadata and Semantics, pp. 433–444. Springer, Boston, MA (2009). https://doi.org/10.1007/978-0-387-77745-0_42

12. Klarman, S., Britz, K.: Ontology learning from interpretations in lightweight description logics. In: International Conference on Inductive Logic Programming, pp. 76–90 (2015)

13. Lisi, F.A.: A declarative modeling language for concept learning in description logics. In: International Conference on Inductive Logic Programming, pp. 151–165 (2012)

14. Martínez-Gómez, P., Mineshima, K., Miyao, Y., Bekki, D.: ccg2lambda: a compositional semantics system. In: Proceedings of ACL-2016 System Demonstrations, pp. 85–90 (2016)

15. Ozaki, A.: Learning description logic ontologies: Five approaches. where do they stand? KI-Künstliche Intelligenz **34**(3), 317–327 (2020)

16. Petrucci, G.: Information extraction for learning expressive ontologies. In: European Semantic Web Conference 2015, pp. 740–750 (2015)

17. Unger, C., Cimiano, P.: Pythia: compositional meaning construction for ontology-based question answering on the semantic web. In: Muñoz, R., Montoyo, A., Métais, E. (eds.) NLDB 2011. LNCS, vol. 6716, pp. 153–160. Springer, Heidelberg (2011). https://doi.org/10.1007/978-3-642-22327-3_15

18. Völker, J., Hitzler, P., Cimiano, P.: Acquisition of owl dl axioms from lexical resources. In: European Semantic Web Conference, pp. 670–685 (2007)

Enterprise Modeling at Work

Enterprise Modelling Can Be Used as a Research Method: An Application to Sustainability Reporting Research

Sergio España[1,2]([✉]) [ID], Gudrun Thorsteinsdottir[2], Vijanti Ramautar[2] [ID], and Oscar Pastor[1] [ID]

[1] Valencian Research Institute for Artificial Intelligence,
Universitat Politècnica de València, Valencia, Spain
{sergio.espana,opastor}@dsic.upv.es
[2] Utrecht University, Utrecht, The Netherlands
{s.espana,v.d.ramautar}@uu.nl

Abstract. Enterprise modelling (EM) refers to eliciting and documenting knowledge about an organisation from several interrelated perspectives. Often EM is industrially applied and scientifically researched
within the fields of enterprise and information systems (IS) engineering.
In this paper, we put forward that EM constitutes a sound and valid
research method that could be used outside these disciplines. Its systematic elicitation and modelling techniques lend themselves to rigorous
empirical investigations. We report on our experience in applying an EM
method as a research method in a project exploring the relationships
between sustainability reporting and strategic management practices.
The results were rich in high-quality, detailed research data, that allowed
drawing strong evidence-based conclusions. If EM were known in other
scientific fields interested in phenomena taking place inside or around
enterprises, these research communities would benefit from a structured
and rigorous approach to investigate aspects related to the organisational
structure, processes, communications and information, motivations, and
relationships among these, which are core constructs in EM methods.

Keywords: Enterprise Modelling · Research Methodology ·
Sustainability Reporting · Environmental · Social and Governance ·
Ethical · Social and Environmental Accounting

1 Introduction

In many scientific fields, research projects require the investigation of phenomena related to organisations. Sometimes it refers to quantitative data, such as
correlations or causal effects between certain organisational practices and organisational performance (e.g. [12]). Other times, the investigation is qualitative

Sergio España is supported by a María Zambrano grant of the Spanish Ministry of
Universities, co-funded by the Next Generation EU European Recovery Plan.

and, for instance, relates to attitudes towards some organisational aspect (e.g. [40]). In some of the latter cases, the research involves discovering structural or behavioural elements of the organisation (e.g. [20]); and it is precisely the scope of enterprise modelling (EM) the elicitation and documentation of knowledge about an organisation from several interrelated perspectives. The application of EM in research is typically confined to a small set of fields, but hereby we argue that EM should be regarded as a useful and valid research method within disciplines outside enterprise and IS engineering. EM should come to the mind of researchers while conceiving their research approach, when enterprise knowledge is key to their project, and it should be accepted by reviewers and readers of the resulting papers as a valid approach to eliciting and documenting phenomena related to enterprises.

In this paper, we report on the use of EM within a research project that investigates the mutual influences between ethical, social and environmental accounting (a.k.a. sustainability reporting) and strategic management within large enterprises. The contributions of this paper are: (i) we report on the use of EM as a research method within a project outside the conventional realm of EM applications, (ii) we discuss the effectiveness, strengths and weaknesses of such use, also offering advice for researchers willing to use EM within their research projects. In Sect. 2, we present background knowledge, that allows us to properly define the research method, in Sect. 3. We then proceed with problem investigation (Sect. 4), demonstrating the applicability of EM as a research method (Sect. 5), and discussing the results (Sect. 6). Finally, Sect. 7 concludes the paper.

2   Background Knowledge

On the Purposes of EM Methods. Many authors have elaborated on the purposes of EM. The list is large, so we sample a few (find more details in the companion technical report [15]): diagnosing disorders of the enterprise [51], re-engineering the enterprise [31,38,51], communicating among stakeholders [38,42], achieving proper integration (e.g. information system interoperability) within the enterprise and with external actors [24,51], as a reasoning tool for evaluating the application of new technology to the enterprise [31], developing IS that are aligned with the enterprise [38,42,51]. Some purposes are related to investigation and research; e.g. understanding of how the enterprise should work and how it really works [51], acquiring knowledge about the enterprise from different stakeholders [38]. However, we have not found any explicit recognition of the suitability of EM as a research method capable of yielding knowledge outside of the traditional disciplines that use EM methods and tools.

On the Use of EM Methods for Research Purposes. We found the work by Kirikova [28] on the representational and explanatory capabilities of EM enlightening; while her paper does not explicitly characterise EM as a research method, it does perform a theoretical examination of the capabilities of enterprise

models from the perspective of Aristotle's explanatory principles. We have found
some examples of papers outside enterprise and IS engineering that have applied
(fragments of) EM methods as research methods, with or without explicit recognition of this fact. For instance, Shukla et al. [44] propose the use of Role Activity
Diagrams [35] to elicit and document detailed healthcare pathways and use the
models as input for problem identification, decision making modelling, pathway variation analysis, and simulation. Sawitria et al. [43] have used Business
Model Canvas[1] [34] to investigate product diversification strategies in Indonesian
enterprises of the food sector. Gerber et al. [20] adopt Zachman Framework for
Enterprise Architecture (ZFEA) as an explanatory IS theory. They apply ZFEA
in seven case studies with South African enterprises, to structure the interview
protocol. They recorded and transcribed the interviews, and later coded them
in Atlas.TI using ZFEA elements as a base reference as well as relevant themes
that emerged from the interviews. In this way, each transcript was mapped to
the different elements of the ZFEA, facilitating the identification of possible patterns of focus during enterprise growth. They also aggregated results to produce
heatmap and identify how knowledge about the holistic organisation and its
underlying parts is relevant for growth. Herein, we will refer to an EM method
used as a research method as enterprise modelling research method (EMRM).

On Sustainability Reporting and Its Links to Strategic Management.
Enterprises are increasingly interested in assessing and reporting their performance on ethical, social and environmental topics. Such process is referred to
with many names; e.g. social (and environmental) auditing [23], sustainability
accounting [2], social audits [36], integrated reporting [13], environmental, social
and governance (ESG) reporting [8]. We will use either the term *sustainability
reporting, ch10hahn2013determinants* (because it is by far the most widespread
both in academia and industry) or the term *ethical, social and environmental
accounting* (ESEA) [16,17] (because we find it the most accurate). There exist
many methods and standards guiding ESEA [16]; e.g. B Impact Assessment,
Common Good Balance Sheet, REAS Social Balance, ISO 26000, ISO 14000,
GRI Standards, Integrated Reporting framework. The motivations for conducting sustainability reporting are diverse; e.g. attracting funding [27] or human
resources [4], obtaining a certification [45], improving the enterprise [23], using
the results in marketing [50], reacting to public pressure [48]. Furthermore, there
is an increasing research interest in the use of ESEA data to inform strategic
management decisions and processes [1,3,5,23,30,32,39], but the authors merely
advocate for the need to establish a strong link between both practices or, when
they claim that such link exists, the evidence is anecdotal or based on manager surveys. There is a need for case-study research that shows how many links
between ESEA and strategic management appear in real enterprises and how

---

[1] While not a full-fledged enterprise modelling method, we considered the authors'
research approach representative of the intentions we pursue in championing EM as
a research method.

these links are operationalised. It is in this research context that we experienced the need of applying EM as a research method.

3 Research Method

The research questions addressed by this paper are the following:

- **RQ1**: How can we use an enterprise modelling (EM) method with the purpose of researching a domain unrelated to enterprise or IS engineering? We intend to design an enterprise modelling research method (EMRM) and report on the experience.
- **RQ2**: What are the benefits and drawbacks of applying an enterprise modelling method for such purpose? We aim at applying the EMRM within a research project and report on its performance.

In this research, we define an EMRM and acquire new knowledge about its performance in a practical setting. Such combination of practical and knowledge problems lends itself to enacting the Design Science cycle [55], as follows.

Problem Investigation. To understand the phenomenon under study, we perform a literature review on sustainability reporting and its relation to management practices (reported in Sect. 2). We also conduct six literature-based case studies (Sect. 4), in which we analyse six enterprises that have disclosed links between their ESEA and strategic management. The sources comprise a variety of scientific and grey literature, such as papers (e.g. [52]) and thesis reports performing case studies that we analyse through a different lens (e.g. [11]), sustainability reports (e.g. [19]), corporate websites and communications (e.g. [37]). During this phase, we soon felt the need for a rigorous modelling approach that would guide the knowledge elicitation and documentation, and that would provide a structured representation that facilitated data aggregation to generalise the results: it became clear to us that EM could assist in our research. The sources are coded in the QSR Nvivo tool for qualitative analysis, starting with a minimal coding scheme (a.k.a. node tree) based on our anecdotal evidences in the domain, and later adding more codes when deemed necessary.

Treatment Design. We use the results from the problem investigation to define the requirements for the EMRM. We then design the EMRM through method engineering [9]. The overall approach is a method integration [22], which we operationalise as a metamodel integration [26], using UML Class Diagram.

Treatment Validation. We apply the EMRM while we conduct observational case studies in five large enterprises, selected through convenience sampling across several industry sectors (find more demographic details in the report [15]). For each case study, we (1) Gather and analyse publicly available documents about the enterprise (e.g. websites, sustainability reports, mission statements), (2) Conduct a semi-structured interview to elicit: ESEA methods applied, how they use accounting results for management and strategic planning, how strategic management needs influence the accounting practices, (3) Request internal documentation about the enterprise structures, processes and strategies mentioned during the interview, (4) Transcribe and code data, (5) Analyse input and output information flows, (6) Create detailed models of the relevant processes (e.g. when sustainability reporting methods are adapted based on request from strategic managers). Contrasting several sources (external and internal documentation, and interviews) allows us to triangulate the data and verify its accuracy. During and after the case studies, we collect evidences about the performance of the EMRM, which allows us to analyse and reflect on the results of applying an enterprise modelling method as a research method.

4   Analysing the Problem to Design the EMRM

The main stakeholders are researchers who need to investigate phenomena related to enterprises, within projects that fall outside the conventional realm of EM; that is, research projects unrelated to enterprise and IS engineering. They often resort to interviews and surveys, but they rarely structure their data collection protocols with a holistic view of the constituents of an enterprise, nor do they resort to modelling languages that allow them to document the elicited data unambiguously and with a level of detail that adapts to the needs of the investigation. This also complicates the validation of the data to ascertain that it is accurate and faithfully represents the phenomena they are set to investigate. The problem is, thus, the lack of a guidance in eliciting and documenting data from enterprises, leading to sub-optimal results in terms of research process rigour, and results completeness and validity.

As argued above, we faced that precise problem as part of a research into the relationships between ESEA and strategic management practices. When we analyse the keywords of the publications and the areas of expertise of their authors, it becomes evident that this research goal is outside the disciplines where EM is commonly applied; e.g. accounting, corporate social responsibility, sustainability reporting, sustainability management control, policy-making (see a detailed analysis in the report [15]). We wanted to find strong evidences of the relationships, and understand the mechanisms in play so, for us, EM became an evident research approach. The literature-based case studies have revealed links between ESEA practices and strategic management. While the level of detail of the sources does not allow for a thorough understanding of the links or a detailed specification of the mechanisms in play, it encouraged a deeper investigation.

The coding of literature from the domain and the sources used within the literature-based case studies (e.g. [7,23,47]) allows us to identify which constructs are key to investigate the phenomena. In Fig. 1 we depict a metamodel with such constructs. The background colour denotes how frequently the constructs or instances of them are mentioned in the literature. For instance,

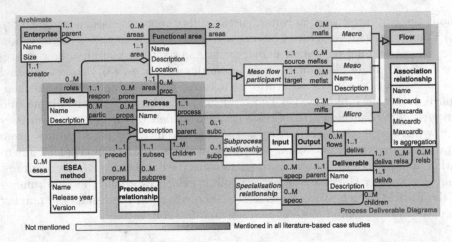

Fig. 1. Metamodel containing the constructs resulting from the qualitative analysis of the sources. The background colour of the metaclass header denotes the frequency with which the construct appears. The greyish classes with their name in italics were added afterwards, to better structure the model.

Functional areas are mentioned in nearly all the sources, whereas **Precedences** among processes are barely indicated (at least explicitly).

After the literature-based case studies, we also define some requirements for the EMRM (see Table 1). Firstly, we considered it was important to be able to represent the investigated phenomena with different levels of detail; in some literature-based case studies, the sources had abstract or coarse-grained descriptions of (parts of) the organisational practices, and we expected something similar during the observational case-studies. We aim at specifying the findings with great detail, but we rather not reject any evidence, even if the details are not fully known. We decided to follow a three-tier approach, following suggestions by Dopfer et al. [10], who conceive an analytical framework for evolutionary eco-

Table 1. Requirements for the enterprise modelling research method, defined after the problem investigation

Id	Requirement
R1	The EMRM should allow us to define the links between ESEA and managerial practices at different levels of detail, allowing for different depths of analysis, depending on the amount of information that the case studies provide
R2	The models resulting from applying the EMRM should be understandable by stakeholders, to a degree that allows them to provide feedback
R3	The EMRM can be made of fragments of existing EM methods
R4	The resulting EMRM or its constituent fragments, should be compatible with our competencies and earlier research we have conducted in the field of ESEA

nomics with a tiered architecture. In the **macro tier** we seek to determine the organisational structure, setting the context for understanding the relationship between ESEA and managerial practices within functional areas in enterprises. Even when the details of the relationship are not known, we intend to specify any evidences of strategic managers using inputs from or, providing instructions to, the (ESEA) accounting department. In the **meso tier**, we review the information flow between IS supporting ESEA and IS supporting managerial practices; this clarifies the information being exchanged among the functional areas. In the **micro tier**, we further gain a deeper understanding of the exact processes followed (i) by the managers defining strategies within functional areas, based on the results of the ESEA, or (ii) by the accountants adapting the ESEA methods to the needs and wishes of the strategic managers. We aim at specifying the activities and products of such processes in detail.

We decide to create an ad-hoc EMRM integrating fragments of two existing methods (R3); namely, ArchiMate [29] and Process Deliverable Diagram (PDD) [53]. ArchiMate is a visual EM language that allows describing, analysing, and communicating enterprise-related phenomena. PDD is a language aimed at modelling methods so as to support situational method engineering endeavours[2]; it integrates a UML Activity Diagram that represents the process aspects and a UML Class Diagram that specifies the initial, intermediate and resulting products. The resulting EMRM allows us to express the phenomena at different levels of detail (R1): we use ArchiMate to elicit and document the macro and meso tiers, and PDDs to elicit and document the micro tier. See the mapping between the EMRM metamodel constructs and EM primitives in Table 2).

Also, we expect the stakeholders to understand the ArchiMate models well, and to understand the PDDs sufficiently (R2); earlier experience showed us that interviewees can understand the process part of PDDs and that, while they have trouble understanding the deliverable part in full, they can at least validate those UML classes that represent business forms, documents and tools. While we could have represented fine-grained processes with ArchiMate as well, instead of resorting to PDDs, in earlier research we have produced very detailed PDDs of the most widespread ESEA methods in the market, and these models have also been validated by ESEA accountants and consultants, so they can be considered accurate representations of industrial practice. So far, we have 33 of such PDDs available in an online repository [14]. We found that using PDDs for the micro tier was convenient (R4).

5   Applying the EMRM

To get acquainted with the EMRM, we first modelled the results of the literature-based case studies. Find the models in the technical report [15]. The experience confirmed that (i) we could create models at the macro, meso or micro level, depending on the amount of information we could extract from the sources,

---

[2] Originally intended for IS development methods, it is currently used for other types of methods and processes (e.g. we have used it to model many ESEA methods [16]).

Table 2. Mapping of EMRM metamodel constructs to EM language primitives. This mapping also determines the two shapes in the background of Fig. 1 where blue represents the ArchiMate EM method fragment, red refers to Process Deliverable Diagrams, and purple represents both.

Metamodel construct	ArchiMate	Process Deliverable Diagram
Enterprise	Business actor	
Functional area	Business actor	
Role	Business actor	Role
Process	Business process	Activity
Flow	Flow	Process-deliverable arrow
Precedence		Activity edge
Deliverable		Class
Relationship		Association relationship
Specialisation		Specialisation relationship

(ii) the models showed clearly the links between ECG accounting and strategic management, pointing towards a good direction of the research. However, no case had sources which were detailed enough to allow understanding the intricate mechanisms through which the sustainability reporting results were integrated within strategic management or how exactly strategic managers had an effect on sustainability reporting practices (beyond participating in the selection of the ESEA method to apply).

We then proceeded with the observational case studies. The possibilities to conduct interviews with ESEA accountants and CSR managers, and ask them for company documentation (typically under some confidentiality agreements) helped us collect rich information that deepened into the mechanisms mentioned above. Not only we again found evidences of the relationship between ECG accounting and strategic management, but we could also perfectly understand how those interactions take place in the enterprises. Rather than guiding our interviews (it did not affect the coarse-grained outline of the interview protocol), the EMRM gave structure to the discussions every time the topic deepened into the investigated relationships. The EM primitives associated with the metamodel constructs in Fig. 1, served as a checklist to identify what details we were still missing to paint the full picture of the case (i.e. to create the EM models).

It is beyond the scope of this paper to report in detail on the results of the research project focused on sustainability reporting. However, we include a sample of the EM models that were produced during case study D, to illustrate the use of the EMRM in this context, and discuss what types of insights and research results they enabled. Figure 2 shows part of the organisational structure of the enterprise that falls within the scope of the case study, depicting the functional areas, and the core processes within each area. Other models at the macro tier provide a more comprehensive view of the organisational structure, but we omit them for reasons of space (the reader can find all models in the technical report [15]). The figure also depicts the meso-tier flows that represent relationships between ESEA and strategic management practices. Overall, the Governance Department influences the ESEA by informing the selection of material topics; i.e. those that are relevant enough to have their impact monitored. Most functional areas have shown evidences of using the results of the ESEA to inform their own strategic management processes. The model shows the meso-tier flows received by the Supply Chain Department, each flow representing a specific ESEA indicator. We further inquired the interviewee about them until fully understanding how the department used the information. For instance, the Total amount, in CO2 equivalents, for Scope 3 is used to inform the strategic management decisions related to waste management, packaging optimisation, and overall actions to reduce carbon emissions. Finally, Fig. 3 refines the relationship between the Governance Department and the Accounting Department. It depicts the process whereby the executive board defines a company-wide strategy that influences the application of the SDGc ESEA method by informing the prioritisation of SDGs. The result then informs the sustainability vision defined by the executive board (which further influences the functional and modular strategies). The process continues with the executive board, functional managers and the ESEA manager jointly defining the set of categories and metrics to be used during the application of the ESG reporting 2.0 method.

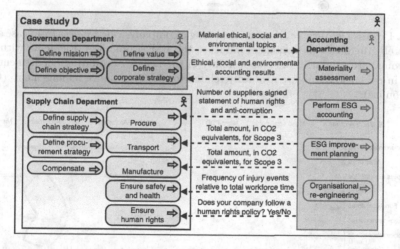

Fig. 2. ArchiMate model depicting the meso-tier information flows from and to the Accounting Department that relate ESEA practices to managerial practices, with the focus put on the Supply Chain Department.

Overall, across all literature-based and observational case studies, we have created 12 macro-tier, 17 meso-tier and 17 micro-tier models (additionally, 5 micro-tier PDD were created to specify off-the-shelf ESEA methods, but these are not considered in the overview that follows). Figure 4 shows, on the left, the

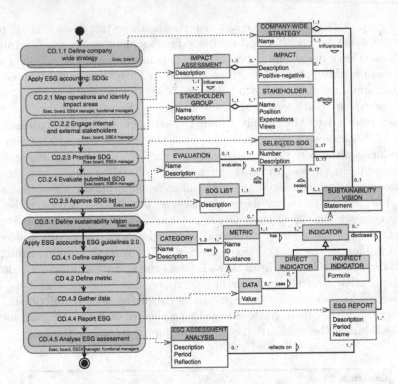

Fig. 3. Process Deliverable Diagram depicting a company-wide process from case study D whereby the strategic managers influence the ESEA practices. Elements with blue background are primarily the responsibility of the ESEA Accounting department, elements in red background are primarily related to the Governance management. (Color figure online)

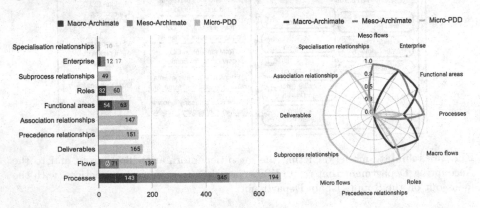

Fig. 4. Overview of the use of EMRM metamodel constructs across the models of the three tiers created during this research. Left: stacked barchart showing the total number of instances of each construct considering all models. Right: radarchart representing how each tier focuses on a subset of the constructs; scores are calculated using normalised averages of the number of instances of each construct per model.

total number of instances of each construct of the EMRM metamodel (see Fig. 1) in all models from all case studies. The two most frequent elements in the models are processes and flows, which is a reasonable result given that the investigation was looking into links (i.e. flows) between strategic management and ESEA practices (i.e. processes). The rest of the elements provide the necessary context and details to properly understand the phenomena under study. To the right of Fig. 4, a radar chart shows the shapes that characterise the scope of each of the three tiers we defined. As intended and described in Sect. 4, the macro tier mostly focuses on the structural aspects, and thus models the enterprise, its functional areas, some relevant roles and processes, and macro flows. The focus of the meso tier is similar, but does not include roles and contains meso flows instead of macro flows. The micro tier deepens into the mechanisms of the investigated links, and specifies processes in detail, thus covering processes and precedences on the dynamic perspective, and classes with their association and specialisation relationships on the static perspective; plus micro flows.

On the one hand, unlike macro and meso flows, which focus exclusively on the investigated links, not all micro flows are relevant to the research goal, since PDDs use flows to specify the relationships from process activities to their input and output deliverables (i.e. classes). Only 23% of the micro flows constitute evidence of the links under study: 15 micro flows represent information departing from strategic management and arriving to the accounting department, and 17 signal the opposite direction (see Fig. 5). On the other hand, micro flows are part of a detailed description of the link, so they provide valuable qualitative information that reinforces the findings.

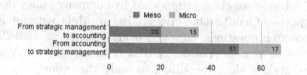

Fig. 5. Flows that contribute evidence of the links between ESEA and strategic management practices.

6   Discussion of the Results

Earlier research has highlighted the value of sustainability reporting results for strategic management or the effect of strategic management practices in shaping the firm's sustainability agenda, in the areas of supply chain management, human resource management or marketing (see, for instance, [33,41,46], respectively). Our results complement theirs by showing how enterprises perform the processes that link both areas, and depict in models the exact mechanisms that earlier papers discuss broadly or merely hypothesise. Such a contribution was only possible through the use of the EM, the reason why we claim that the

EMRM was effective. It provided detailed models, rich in qualitative information, that allowed to deepen into the investigated phenomena and reveal non-evident links. The main strengths are the structure that the EM method provides during elicitation and the expressiveness of the EM languages. The main weakness is the difficulty to formulate quantitative hypotheses. In scientific disciplines such as cleaner production, sustainability reporting, or strategic management, reviewers and readers are used to quantitative research (e.g. structural equations or multiple regression models). The effort to obtain sufficient data points through EM would be prohibitive. Convincing the audience of the validity of en EMRM as a qualitative research method within these disciplines might prove a challenge. Nonetheless, assuming that the researchers are willing to overcome resistance to conventions in the field, we provide the following advice to select and apply EM as a research method. **Select an EMRM** (i) whose underlying ontology (e.g. metamodel) is suitable for the intended investigation, (ii) that is compatible with earlier research results and competences of the research team, (iii) that is understandable by your stakeholders and research participants (e.g. interviewees). **Feel free to engineer a research method based on EM method fragments**, but consider whether the resulting combination of languages has the proper quality [21] and allows creating a set of models that is coherent [6]. **Elicit the information** through your preferred requirements or EM elicitation technique (e.g. interviews, focus groups, document analysis), taking into account the availability and confidentiality of sources. It is not unlikely to be required to sign a non-disclosure agreement preventing some details from being published (e.g. name or location of the enterprise). **Triangulate** the findings when possible, by checking consistency across different sources referring to the same phenomena (e.g. interviewee claims supported by company policy documents or sustainability reports). **Create the enterprise models** without losing focus of the original research questions, to avoid overkills such as modelling beyond the area of interest or at a level of detail that does not pay off. **Validate the models** when the stakeholders are willing to make that effort.

This work has some limitations and threats to the validity. We could have opted for other modelling languages for specifying the metamodel or the deliverables of PDDs (e.g. Entity-Relationship Diagrams [18]), and this could have influenced the results (e.g. readability). We have used the same ArchiMate primitive **Business actor** to represent three EMRM constructs (i.e. **Enteprise**, **Functional area** and **Role**. We acknowledge that this ontological overload is not ideal, but served our purposes. We have only applied the EMRM in a single research project within sustainability reporting, so we cannot yet make general claims. The actual value of EM as a research method will (likely) become evident when more researchers from outsider disciplines apply such an approach. The selection of the appropriate EM method for a given project is sensitive to the results of the initial problem investigation, as well as to the modelling skills of the researcher. EM is not part of most curricula in Economics, Industrial Engineering, etc. It might become necessary to provide guidance to researchers who are inexperienced with EM, before they can fully tap into its potential.

7   Conclusions

In this paper, we champion enterprise modelling (EM) as a valid research method outside the scientific disciplines where it is traditionally applied; namely, enterprise and information systems engineering. We have showcased how an EM method was applied in the context of sustainability reporting research. The approach has yielded valuable results, providing evidences of the links between sustainability reporting and strategic management practices, at a level of detail previously inexistent in the scientific literature of the area. As future work, we aim at applying EM as a research method in more research projects, and also within other domains and with different types of research questions. To test means of generalising the results obtained through an EM research method, we would attempt techniques such as the method comparison approach [54] or the inductive reference enterprise architecture modelling [49], which allow producing reference models from case models. We consider that EM constitutes an untapped potential for researchers from a diverse set of disciplines, who could incorporate it in their research methods toolkit. We hope to soon find that enterprise modelling becomes a known and accepted research method and we encourage researchers to share their experiences.

References

1. Adams, C.A., Frost, G.R.: Integrating sustainability reporting into management practices. Acc. Forum **32**(4), 288–302 (2008)
2. Adams, C.A., Larrinaga-González, C.: Engaging with organisations in pursuit of improved sustainability accounting and performance. Acc. Audit Acc. J. **20**(3), 333–355 (2007)
3. Adams, C.A., McNicholas, P.: Making a difference: sustainability reporting, accountability and organisational change. Acc. Audit Acc. J. **20**(3), 382–402 (2007)
4. Barrena-Martínez, J., López-Fernández, M., Márquez-Moreno, C., Romero-Fernández, P.M.: Corporate social responsibility in the process of attracting college graduates. Corp. Soc. Responsib. Environ. Manag. **22**(6), 408–423 (2015)
5. Bebbington, J.: Accounting for sustainable development performance. Elsevier (2007)
6. Bjekovic, M., Proper, H., Sottet, J.S.: Towards a coherent enterprise modelling landscape. In: PoEM 2012, Short Papers (2012)
7. Bonn, I., Fisher, J.: Sustainability: the missing ingredient in strategy. J. Bus Strategy **32**(1), 5–14 (2011)
8. Bose, S.: Evolution of ESG reporting frameworks. In: Esty, D.C., Cort, T. (eds.) Values at Work, pp. 13–33. Springer, Cham (2020). https://doi.org/10.1007/978-3-030-55613-6_2
9. Brinkkemper, S.: Method engineering: engineering of information systems development methods and tools. Inform Softw. Tech **38**(4), 275–280 (1996)
10. Dopfer, K., Foster, J., Potts, J.: Micro-meso-macro. J. Evol. Econ. **14**, 263–279 (2004)
11. Drawbridge, J.E.: Going Off Course: a case study on the marketing strategy of Patagonia. Master's Thesis, California Polytechnic State University (2018)

12. Ducassy, I.: Does corporate social responsibility pay off in times of crisis? An alternate perspective on the relationship between financial and corporate social performance. Corp. Soc. Responsib. Environ. Manag. **20**(3), 157–167 (2013)
13. Dumay, J., Bernardi, C., Guthrie, J., Demartini, P.: Integrated reporting: a structured literature review. Account Forum. **40**, 166–185 (2016)
14. España, S., Ramautar, V.: Open repository of ethical, social and environmental accounting methods (2023). https://osf.io/4av3s/
15. España, S., Thorsteinsdottir, G., Ramautar, V., Pastor, Ó.: Investigating the links between ethical, social and environmental accounting and strategic management practices through enterprise modelling: technical report. Tech. Rep., OSF Preprints (2023). https://doi.org/10.31219/osf.io/xv529
16. España, S., Bik, N., Overbeek, S.: Model-driven engineering support for social and environmental accounting. In: RCIS 2019, pp. 1–12. IEEE (2019)
17. España, S., Ramautar, V., Overbeek, S., Derikx, T.: Model-driven production of data-centric infographics: an application to the impact measurement domain. In: Guizzardi, R., Ralyté, J., Franch, X. (eds.) Research Challenges in Information Science. RCIS 2022. LNBIP, vol. 446. Springer, Cham (2022). https://doi.org/10.1007/978-3-031-05760-1_28
18. Fidalgo, R.N., Alves, E., España, S., Castro, J., Pastor, O.: Metamodeling the enhanced entity-relationship model. J. Inf. Data Manage. **4**(3), 406 (2013)
19. Fireclay: Proud to be a B Corp (2023). https://www.fireclaytile.com/b-corp
20. Gerber, A., Le Roux, P., Van der Merwe, A.: Enterprise architecture as explanatory information systems theory for understanding small-and medium-sized enterprise growth. Sustainability **12**(20), 8517 (2020)
21. Giraldo, F.D., España, S., Giraldo, W.J., Pastor, O.: Evaluating the quality of a set of modelling languages used in combination: a method and a tool. Inform. Syst. **77**, 48–70 (2018)
22. Goldkuhl, G., Lind, M., Seigerroth, U.: Method integration: the need for a learning perspective. IEE Proc. Softw. **145**(4), 113–118 (1998)
23. Gray, R.: Current developments and trends in social and environmental auditing, reporting and attestation: a review and comment. Int. J. Audit. **4**(3), 247–268 (2000)
24. Grunninger, M.: Enterprise modelling. In: Bernus, P., Nemes, L., Schmidt, G. (eds.) Handbook on Enterprise Architecture. International Handbooks on Information Systems. Springer, Heidelberg (2003). https://doi.org/10.1007/978-3-540-24744-9_14
25. Hahn, R., Kühnen, M.: Determinants of sustainability reporting: a review of results, trends, theory, and opportunities in an expanding field of research. J. Clean. Prod. **59**, 5–21 (2013)
26. Henderson-Sellers, B., Ralyté, J., Ågerfalk, P.J., Rossi, M.: Situational Method Engineering. Springer, Heidelberg (2014). https://doi.org/10.1007/978-3-642-41467-1
27. Ioannou, I., Serafeim, G.: The consequences of mandatory corporate sustainability reporting. Report (2017)
28. Kirikova, M.: Explanatory capability of enterprise models. Data Knowl. Eng. **33**(2), 119–136 (2000)
29. Lankhorst, M.M., Proper, H.A., Jonkers, H.: The anatomy of the ArchiMate language. Int. J. Inf. Syst. Model Des **1**(1), 1–32 (2010)
30. Lokuwaduge, C.S.D.S., Heenetigala, K.: Integrating environmental, social and governance (ESG) disclosure for a sustainable development: an Australian study. Bus Strategy Environ. **26**(4), 438–450 (2017)

31. Loucopoulos, P., Kavakli, E.: Enterprise modelling and the teleological approach to requirements engineering. Int. J. Coop Inf. Syst. **4**(01), 45–79 (1995)
32. Maas, K., Schaltegger, S., Crutzen, N.: Integrating corporate sustainability assessment, management accounting, control, and reporting. J. Clean Prod. **136**(A), 237–248 (2016)
33. Morali, O., Searcy, C.: A review of sustainable supply chain management practices in Canada. J. Bus. Ethics **117**, 635–658 (2013)
34. Osterwalder, A., Pigneur, Y.: Business model generation: a handbook for visionaries, game changers, and challengers, vol. 1. Wiley (2010)
35. Ould, M.A.: Business process management: a rigorous approach. Meghan-Kiffer Press (2005)
36. Owen, D.L., Swift, T.A., Humphrey, C., Bowerman, M.: The new social audits: accountability, managerial capture or the agenda of social champions? Eur. Account Rev. **9**(1), 81–98 (2000)
37. Patagonia: Patagonia's mission statement (2023). https://eu.patagonia.com/es/en/core-values
38. Persson, A., Stirna, J.: Why enterprise modelling? An explorative study into current practice. In: Dittrich, K.R., Geppert, A., Norrie, M.C. (eds.) CAiSE 2001. LNCS, vol. 2068, pp. 465–468. Springer, Heidelberg (2001). https://doi.org/10.1007/3-540-45341-5_31
39. Pfeffer, J.: Business and the spirit. Management Practices That Sustain Values, pp. 27–43. Routledge (2010)
40. Rodrigo, P., Arenas, D.: Do employees care about CSR programs? A typology of employees according to their attitudes. J. Bus Ethic **83**, 265–283 (2008)
41. Rutkauskas, A.V., Lapinskaitė, I.: Marketing as core instrument to implement sustainability strategy for a business world. the case of fast moving consumer goods. In: 7th International Science Conference Business and Management, vol. 11, pp. 162–172 (2012)
42. Sandkuhl, K., et al.: Enterprise modelling for the masses – From elitist discipline to common practice. In: Horkoff, J., Jeusfeld, M.A., Persson, A. (eds.) PoEM 2016. LNBIP, vol. 267, pp. 225–240. Springer, Cham (2016). https://doi.org/10.1007/978-3-319-48393-1_16
43. Sawitria, D., Suswatib, E.: Trenggalek Typical food diversification strategies for increasing competitiveness in the SDGS era by using a business model canvas. Int. J. Innov. Creativity Chang. **9**(4), 259–272 (2019)
44. Shukla, N., Lahiri, S., Ceglarek, D.: Pathway variation analysis (PVA): modelling and simulations. Oper Res. Health Care **6**, 61–77 (2015)
45. Silva, V., Lima, V., Sá, J.C., Fonseca, L., Santos, G.: B impact assessment as a sustainable tool: analysis of the certification model. Sustainability **14**(9), 5590 (2022)
46. Sroufe, R., Liebowitz, J., Sivasubramaniam, N., Donahue, J.: Are you a leader or a laggard? HR's role in creating a sustainability culture. People Strat. **33**(1), 34–42 (2010)
47. Tate, W.L., Ellram, L.M., Kirchoff, J.F.: Corporate social responsibility reports: a thematic analysis related to supply chain management. J. Supply Chain Manag. **46**(1), 19–44 (2010)
48. Tilt, C.A.: The influence of external pressure groups on corporate social disclosure. Acc. Audit Acc. J. **7**(4), 47–72 (1994)
49. Timm, F., Klohs, K., Sandkuhl, K.: Application of inductive reference modeling approaches to enterprise architecture models. In: BIS 2018, pp. 45–57 (2018)

50. Vasilieva, T., Lieonov, S., I., M., Sirkovska, N.: Sustainability information disclosure as an instrument of marketing communication with stakeholders: markets, social and economic aspects. Int. Mark Manag. Innov. **4**, 350–357 (2017)
51. Vernadat, F.: UEML: towards a unified enterprise modelling language. Int. J. Prod. Res. **40**(17), 4309–4321 (2002)
52. Waller, R.L., Conaway, R.N.: Framing and counterframing the issue of corporate social responsibility: the communication strategies of nikebiz.com. Int. J. Bus Commun. **48**(1), 83–106 (2011)
53. van de Weerd, I., Brinkkemper, S.: Meta-modeling for situational analysis and design methods. In: Handbook Of Research on Modern Systems Analysis and Design Technologies and Applications, pp. 35–54. IGI Global (2009)
54. van de Weerd, I., de Weerd, S., Brinkkemper, S.: Developing a reference method for game production by method comparison. In: SME 2007, pp. 313–327 (2007)
55. Wieringa, R.J.: Design Science Methodology for Information Systems and Software Engineering. Springer, Heidelberg (2014). https://doi.org/10.1007/978-3-662-43839-8

Using the Business Motivation Model as an Organising Principle to Clarify Public Policy

Helena Zhemchugova(✉) ⓘ, Friederike Stock ⓘ, and Lutho Madala ⓘ

Stockholm University, Borgarfjordsgatan 12, 164 07 Kista, Sweden
helena.zhemchugova@dsv.su.se, stofrie@gmail.com, madalalutho@gmail.com

Abstract. Public policies use constructive ambiguity as a linguistic and diplomatic tool to manage the conflicting views of stakeholders and facilitate policy implementation in the presence of tensions. However, the ambiguity of policy content is a knowledge problem. It can lead to misunderstandings of its ends and means and may result in failed mitigation measures for societal crises. The Business Motivation Model (BMM) combined with the UML attribute elements can solve this problem by structurally decomposing the policy content into a BMM representation. This representation is an epistemic artefact that generates meta-knowledge about the policy by clarifying its intentions and conceptual structure, thus decreasing the likelihood of it being misunderstood. We present the case of the Aviation Chapter of the Greenhouse Gas Emissions Trading System (EU ETS), where we clarify its prescriptions for the European Commission (EC), Member States, and aircraft operators using BMM concepts and relationships as deductive coding patterns. The artefact has undergone artificial empirical evaluation by expert opinion ($n = 15$). Possible use scenarios were discussed with enterprise modellers, climate policy researchers, and aircraft industry experts concerned with EU ETS enforcement, implementation, and auditing. The BMM representation presented advantages over the policy's textual form and improved the aviation industry experts' understanding of the Chapter. Future research could look into increasing the analytical capabilities of the notation to address the needs of policy researchers working with gap analyses and co-development of policy revisions with stakeholders. Other modelling and diagramming tools should be examined to enable model durability and robustness.

Keywords: Business Motivation Model · Policy Content Analysis · EU ETS · Knowledge Problems · Design Science Research

© IFIP International Federation for Information Processing 2024
Published by Springer Nature Switzerland AG 2024
J. P. A. Almeida et al. (Eds.): PoEM 2023, LNBIP 497, pp. 177–192, 2024.
https://doi.org/10.1007/978-3-031-48583-1_11

1   Introduction

Policy systems consist of interconnected public policies with webs of actors, processes, rules, and decisions that guide and govern administrative action within and across international borders [1]. Their governance mechanisms can rely on hierarchies, markets, or networks (cf [2]). A *public policy* is a documented decision made by a government to do or not do something about a problem perceived by the public [3]. It comprises objectives and strategies for achieving them.

Managing a policy system is similar to managing a large and complex enterprise. In both cases, there is a need to oversee and manage numerous parts of the entire whole that collectively influence the outcomes. Achieving the *desired outcomes* depends on *knowledge* about the system and its environment, a foundation for decision-making, strategic planning, operational efficiency, and innovation. However, public policies use *constructive ambiguity*, i.e., deliberately ambiguous language, in their strategies and objectives to manage conflicting interests among actors concerning sensitive issues [4–6]. This ambiguity may complicate the interpretation and implementation of individual policies and mislead conclusions regarding their performance (cf [3]).

This paper focuses on the EU Greenhouse Gas Emissions Trading System (EU ETS) [7]. This policy system intends to limit large industrial polluters, such as the aviation industry, from using fossil fuels through market-based mechanisms. Actors can buy emission allowances, invest in cleaner technologies to lower their compliance costs, and sell excess allowances to make a profit. Parts of the EU ETS contain constructive ambiguity [5]. Despite efforts to eliminate it through harmonisation, Member States may still have differing views of its content. This lack of consensus constitutes a *knowledge problem*.

Research suggests that knowledge problems of this type can be resolved by allowing external interpretations to reframe ambiguous information into something more coherent and concrete [8]. In the domain of policy analysis, content analysis of policy documents clarifies who says what, to whom, and with what effect and provides the possibility to quantify the data for use in simulations [9,10]. We propose that enterprise modelling notations, such as the Business Motivation Model (BMM) [11], can enhance the clarifying function of policy content analysis as an external organising principle and a stable conceptual foundation for understanding the ends and means of a given policy. Similarly, relevant domain theories are commonly employed as conceptual frameworks for supporting data analysis within a given domain.

In this paper, we analyse the Aviation Chapter [7, pp. 5-10] of the EU ETS to answer the question: *How can we disambiguate the content of the policy governing the reduction of CO_2 emissions by the aviation industry using the tools of enterprise modelling?* The analysis aims to clarify the Chapter's prescriptions for ends and means using the BMM notation, thereby reducing ambiguity. The delimitation by industry is motivated by the fact that in 2021, the European Commission (EC) solicited the input of citizens, researchers, and think tanks to assist in revising the EU aviation legislation, as well as by the importance of the aviation industry for climate neutrality, as it accounts for almost four per cent of the EU's CO_2 emissions [12]. The outcome of this work is a diagrammatic representation of the Aviation Chapter of the EU ETS, i.e., its conceptual model. It shows its structure, the dependencies between its elements, and an overview of its content to simplify its understanding for those without a legal background.

2 Relating Policy Intention with Business Motivation

2.1 Enterprise Modelling Languages and Notations

The intentionality of government action embedded in public policy is reflected in the motivation layer of established goal-oriented enterprise modelling languages and notations such as iStar (i*) [13], ArchiMate [14], and BMM [11]. i* is a goal-oriented modelling language representing actors' intentions and their relationships within a system. Its application to policy analysis examines how stakeholders' motivations and relationships affect policymaking and policy outcomes. Its focus on social modelling makes it less suitable for analysing policies employing market-based governance mechanisms such as the EU ETS, but could fit those focusing on networks. ArchiMate, an open standard for enterprise architecture and modelling, has recently been extended with a motivation layer [15]. Though promising, it needs to be supported by other notations to provide accurate representations [16]. BMM is an established conceptual framework and a standardised notation for modelling and analysing an enterprise's business motivation and strategic goals. It can represent its structure in terms of business elements that direct organisational action. Although we have not found any research on using BMM for public policy content analysis, we see many structural and semantic intersections between policy elements and BMM concepts. For example, both are concerned with *ends*, such as goals, and *means*, such as actions to be taken to achieve them. Moreover, the BMM notation is simple enough to be understood by non-specialists after a short introduction. It thus presents a practical advantage over more elaborate modelling techniques to clarify the content of public policy.

2.2 Policy Content Analysis

A public policy is a formal statement or guideline a government or public authority adopts to achieve specific societal goals, promote the public interest, or regulate specific activities. It employs the following terms: *Intention* - the purpose of government action; *Goal* - the end to be achieved; *Plans* and *Proposals* - proposed means for pursuing the *Goal*; *Programs* - authorised means for pursuing the *Goal*; *Decisions* and *Choices* - specific actions taken to set *Goals*, develop *Plans*, and implement *Programs*; and *Influencers* - things and circumstances affecting the decisions [3,4]. These terms are often unclear and difficult to identify in policy documents [4]. Policy content analysis systematically examines the written content of policy documents to understand their objectives, strategies, provisions, and implications [10]. It looks into the specific language and textual elements of policy and can be qualitative, focusing on contextual understanding, or quantitative, focusing on counting occurrences of predefined categories or other elements in the content. Subjectivity in coding and categorising limits both approaches. Enterprise modelling languages and notations supporting business motivation could enhance policy analysis with an adaptable conceptual roadmap for coding and categorising the policy content. Business motivation is concerned with the drivers of the actions and decisions of an enterprise. Akin to public policy, it involves setting objectives and developing strategies to achieve them.

2.3   Linkages Between BMM Concepts and Policy Elements

We found that the elements and terms constituting a public policy resemble those of BMM, making the notation well-suited for analysing its content. Perhaps even more so for policies employing market-based governance mechanisms such as the EU ETS, which leverages value-driven economic incentives to influence the behaviour of actors to achieve policy goals. In its native domain of business management and strategic planning, BMM seeks to visually represent the structure of the enterprise from a business perspective [17] grounded in value-driven motivations.

The main concepts used for creating representations are *end, means, Influencer*[1], and *assessment* [18]. *Ends* include *Vision* and *Desired Result*. *Vision* represents the overall purpose, or motivation of the enterprise; we relate it to *Intention* in policy (see Sect. 2.2). *Desired Result* in BMM is similar to *Goal* in policy, representing what an enterprise aims to achieve. BMM divides *Desired Results* into *goals* (abstract desired outcomes) and *objectives* (time-bound and concrete milestones). *Objectives* are not distinguished as a stand-alone conceptual element in policy, meaning that the BMM notation adds expressive power. *Means* in BMM refer to activities the enterprise will employ to achieve the *ends* and include *mission, Course of Action*, and *Directive*. In policy, they are *Plan, Proposal*, and *Program*. *Course of Action* is specialised into *strategy* (plan of action) and *tactic* (concrete action), while *Directive* includes *business policy* and *business rule* (guidelines and rules regulating the plans). The conceptual homonymity of the term "policy" presents a complication for modelling a *business policy* within a policy. A surrogate term such as, for example, *guideline* can be used to disambiguate the terms. Policy *Decisions* and *Choices* cannot be modelled in BMM and require supplementary notation. An *Influencer* in BMM is similar to *Influencer* in policy and denotes a factor that affects the employment of the *means* or the achievement of the *ends*. As a neutral entity, it can produce a positive or negative impact on *ends* and *means*, which is determined through *assessment* not present in policy, meaning that the BMM notation adds expressive power. *Assessment* judges the impact of an *Influencer* using a SWOT analysis [17] and can render it as a *strength*, a *weakness*, an *opportunity*, or a *threat*.

---

[1] We capitalise all policy terms and the five core BMM concepts we use to represent them during the analysis; sub-concepts and general concepts such as *ends* and *means* are not capitalised.

3   Methodological Overview

3.1   Case: How the EU ETS Governs Aviation

In 2012, the Aviation Chapter[2] [7, pp. 5-10] was added to the EU ETS to regulate emissions from certain types of flights. The Chapter defines the scope of the aviation activities addressed by the policy and prescribes the quantity of allowances to be distributed, the method of their allocation, and the guidelines for monitoring and reporting the data. Different Member States implement the policy slightly differently. In addition, there are procedural differences with regard to sanctions and penalties for non-compliance, whether certain services are subject to fees, and what happens to the revenue from sales of allowances [19]. As the EC and the informed public advocate for more sustainable aviation, government officials and academics believe airlines should be subject to stricter regulations. In turn, the aircraft industry would like fewer restrictions and a free allocation of allowances [19] and may seek out legitimate means to avoid compliance constraining its operations. Due to these conflicting interests and strong lobbying from the airline industry, changes in the policy are likely to be slow and difficult to enforce, making it all the more important to disambiguate its content.

The Chapter consists of seven articles that first cover its scope (Article 3a) and provide information about the aviation activities referred to in the articles that follow (Article 3b), and further prescribe how the allowances should be calculated (Article 3c), auctioned (Article 3d), allocated free of charge (Article 3e) and to new or fast-growing aircraft operators (Article 3f), as well as how the emissions data should be monitored and reported (Article 3g).

3.2   Design Science Research Methodology

The BMM representation of the Aviation Chapter of the EU ETS was developed using the design science research methodology (DSR) (cf [20,21]) as shown in Fig. 1.1.

Problem and Requirements. The knowledge problem posed by the *ambiguity* and *complexity* of policy texts was identified using a scoping literature review. It identified the need for a conceptual representation of policy content that reduces ambiguity and allowed us to estimate its effectiveness as a potential solution [21]. The functional requirement defined the primary purpose of the model. It was set to create epistemic value (cf [??]) by supporting the understanding of policy, i.e., the entity it represents, by three user groups: airline industry practitioners, climate policy researchers, and the informed public without legal background or background in BMM. The structural and generic design requirements were shortlisted by consulting the literature on quality assurance of conceptual models (cf [23–27]) regarding how well they supported the model's purpose.

---

[2] Chapter II of the Directive 2003/87/EC of the European Parliament and of the Council of 13 October 2003 Establishing a Scheme for Greenhouse Gas Emission Allowance Trading Within the Community and Amending Council Directive 96/61/EC (Text With EEA Relevance).

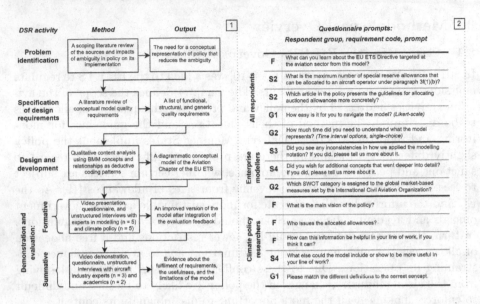

Fig. 1. 1. An overview of our design science research process. 2. A breakdown of evaluation questionnaire prompts by requirements and respondents; requirement S1 was not included because its evaluation does not depend on expert judgement.

Design and Development. The BMM representation of the Aviation Chapter was created using a deductive, theory-driven approach to qualitative content analysis originally proposed by [28]. It is systematic and language-oriented, focusing on form and content instead of subjective experiences, thereby mitigating some validity and reliability issues typical of qualitative research. Our approach included the following steps: 1. Familiarise oneself with the text; 2. Markup the text segments to be coded with unique identifiers for traceability management; 3. Develop deductive coding patterns, i.e., repeatable language structures that organise the data points within segments for translating them into BMM concepts; 4. Choose a modelling tool; 5. Create the model while coding the text.

The coding process began with identifying the high-level BMM concepts – *ends*, *means*, and *Influencers*. The *ends* and *means* were further specialised into *Vision*, *Desired Results*, *Courses of Action*, *Directives*, as well as *assessments* of *Influencers* were made. *Vision* is the overall intention of the policy, expressed in abstract terms. *Desired Results* are "what" should happen to operationalise different aspects of the policy intention, expressed in general terms and specified into an abstract *goal* or a concrete and measurable *objective*. *Courses of Action* are "how" the operationalisation should happen, expressed in concrete terms and specified in a long-term *strategy* or a short-term *tactic*. *Directives* are prescriptions that apply when making it happen. They are specified in a *policy* that bears no formal obligation to comply or a *rule* with sanctions or penalties for non-compliance. Influencers are current circumstances (internal or external) that can affect the "what" and the "how" either positively (*strength, opportunity*) or negatively (*weakness, threat*). Finally, we identified the relationships between the elements using BMM connectors.

Demonstration and Evaluation. The model was evaluated for fitness for purpose against the established requirements using expert opinion [29] in an artificial setting. As an *epistemic artefact* [30,31], its purpose was to convey and constitute knowledge to assist in the understanding of the entity it represents [32], i.e., the policy document. A series of formative evaluations supported the improvement of the initial version of the model, while summative evaluations provided insights into its perceived value as a source of knowledge among potential users. An asynchronous demonstration of the model via a pre-recorded video preceded each expert consultation. The video briefly introduced conceptual modelling, BMM concepts, and the model's structure, allowing participants to understand and navigate the model independently.

Further, expert interviews were employed to collect the evaluation data and were unstructured [33] to reduce researcher bias and facilitate the discovery of new knowledge. They were held in person or through video conferencing, with the data collected through note-taking. In addition, we used a web-based questionnaire that prompted the experts to interact with the model to answer a few questions about the fulfilment of specific requirements relevant to their expertise (see Fig. 1.2) to corroborate the interview data. Informed consent regarding handling the interview and questionnaire data was obtained as part of email communication and duplicated in the questionnaire form. In total, 15 unique opinions were obtained by non-probabilistic purposive sampling [34], which provided data saturation [35] as a measure of the quality of findings in qualitative research.

Formative feedback was provided by five experts in *enterprise modelling and architecture* with affiliations at Stockholm University, Sweden; University of the Witwatersrand, South Africa; Riga Technical University, Latvia; and the University of Rostock, Germany; and five experts in *climate policy research* with affiliations at Stockholm Resilience Centre (SRC) and Södertörn University, Sweden; ETH Zürich, Switzerland; and the International Institute for Applied Systems Analysis (IIASA), Austria. Summative input was supplied by two experts in *climate policy research* with affiliation at IIASA, Austria; one expert in *EU ETS enforcement* via trading emission rights at the Swedish Environmental Protection Agency (Naturvårdsverket), Sweden; and two aviation industry experts specialising in *EU ETS implementation* (a non-EU aircraft operator) and *EU ETS auditing* (a global EU ETS verifier).

4 Specification of Requirements

Seven requirements have supported the development of the model. One functional requirement (F) specifies the main *purpose* of the model - it shall clarify the structure of the content of the policy to support its understanding and communication by stakeholders [22,24]. Further, four structural requirements (S)

address the internal composition of the model, and two generic quality requirements (G) address the user's perspective and experience of the model. Specifically, the structural quality requirements are *Completeness* (S1) [14, 23, 24, 26, 27]
- the model should represent all relevant policy text to show the entity it clarifies
accurately; *Integration* (S2) [23–25] - the model should refer each element to the
original policy text to support the structural integrity of the representation and
the traceability of analysis; *Correctness* (S3) [24, 27] - the model should follow the
rules of BMM notation; and *Simplicity* (S4) [23, 24] - the model should use only
a few core BMM concepts to make it easier to understand and use the model.
Finally, the generic quality requirements are *Understandability* (G1) [23, 24, 26] -
the model should be easy to understand to retain its function for users with and
without a background in BMM; and *Usability* (G2) [14, 23, 25] - the model should
make finding information easy and quick to present the advantage over reading
the original policy text, lessen the learning curve, and increase user acceptance.

5   The Model of the Aviation Chapter of the EU ETS

The following coding patterns were adopted for modelling the text of the Aviation
Chapter with BMM concepts: *Vision – this large-scale abstract thing should be
achieved*, e.g., "Climate change should be tackled"; *Desired Result – this smaller-
scale abstract thing should be done*, e.g., "The special reserve should be set";
Course of Action – do this concretely, e.g., "Auction leftover allowances"; *Directive – apply this prescription when doing X"*, where the modal verb *shall* is used
to indicate obligation, e.g., "Information obligation rules shall be applied when
using revenues"; and *Influencer – this exists* or *this is ongoing*, e.g., "There exists
data on historical aviation emissions". To disambiguate the BMM notation from
the language of EU legislation, *Directive* was renamed into *Instruction*, *policy*
into *guidance*, and *rule* into *mandate*. We found that while the policy contained
many *guidances*, there was only one *mandate* (in Article 3d). Neither of these
explicitly mentioned consequences for actors for non-compliance.

Figure 2 presents an overview[3] of the model structure. This diagrammatic
policy breakdown categorises its prescriptions into what should be done, by
whom, and how. The model features horizontal lanes, analogous to business
process modelling diagrams, to show the hierarchical interplay between actors.
For example, it highlights that Article 3d contains a lot of information about
how the allowances ought to be auctioned – categorised as *Instruction* – by the
Member States, and that the Commission and the Member States are intended
to share the responsibility for the *Desired Result*.

A Miro 'Board' [36] was used to create a detailed representation of the policy
and Miro 'Frame' – to encompass articles of the policy. In the actor lanes, Miro
'Card' was used to represent policy elements with a coded summary of the content, BMM concept tags, and extended quotes from the original policy text. The
model can be read clockwise starting from Article 3c, or the article of interest

---

[3] A full-size model with searchable content is available at https://shorturl.at/ahBZ5
in view-only mode.

by following the section names. Figure 3 provides an example of how we coded the policy text with BMM concepts and UML attribute elements. Each coded portion of text received a unique identifier (ID) that includes original article numbering, paragraph numbers in Arabic numerals, and sentence numbers in Roman numerals. For example, the code with ID "3c(2-ii)" in Fig. 3.3 refers to the second sentence ("ii") in the second paragraph ("2") in Article 3c.

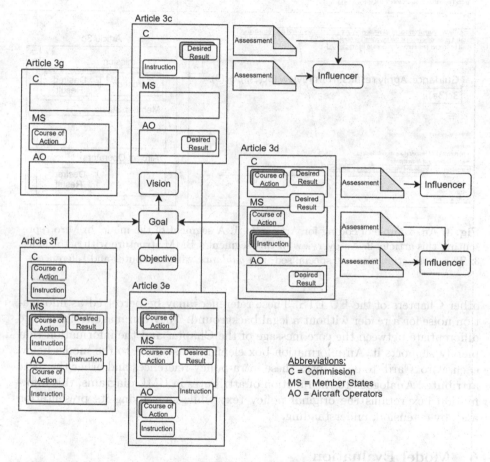

Fig. 2. An overview of the model structure for the Aviation Chapter of the EU ETS.

To increase the understandability of the model and the relationships between its elements, we added induced elements, distinguishing them from the rest and providing external references to mitigate the bias. They are *Influencers*, the *Vision* of "tackling climate change", the *goal* of "reducing greenhouse gas emissions" that amplifies the *Vision*, and the *objective* that quantifies it. Further, the Aviation Chapter contains numerous references to its articles and the articles in

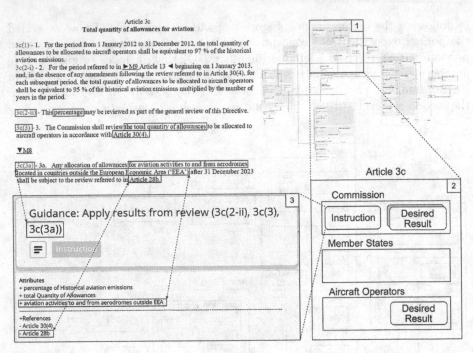

Fig. 3. An example of coding for Article 3c. 1. A segment of the model in Miro representing this article. 2. An overview of this segment's BMM structure with actor lanes. 3. The *Instruction* element specialised into *guidance* with attributes and references.

other Chapters of the EU ETS. These references may be perceived as information noise for a reader without a legal background. They can make it difficult to differentiate between the core message of the Chapter and the information that merely supports it. An information box element was added to the model below each Miro 'Card' to encompass these intra-policy references and other thematic attributes. Analogous to the function of attributes in UML diagrams, this information box retains the original policy text while simplifying its presentation and, by extension, understanding.

6   Model Evaluation

6.1   Fulfilment of Requirements

All requirements were evaluated for fulfilment to determine the model's quality and fitness for purpose. *Purpose* (F) – fulfilled: the data showed that the model could assist all expert groups in their understanding of the policy. *Completeness* (S1) – fulfilled: all relevant policy text was modelled except for Articles 3a and 3b, which merely scoped the content of the Chapter and did not provide details on governing the allocation of allowances, and the second sentence in paragraph 3c(4) that only impacted Article 23(1) which was outside of the scope of our analysis. *Integration* (S2) – fulfilled: all user groups could successfully use the reference system that links the model elements to the policy text. *Correctness* (S3) – partially fulfilled: minor modifications were made to the BMM notation to increase its expressive power and disambiguate its concepts from the EU's legal language. *Simplicity* (S4) – fulfilled: the model uses only five core BMM concepts. *Understandability* (G1) – fulfilled: it took 15 to 20 min for all user groups to understand the model. *Usability* (G2) – partially fulfilled: while all user groups could successfully interact with the model to find information and solve problems posed in the questionnaire, some participants had minor difficulties navigating the Miro 'Board'.

6.2   Expert Opinion

Enterprise Modelling and Architecture. The modelling experts regarded the model and the modifications made to the BMM notation - disambiguating the BMM concepts under *Directive* and integrating the UML attribute element - positively. The use of actor lanes was noted to be advantageous as they allowed one to see the actors involved and responsible for each element. During the interviews, understanding what the model shows was assessed as easy, with questionnaire responses confirming that it took this group 15 min on average. The choice of the tool was regarded as a limitation. It was suggested that the task could be handled by other specialised modelling tools, such as Enterprise Architect [37], which could increase the model's robustness and display its different dimensions at a glance. One participant argued that some portions of the text could have been modelled differently. For example, the element 3e(5), modelled as an *objective*, could have been interpreted as a *Course of Action*. Although different interpretations of policy content are possible, the analysis was deliberately constrained by semantic boundaries. Our established concept definitions and the resulting coding patterns determined our coding decisions. The outcome of the analysis can be slightly different should the concepts be defined differently. As for possible use scenarios, the modelling experts proposed project-based analytic assignments where creating a holistic overview of the content of the policy is necessary for making correct judgements about it. A small interdisciplinary team of modelling and domain experts can undertake this modelling task.

Climate Policy Research. All climate policy researchers engaged in this study assessed the structural, diagrammatic representation of policy as the main benefit of the model. They claimed it made understanding the policy easier and quicker than reading the text directly. However, the questionnaire data showed their average understanding time to be 20 min, i.e., slightly longer than in the group of enterprise modellers. Such a positive assessment may not be unique to our use of BMM, and other modelling notations could have yielded comparable results. The model was further assessed as beneficial for providing an overview of operational aspects, such as key decision hubs and the actors involved or responsible. Some experts expressed that the model could be more valuable if it could actively support the process of identifying gaps and coming up with recommendations, as well as show the temporal aspect and indicate how, when, and where the policy was changed or amended. It was noted that an overview of the history of changes could show which parts of the policy are considered by decision-makers most actively. This group found it challenging to navigate the model, which was corroborated by mistakes in answers to problem-solving prompts in the questionnaire. We attribute the challenge to both the tool's limitations and the participants' unfamiliarity with this type of conceptual modelling.

Several alternatives were suggested by this group of participants regarding possible use scenarios. The model could be used as an analytical tool in policy analysis due to its ability to show the content at different levels of detail. However, it was noted that to provide the most analytical value, the policy system would need to be modelled in its entirety, making the policies it contains comparable. In addition, the model was seen as capable of informing the public about the EU ETS and helping them learn about its objectives and strategies. Nevertheless, in this scenario, a BMM representation may not be directly usable by the public and would need to be supplemented with a list of key insights. For scientists, environmental lobbyists, journalists, and business consultants, the model could provide an overview of how different actors can be affected by the policy. The model may not be helpful for policymakers and lawyers because it conceals the text unless the model elements are expanded, as this group of experts may prefer working with full-length texts over overviews.

EU ETS Enforcement, Implementation, and Auditing. The expertise in this group ranged from trading with emission rights to managing and supporting airline operations, flight and fuel planning, and emissions reporting. The group included one expert affiliated with a non-EU airline. Non-EU airlines get to work with the EU ETS if they manage flights that take off and land in Europe, as they have to monitor and record their CO_2 emissions while in the European airspace. It was brought to our attention that airlines use EC guidebooks to prepare internal policy manuals when working with the EU ETS, meaning that several layers of interpretation may be added beyond the ambiguity of the original texts. Similar to the climate policy researchers, all experts in this group found the diagrammatic view to be superior to EC guidebooks in presenting information and expressed that it simplified its understanding. They were able to assess the consequences of decisions for some stakeholders, suggesting that although BMM does not explicitly express *Decisions* and *Choices*, they could be inferred from the model's structure.

Concerning possible use scenarios, this group presented several practical considerations. To increase the usefulness of the model, it was suggested to supplement it with a "resource hub" dashboard. The following resource items were proposed for inclusion in the dashboard: a list of flights the policy addresses, a sample of the monitoring plan and an emissions report, a list of traders, a link to the latest prices for allowances, and general information on where and how to buy them. It was brought to our attention that working with the EU

ETS as intended may not always be possible for smaller airlines. Trading with allowances has similarities to trading with stocks, and to be able to do it, airlines may be dependent on employing financial specialists who are also knowledgeable in legal matters. Without specialist staff, the EU ETS would be difficult to navigate, resulting in various forms of inadvertent non-compliance. Although the experts in this group found the BMM representation helpful in this regard, they found that it would be more useful if supplemented with advice for implementing the *tactics*, as well as included deadlines and recent updates to the policy. Although implementing these suggestions is beyond the scope of our analysis, they point to knowledge gaps surrounding the EU ETS implementation in the aviation industry.

7   Discussion and Conclusions

This paper aimed to clarify the prescriptions for ends and means in the Aviation Chapter of the EU ETS [7, pp. 5-10] to increase its understanding by reducing ambiguity. The BMM notation supported qualitative content analysis through *systematic conceptual simplification*. BMM concepts and relationships were used as coding patterns for organising and rearranging the text of the policy to reveal its conceptual structure rather than manipulate its meanings and implications.

Before information can be converted to actionable knowledge, it must be understood, and "understanding involves seeing how the parts (...) fit together" [22, p. 68]. Structural representation of information contained in a policy using BMM clarifies it and helps its user understand it, similar to how a map clarifies the layout of a city to help its user navigate the city environment. It can, therefore, be *seen as a solution to the ambiguity problem as it can support policy users in navigating it to extract knowledge more straightforwardly*.

A modelling notation merely provides a form of expression of reality. It cannot perform analysis without an analyst, similar to how spoken language expresses analytical thought and does not constitute the analysis itself. However, notations differ by what they can enable us to see and express. Even though BMM proved to be fit for this particular application, it could not identify gaps, tensions, and consequences for specific stakeholders. Other modelling notations, such as Archi-Mate, should be explored in future research to improve the analytical capability of the approach and facilitate structural representations of policy systems.

Although several established tools can support enterprise modelling (cf [37,38]), the choice should be contingent on their ability to enable effective communication in the context of their intended use. Miro [36], a web-based collaborative platform, was chosen for its ease of use and understanding by non-specialists. However, this tool has clear disadvantages regarding the model's durability, robustness, and maintenance. Tools that balance ease of use and durability should be considered in future research.

This analysis demonstrates conceptual transferability between "intention" in policy and "motivation" in business. It has the potential to assist diverse groups of stakeholders as end-users in understanding and communicating the policy content. The diagrammatic view separates policy prescriptions from supporting information, which presents an advantage over reading the original policy text. In its current form, the model has been assessed to be usable as a *knowledge tool* for supporting operations within EU ETS enforcement, implementation, and auditing, as an *analytical tool* within climate policy research, and as a *basis for further research* within enterprise modelling. Due to limited access to stakeholders, we could not obtain opinions from EC policymakers at this time. In addition, we acknowledge that, due to our limited knowledge of legal terms in policy systems, we may have misclassified some of the terms when translating them into the BMM concepts. Collaborating with policy experts when developing conceptual representations of policies is recommended to avoid this limitation in the future.

BMM is commonly used for modelling complex organisational systems in the domain of business strategy. Our application of BMM to policy content analysis adds to the existing body of knowledge by introducing a new way of using the notation outside of its native domain. It provides a new perspective on policy analysis. We have demonstrated that while the BMM notation alone may not be sufficient for policy content analysis, this systematic approach can be adapted to the target domain using modifications and extensions. The applicability of BMM to this type of analysis may depend on the governance mechanisms used in the target policy. The EU ETS is market-based, which may be more compatible with the intended use of this notation. Investigating BMM's applicability to analysing policies that employ hierarchy- and network-based governance mechanisms is another possible direction for future research. The temporal aspect could be modelled to illustrate policy evolution over time, highlighting less stable components. Future research could also investigate whether this can be represented using elements of, e.g., UML, Business Process Model and Notation (BPMN), or ArchiMate. Finally, a general guide for applying and adapting the BMM notation for policy content analysis could be developed, as could the solutions for automating parts of the modelling process.

References

1. Magro, E., Wilson, J.R.: Complex innovation policy systems: towards an evaluation mix. Res. Policy. **42**, 1647–1656 (2013). https://doi.org/10.1016/j.respol.2013.06.005

2. Ostrom, E.: Governing the Commons: The Evolution of Institutions for Collective Action. Cambridge University Press (1990)

3. Kraft, M.E., Furlong, S.R.: Public Policy: Politics, Analysis, and Alternatives. CQ Press (2021)

4. Capano, G., Howlett, M. eds: A Modern Guide to Public Policy. Edward Elgar Publishing (2020)

5. Jegen, M., Mérand, F.: Constructive ambiguity: Comparing the EU's energy and defence policies. West Eur. Politics **37**, 182–203 (2014). https://doi.org/10.1080/01402382.2013.818325

6. Berridge, G., James, A.: A Dictionary of Diplomacy. Palgrave Macmillan UK (2003)

7. European Parliament and Council: Directive 2003/87/EC of the European Parliament and of the Council of 13 October 2003 establishing a scheme for greenhouse gas emission allowance trading within the Community and amending Council Directive 96/61/EC (Text with EEA relevance). https://eur-lex.europa.eu (2023)
8. Zack, M.H.: If managing knowledge is the solution, then what's the problem. In: Malhotra, Y. (ed.) Knowledge Management and Business Model Innovation, pp. 16–36. IGI Global (2001). https://doi.org/10.4018/978-1-878289-98-8.ch002
9. Vaismoradi, M., Turunen, H., Bondas, T.: Content analysis and thematic analysis: implications for conducting a qualitative descriptive study. Nurs. Health Sci. **15**, 398–405 (2013). https://doi.org/10.1111/nhs.12048
10. Fischer, F., Miller, G.J.: Handbook of Public Policy Analysis: Theory, Politics, and Methods. Taylor & Francis Group, Baton Rouge, United States (2006)
11. The Business Rules Group: The Business Motivation Model: Business Governance in a Volatile World (2010)
12. European Commission: Reducing emissions from aviation. https://climate.ec.europa.eu. Accessed 23 Jul 2023
13. Yu, E.S.K.: Modelling Strategic Relationships for Process Reengineering. Thesis (Ph.D.), University of Toronto (1995)
14. Lankhorst, M.: Enterprise Architecture at Work: Modelling, Communication and Analysis. Springer Science & Business Media (2009)
15. Walters, E., Plais, A.: Using ArchiMate(R) Modeling Language with BMM(TM): Representing the Concepts of the Business Motivation Model (BMM) using the AchiMate 3.0 Specification. https://www.tud.ttu.ee (2017)
16. Bhattacharya, P.: Synthesis of Business Motivation Model (BMM) and ArchiMate: Towards a New Modelling Technique for Strategic Alignment of Business and IT. In: MCIS 2018 Proceedings. AIS (2018)
17. Rekik, M., Boukadi, K., Ben-Abdallah, H.: A decision-making method for business process outsourcing to the cloud based on business motivation model and AHP. Int. J. Cloud Comput. **4**, 47–62 (2015). https://doi.org/10.1504/IJCC.2015.067709
18. Object Management Group: Business Motivation Model (2015)
19. Efthymiou, M., Papatheodorou, A.: EU emissions trading scheme in aviation: policy analysis and suggestions. J. Clean. Prod. **237**, 117734 (2019). https://doi.org/10.1016/j.jclepro.2019.117734
20. vom Brocke, J., Hevner, A., Maedche, A.: Introduction to design science research. In: vom Brocke, J., Hevner, A., Maedche, A. (eds.) Design Science Research. Cases. PI, pp. 1–13. Springer, Cham (2020). https://doi.org/10.1007/978-3-030-46781-4_1
21. Dresch, A., Lacerda, D.P., Antunes, J.A.V.: Design Science Research. Springer, Cham (2015). https://doi.org/10.1007/978-3-319-07374-3
22. Zagzebski, L.: Recovering Understanding. In: Zagzebski, L. (ed.) Epistemic Values: Collected Papers in Epistemology, pp. 57–77 (2020). https://doi.org/10.1093/oso/9780197529171.003.0004
23. Stirna, J., Persson, A.: Enterprise Modeling: Facilitating the Process and the People. Springer (2018). https://doi.org/10.1007/978-3-319-94857-7
24. Sandkuhl, K., Stirna, J., Persson, A., Wißotzki, M.: Enterprise Modeling. TEES, Springer, Heidelberg (2014). https://doi.org/10.1007/978-3-662-43725-4
25. Johannesson, P., Perjons, E.: An Introduction to Design Science. Springer, Cham (2014). https://doi.org/10.1007/978-3-319-10632-8
26. Nelson, H.J., Poels, G., Genero, M., Piattini, M.: A conceptual modeling quality framework. Softw. Qual. J. **20**, 201–228 (2012). https://doi.org/10.1007/s11219-011-9136-9

27. Wand, Y., Weber, R.: Research commentary: information systems and conceptual modeling – a research agenda. Inf. Syst. Res. **13**, 363–376 (2002). https://doi.org/10.1287/isre.13.4.363.69

28. Selvi, A.F.: Qualitative content analysis. In: Rose, H. and McKinley, J. (eds.) The Routledge Handbook of Research Methods in Applied Linguistics, pp. 440–452. Taylor & Francis Group (2019). https://doi.org/10.4324/9780367824471-37

29. Walton, D.: Appeal to Expert Opinion: Arguments from Authority. Penn State Press (2010)

30. Gelfert, A.: The ontology of models. In: Magnani, L., Bertolotti, T. (eds.) Springer Handbook of Model-Based Science. SH, pp. 5–23. Springer, Cham (2017). https://doi.org/10.1007/978-3-319-30526-4_1

31. Knuuttila, T.: Models as Epistemic Artefacts: Toward a Non-Representationalist Account of Scientific Representation. University of Helsinki, Department of Philosophy (2005)

32. Houy, C., Fettke, P., Loos, P.: Understanding understandability of conceptual models – what are we actually talking about? In: Atzeni, P., Cheung, D., Ram, S. (eds.) ER 2012. LNCS, vol. 7532, pp. 64–77. Springer, Heidelberg (2012). https://doi.org/10.1007/978-3-642-34002-4_5

33. Zhang, Y., Wildemuth, B.M.: Unstructured interviews. Applications of social research methods to questions in information and library science, pp. 222–231 (2009)

34. Etikan, I., Musa, S.A., Alkassim, R.S.: Comparison of convenience sampling and purposive sampling. Am. J. Theor. Appl. Stat. **5**, 1 (2016). https://doi.org/10.11648/j.ajtas.20160501.11

35. Fusch, P.I., Ness, L.R.: Are we there yet? Data saturation in qualitative research. Qual. Rep. **20**, 1408–1416 (2015)

36. Miro.com: The visual collaboration platform for every team: Miro. https://miro.com/. Accessed 26 July 2023

37. Sparx Systems: Enterprise architect. https://sparxsystems.com/products/ea/. Accessed 26 July 2023

38. ADOxx.org: Introduction to ADOxx. https://www.adoxx.org/live/introduction-to-adoxx. Accessed 21 June 2023

A Study on the Impact of the Level of Participation in Enterprise Modeling

Anne Gutschmidt[1]([envelope]) [iD], Charlotte Verbruggen[2][iD], and Monique Snoeck[2][iD]

[1] University of Rostock, Albert-Einstein-Str. 22, 18059 Rostock, Germany
anne.gutschmidt@uni-rostock.de
[2] KU Leuven, Naamsestraat 69, 3000 Leuven, Belgium
{charlotte.verbruggen,monique.snoeck}@kuleuven.be

Abstract. Participatory enterprise modeling (PEM) is presumed to have a positive impact on commitment, ownership feelings and further appraisals by domain experts with respect to the model. Whether PEM actually produces the desired effects, however, has been little studied. In this paper we report on an investigation of the effects of three different participatory settings: an overall model was created 1) from four individual interviews, 2) from four individual models, or 3) in a joint meeting of domain and modeling experts. The results show that the non-participatory interview setting led to less favorable appraisals, e.g., the level of participation was perceived as lower and the contribution of the modeling experts was perceived as higher. Our findings should help practitioners in weighing possible benefits of participatory enterprise modeling against the organizational and monetary effort it involves.

Keywords: Participatory Enterprise Modeling · Experiment · Participation · Conceptual Modeling

1 Introduction

In participatory enterprise modeling (PEM), enterprise models are created by actively involving stakeholders in the creation process. They jointly participate in modeling sessions in which they, themselves, work on the models, supported by method experts that master the modeling method [26]. A particular added value of PEM arises when the contents of the models have to be coordinated, i.e., when domain experts exchange their different knowledge, possible conflicts or approaches to solutions are discussed, and a consensus has to be found among the participants [29]. Higher model quality is cited as a particular advantage of PEM [24,30]. In addition, authors also mention acceptance and commitment to the resulting models, identification and feelings of ownership [11,25,28,30], consensus between the stakeholders [24,30], and learning or better understanding of the model and the notation [6,7,16] as further benefits. Both model quality

We thank all the students that helped conducting the study and all the persons who took part in the experiment.

© IFIP International Federation for Information Processing 2024
Published by Springer Nature Switzerland AG 2024
J. P. A. Almeida et al. (Eds.): PoEM 2023, LNBIP 497, pp. 193–208, 2024.
https://doi.org/10.1007/978-3-031-48583-1_12

and appraisals regarding the model are important when it comes to the later use of a model or the implementation of the goals and measures presented in it.

The concept of participation is a much discussed topic in the organizational context, e.g. informing employees or involving them in decisions with regard to their company, or financially involving them [15]. Whether PEM actually produces the desired effects such as feelings of ownership with respect to the model, however, has been little studied.

Psychological Ownership (PO) reflects the feeling that one owns a certain object (tangible or intangible), which does not necessarily include legal ownership [23]. In our context, it is a matter of whether those that have contributed to the modeling also feel that the model belongs to them. PO is said to have positive effects on affective commitment, the desire to maintain a relationship [19,20], and on extra-role behavior [32]. Extra-role behavior means to not only do one's job, i.e. what is expected of them, but also take on additional tasks or show helping behavior, for example. The basic idea is that human beings generally care for their possessions, e.g. in terms of protecting or nurturing them. In a study, Giordano et al. found that teams that had ownership feelings towards a product they had created were also likely to keep on supporting this product [10]. We are interested in whether PEM promotes the emergence of PO and how this could be explained. We consider PO as important to investigate in the context of PEM because, as mentioned above, we can expect that PO towards the model will lead to a greater extent of commitment. As a consequence, the people involved in the modeling will be more likely to champion the model and the measures contained in it.

The goal of this research is to examine whether a participatory approach in modeling will lead to a greater extent of ownership feelings among the domain experts compared to a consultative approach. In this context, consultative means that method experts interview domain experts to build a final model from the gathered knowledge. Furthermore, we want to explore possible mechanisms that lead to PO in a modeling project. PO is said to emerge when people can control the target of interest, when they are familiar with the target and when they invest their selves into it in terms of time or labor [23]. That is why we additionally investigate the participants' perception of how much they could participate in the process of creating a model (e.g. did they feel heard, were their ideas considered?) and how much they feel they and other domain experts and method experts actually contributed to the model. In order to investigate this, we will formulate seven hypotheses based on existing literature on PEM and PO.

In an experiment, we compared three settings with different modes of involving the domain experts. In particular, we compared the dependent variables perceived level of participation, PO, and the perceived level of contribution by the respective domain experts, the modeling experts and by the other domain experts involved in the creation process. Furthermore, we want to investigate the relationships between the variables listed above in order to examine mechanisms for the emergence of positive effects through participation. E.g. does the perceived level of participation have an impact on PO? Does the perceived individual contribution have an impact on PO? With our findings we want to provide more insight on PEM, so that in practice, decisions in favor of or against PEM might become easier. Eventually, PEM always means organizational and monetary effort, as employees have to be called away from their usual work for joint modeling sessions. This effort has to be weighed against possible advantages that our study should help pointing out.

The next section presents some theoretical background on PEM, participation and PO. In Sect. 3, we will describe our research method and present our results in Sect. 4. We will conclude with a discussion in Sect. 5.

2 Theoretical and Empirical Background

2.1 Participatory Enterprise Modeling

According to Stirna and Persson, enterprise modeling serves a number of different purposes, such as developing visions and strategies, (re-)designing the business, developing information systems, ensuring the acceptance of business decisions and maintaining and sharing knowledge about the business [29]. With enterprise modeling, an organization is able to document an as-is or a future state of affairs in a graphical way, usually based on a formal modeling notation. Depending on a company's goal, they may use different kinds of models that help depicting different perspectives, such as goals, processes or technical components [26].

Enterprise models can be created in a consultative way, i.e., modeling experts, also called method experts, elicit knowledge by interviewing the stakeholders, by observing them or by studying documentation [26, 28]. On the basis of the gathered information, the method experts create the models and present them to the stakeholders for feedback, resulting in several feedback loops. This poses several problems: As the stakeholders have played a passive role in the model creation process, they may not fully understand the model and therefore not be able to provide feedback. This can lead to inaccurate or flawed models resulting in faulty implementations. In addition, the more feedback loops are required, the less trust there will be in the competence of the modelling experts [6].

Modeling methods such as 4EM therefore suggest a participatory approach of knowledge elicitation and model creation [26]. PEM may be seen as a special case of collaborative modeling where several domain experts collaboratively create enterprise models supported by method experts [25]. Additionally, a tool operator may handle the modeling tool and a minute taker documents the session [29]. This approach considers that domain experts do not need to have expertise in modeling, thus the procedure, modeling notation and modeling tool must be chosen accordingly [6, 16, 29, 30].

Frequently mentioned advantages of participatory modeling comprise an increase in model quality [24, 30], acceptance and commitment to the resulting models, identification and feelings of ownership [11, 25, 28, 30], consensus between the stakeholders [24, 30], and learning or better understanding of the model and the notation [6,7,16]. In this paper, we will concentrate on Psychological Ownership. It is claimed to be important if the models and decisions contained in them should be implemented in the organization [28].

2.2   Participation in Organizations and in the Context of Modeling

Even though in this context, we understand participation as the possibility of stakeholders to actively be involved in creating enterprise models, it is worthwhile to take a brief look at organizational participation. Heller et al. (1998) define participation as "a process which allows employees to exert some influence over their work and the conditions under which they work" [15, p. 15]. Several advantages of organizational participation can be directly transferred to PEM. First, decision-making is improved by integrating the knowledge and different views of the persons involved. Moreover, Heller et al. claim that people will be "more likely to implement decisions they helped make themselves than decisions imposed on them from above" [15, p. 10]. Furthermore, besides fostering learning at the organizational level, employees may also acquire new skills on an individual level.

In the context of PEM, the term participation is mostly used in the sense of involving the participants in the modeling process. Several factors have been considered that might facilitate this involvement and ultimately influence the process and the outcome of model creation. In particular, modeling tools [5,14, 24,29], modeling procedure [4,8,11] and modeling language [26] have been in the focus, because they are required to motivate domain experts that most likely do not have modeling expertise.

In our paper, we focus on a general comparison between participatory and non-participatory approaches. Studies presenting such a comparison are very scarce. Sandkuhl and Seigerrot present a retrospective of company cases, comparing conventional and participatory modeling [25]. They did, however, not consider individuals' contributions to the model or their perceptions of the modeling process and the outcome. Luebbe et al. investigated differences between knowledge elicitation per interview versus directly involving the stakeholders in the modeling. They found no difference with regard to commitment, but the domain experts were more likely to suggest corrections, have more fun and learn more [17]. Nevertheless, this experimental comparison was not done with collaborating groups, but with one domain expert interacting with one method expert. Gutschmidt et al. compared a participatory setting with a setting where the domain experts were able to work with a method expert on a model, but did not collaborate with other domain experts. In the latter setting, the final model was built from several individual models and rated by the participants [13]. For PO, the authors did not find any difference, but interviews gave hint that some domain experts, particularly in the individual setting, consider the method experts as co-owners. The experimental design did, however, not include a truly consultative setting, i.e. interviews without direct involvement in the modeling.

We will therefore extend the former experimental setting of Gutschmidt et al. [13] and compare three settings: 1) collaborative/participatory as the "classic"

PEM with several domain experts collaboratively creating a model supported by a method expert, 2) individual/participatory as the setting where method experts built a final model from several models they have co-created with domain experts in individual meetings, and 3) consultative as the setting where method experts created a final model from several individual interviews with domain experts.

First, we are interested in whether a participatory and collaborative setting has an influence on the domain experts' perception of the possibility to participate. Based on the findings of the above-mentioned studies, we believe that when domain experts are interviewed and do not get actively involved in the creation of the model they will rate their possibility to participate as lower. Compared to the collaborative/participatory setting, the individual/participatory setting may cause a lower extent of perceived participation because the final model may not look like the one created in the first meeting. On the other hand, some people may not be able to voice or defend their ideas in a collaborative session. Thus, in this case, we cannot yet hypothesize on specific differences between the three groups, but we formulate the following general hypothesis:

H1: There is a difference between collaborative/participatory, individual/participatory and consultative setting with regard to the perceived possibility to participate in terms of being heard and considered.

Based on this, we believe that a participatory setting will cause the domain experts to consider their own contribution higher compared to a consultative setting. As in the collaborative setting, most of the work is done by the domain experts, they will also consider their own contribution higher compared to those in the individual/participatory setting. We state the following hypothesis:

H2: There is a difference between collaborative/participatory, individual/participatory and consultative setting with regard to the domain experts' perceived extent of contribution to the model.
H2a: In the consultative setting, the domain experts perceive the lowest extent of contribution to the model.
H2b: In the collaborative/participatory setting, the domain experts perceive the highest extent of contribution to the model.

Moreover, we hypothesize that the domain experts in the consultative setting rate the extent of the method expert's contribution as highest because the method experts take on the task of creating the actual model. Similarly, we hypothesize that domain experts in the individual/participatory will acknowledge the method expert's contribution more than in the collaborative/participatory setting because of the more exclusive exchange and the method expert's service of merging several individual models to one model.

H3: There is a difference between collaborative/participatory, individual/participatory and consultative setting with regard to the domain experts' perception of the method experts' contribution to the model.

H3a: In the consultative setting, the domain experts perceive the highest extent of the method experts' contribution to the model.
H3b: In the collaborative/participatory setting, the domain experts perceive the lowest extent of the method experts' contribution to the model.

We will furthermore explore differences in the perception of the extent of contribution made by other domain experts.

2.3 Psychological Ownership

In the context of PEM, authors have repeatedly argued that active involvement of the stakeholders should lead to a sense of ownership of the created models [11,24,28]. That is why we will take a closer look at the construct of PO. PO means that a person feels that he or she owns something, e.g. an object, something intangible such as an idea, or even a person. Consequently, PO does not necessarily involve legal possession [23]. PO is claimed to emerge when a person controls the target, e.g. by being able to manipulate it, when the person becomes very familiar with the target by obtaining intimate knowledge about it, and when the person invests the self into the target, e.g. through labor and time [22,23]. These antecedents may also occur on a collective level, i.e. shared control, collective intimate knowledge, and investment of joint resources, leading to the emergence of collective PO [21]. E.g. Giordano et al. found that teams that showed collective ownership towards a work product they had created were also likely to champion this product [10].

We believe that in a participatory setting, the domain experts have more control over the model compared to a setting where they are just being interviewed. Moreover, in the collective/participatory modeling, the domain experts have a chance to get to know more about others' perspectives and about modeling in general and about the modeling notation. This refers to the antecedent 'intimate knowledge'. Furthermore, in the collective/participatory setting, the modeling session itself will take more time as the participants' contributions have to be discussed and integrated by the domain experts themselves. Consequently we hypothesize:

H4: There is a difference between collaborative/participatory, individual/participatory and consultative setting with regard to the domain experts' feelings of ownership towards the model.
H4a: In the consultative setting, the domain experts perceive the lowest extent of PO towards the model.
H4b: In the collaborative/participatory setting, the domain experts perceive the highest extent of PO towards the model.

The perceived level of being able to participate should have an influence on feelings of ownership as it is connected to giving the participants some control over the model creation process. Moreover, we believe that there is a connection between the extent of individual contribution as perceived by the domain experts and feelings of ownership. The more we contribute to the work, the more it will feel like ours. Thus, we hypothesize:

H5: The perceived level of participation has an influence on the domain experts' feelings of ownership towards the model.

H6: The extent of individual contribution as perceived by the domain experts has an influence on their ownership feelings.

In our analyses, we will consider collective PO and individual PO separately to examine which aspect is more dominant. In a former study [13], we found indications that domain experts might consider the method experts as co-owners. This is in accordance with our hypotheses about the perception of the method experts' contribution to the model corresponding to their actual involvement in each setting. That is why we hypothesize:

H7: The extent of the method expert's contribution as perceived by the domain experts has an influence on the collective PO.

3 Method

3.1 Experimental Setting and Procedure

With our study, we want to examine whether participatory modeling leads to e.g. a higher extent of PO than a consultative approach. In a former study [13], however, we found interesting results for a third modeling approach where, in a first step, domain experts create models with a method expert in individual meetings and, in the second step, the method expert merges all models to one joint model. These domain experts reported in interviews that they considered the final model as "our" model and stressed the contribution of the method experts. We would like to further explore the role of method experts from the domain experts' point of view. Therefore, we came up with three treatment groups as depicted in Fig. 1. Groups of four persons were assigned to one of each treatment group. In treatment group 1, the method expert interviewed four participants separately and built a joint model from the collected material. In treatment group 2, the method expert also met four participants separately, but in each meeting, the respective domain expert was actively involved in the creation of the individual model. Subsequently, the method expert had to merge the four models to one final model. In treatment 1 and 2, we informed the participants that others contributed in the same way to the model and that one final model would be created from our interviews. In treatment group 3, a group of four domain experts met with the method experts and collaboratively created one model. Afterwards, a method expert refined the model, but only with regard to formatting. They did not make any changes to the content itself. To sum up, the experimental design contained one independent variable, the level of participation.

As PEM is particularly beneficial in situations where a consensus has to be found, we decided to set the task of creating a goal model. Other models in which decisions have to be discussed, especially when it comes to the design of a future state, would have been conceivable, e.g. a should-be model of a process. Since

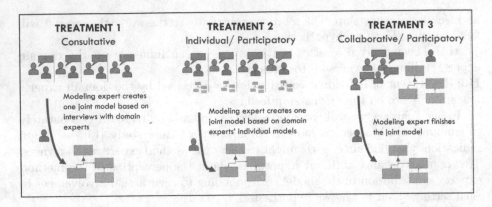

Fig. 1. Experimental design of the study including the three treatment groups.

sufficient samples for an experiment like this are hard to obtain in the industry context we decided to set a task in the university context and recruited students and university teachers as participants. We set the overall goal "To achieve high quality and successful learning and teaching at the university through technology" and asked the participants to draw from their experiences during the pandemic and to develop several sub goals. We used the 4EM modeling notation because it is very intuitive and easy to use for modeling beginners [26]. All the participants were provided with a short video that showed them the basic idea of goal modeling.

We started the study during the pandemic. Consequently we could not conduct the trials in person, but had to arrange video conference meetings. We wanted to create comparable conditions for all groups. That is why we also developed a script that dictated all the work steps during a meeting. In all treatment groups, at first, goals had to be suggested including possible relations, secondly problems and additional relations, thirdly opportunities and additional relations, and, in a last step, all kinds of elements and relations could be added. Although the 4EM notation includes further elements, we did not explicitly ask for those due to the limited time. The domain experts were nevertheless allowed to use them.

We used Miro as a modeling tool that was used in the individual/participatory and the collaborative/participatory setting. Thus, we briefly introduced the participants to Miro before the modeling session started. Miro allows collaborative use, thus, all participants could interact with the tool at the same time. To make the use of the 4EM notation easier, we prepared several elements of each element type that the participants could use to add descriptions etc.

For the collaborative/participatory setting, we followed a procedure recommended by Stirna and Persson [29]. In each work step, the participants had to first write down the goals (or problems or opportunities in the next rounds) for themselves. We prepared the workspace in Miro so that each participant had a personal workspace next to a larger joint workspace. They had three minutes time. Afterwards, the participants presented each element individually to the group by putting the respective element on the joint workspace. The participants had to discuss how to integrate each element into the model and how to summarize redundant elements.

Although the general conditions should be equal in all treatment groups, working collaboratively is fundamentally different from working individually because the participants have to discuss the model and find an agreement. We also expected the interviews to require the least amount of time because no model was drawn during the meetings, and therefore set different time limits: one hour for the collaborative/participatory setting, 30 min for the individual/participatory setting and 20 min for the consultative setting.

All participants were invited to a second meeting a few days after the first meeting. In treatments 1 and 2, the meetings took place individually. In treatment 3, the whole group came together for a second time. In those meetings, we presented the final model of the respective group to the participants. We gave them time to study the model and subsequently asked them to fill out a questionnaire (see Sect. 3.2).

The meetings were facilitated by Master students that were trained in conceptual modeling. In pretests, we made sure to prepare the students particularly for the facilitation in the collaborative/participatory setting. The students helped in developing the above-mentioned script they eventually applied in the trials. They were not part of the sample but part of our research team. In the collaborative/participatory setting, one of these students additionally took the role of the tool operator who supported the participants in handling the modeling tool. Only one collaborative session and two individual meetings were facilitated by one of the authors.

3.2   Measures

As dependent variables, we assessed PO, the perceived level of participation and the perceived level of contribution to the model made by the respective participant, by the method expert and by the other participants that were involved in the model creation. We measured **PO** using a validated questionnaire by [31] and added an item suggested by [2]. For the German version of the questionnaire, we used a validated translation by [18]. We adapted the questionnaire to the modeling context. The following items are contained in the English PO questionnaire: (1) This is MY model, (2) I sense that this model is OUR model, (3) I feel a very high degree of personal ownership for this model, (4) I sense that this is MY model, (5) This is OUR model, (6) Most of the people that have worked on this model feel as though they own the model, (7) It is hard for me to think about this model as MINE (reversed), and (8) I feel that the model is mine, even if others contributed to its development. Each item had to be rated on a Likert scale from 1 (I do not agree at all) to 5 (I totally agree). Past studies give hint that the questionnaire reflects two factors, collective (our) and individual (my) PO [12,13]. We considered this in our analyses.

To measure the **perceived level of participation**, we developed the following set of items: (1) I was asked about information that should be contained in the model, (2) I was asked for my opinion during the task, (3) My suggestions were incorporated into the model, (4) My suggestions were always listened to, (5) I could speak my mind at any time, (6) I could criticize at any time, (7) The model contains items that were included in the model against my explicit will (reversed), (8) I was able to get as involved in model creation as I wanted to be, and (9) All my suggestions were taken into account. The questionnaire was in part inspired by [27]. Again, each item had to be rated on a 5-point Likert scale.

For each construct, an overall value was calculated based on the average value of the corresponding item ratings [1]. Thus we calculated one value for collective PO from the average value of items 2 and 5, and for individual PO from the average value of the remaining PO items. An overall value for the perceived level of participation was calculated from the average value of all the ratings of the items belonging to the above-listed questionnaire.

To measure the different **levels of contribution by the involved parties (oneself, method experts, and other domain experts)** as perceived by the participants, we asked them to give 1 to 5 points to the respective party where 1 means a very low and 5 very high contribution. Thus, we obtained three different contribution scores, one for each party.

3.3 Methods of Data Analysis

For checking validity and reliability of the PO and participation questionnaires, we used exploratory factor analyses. We used principal axis factoring. We used Promax rotation because for PO, we did not expect the factors for collective and individual PO to be independent. We checked for factor loadings greater than 0.6. A reliability analysis additionally helped us looking for problems concerning reliability [9]. Due to the small sample size, we did not conduct a confirmatory factor analysis.

Due to the low sample size, we do not assume normal distribution. That is why we used the Kruskal-Wallis test as a non-parametric test to test for a general difference between the treatment groups. To investigate concrete differences in a pairwise comparison, SPSS provides corresponding post-hoc tests. Moreover, to examine relations between variables, we examined bivariate correlation with Kendall's tau [9].

3.4 Sample

We recruited students and teachers from universities in Germany, Belgium and Russia. On the whole, 55 persons took part in the study (25 female, 29 male, 1 diverse). The participants' average age was 26.8 ($\sigma = 6.4$). We had five teams assigned to the Interview treatment, four teams to the Individual/Participatory treatment, and five teams to the Collaborative/Participatory treatment. Each team should consist of three students and one university teacher. For the collaborative setting, some of the participants had met before in two of the groups, in one group, the participants did not know each other, and in two groups, all participants knew each other before. The students' subject of studies varied from computer science and business information systems to medicine, educational science, biological sciences, economics etc. In one collaborative team, one student did not show up at all, so the trial had to be done with only three participants. In another collaborative team, a participant did not show up in the second meeting and did thus not fill out the questionnaire. Consequently, we gathered 54 questionnaires. We let the participants rate their enterprise modeling expertise on a scale from 1 (novice) to 5 (expert). The average rating was 2.35 ($\sigma = 1.5$).

4 Results

Factor and Reliability Analysis: Considering all items for PO, we found a 2-factor solution. Items 2 and 5 that contained the term "our model" loaded on one factor, i.e., they correlated with this factor. The other items loaded on the other factor with one exception: the item "I feel a very high degree of personal ownership for this model" had high loadings on both factors (0.6 and 0.65). We decided to dismiss this item. The reliability analysis of the items of collective PO (items 2 and 5) resulted in a Cronbach's alpha of 0.926. The reliability analysis of the items of individual items PO (remaining items except item 3) resulted in a Cronbach's alpha of 0.854. We consider the reliability of both sub questionnaires as sufficient [9]. We calculated one value for individual PO and one value for collective PO for each participant based on the average value of the corresponding items' ratings.

For the perceived level of participation, the factor analysis resulted in two factors with an eigenvalue greater than 1 with the second factor having an eigenvalue of 1.072. The scree plot gave, however, hint on one factor. According to Field (2017), the results of the scree plot are more relevant. Consequently, we continued our analysis with one factor which led to factor loadings greater than 0.6 except for items 7 and 8. So, we did not consider these two items when we calculated an overall value for the construct. The reliability analyses for the remaining items resulted in a Cronbach's alpha of 0.969 which is sufficient [9].

Table 1. Mean values and standard deviations for the dependent variables in the treatment groups (PLoPart = perceived Level of Participation, ME = method expert) and p-values for the Kruskall-Wallis test (**$p \leq 0.01$, *$p \leq 0.05$)

	Consultative		Ind./Part.		Coll./Part.		Kruskal-W.
	μ	σ	μ	σ	μ	σ	
PLoPart (H1)	3.1	1.3	4.7	0.3	4.5	0.5	0.002 **
my contribution (H2)	3.4	1.0	3.6	0.9	3.7	0.9	0.517
ME's contribution (H3)	4.6	0.6	3.8	1.5	3.8	1.0	0.039 *
others' contribution (explor.)	3.6	0.8	4.1	0.7	4.1	0.9	0.062
PO collective (part of H4)	3.8	1.3	4.4	0.8	4.3	0.8	0.265
PO individual (part of H4)	2.2	0.8	2.2	0.8	2.7	1.0	0.196

Table 2. Correlations based on Kendall's tau, PLoPart = perceived Level of Participation, ME = method expert, $**p \leq 0.01$, $*p \leq 0.05$

	PO collective	PO individual
PloPart (H5)	0.281 **	0.226 *
my contribution (H6)	0.431 **	0.134
ME's contribution (H7)	0.205	

Examination of Hypotheses: For each dependent variable we present mean value and standard deviation for each treatment group in Table 1. The Table also contains the significance values of the Kuskal-Wallis test. The test shows a significant difference for the perceived level of participation and the method expert's contribution as perceived by the participants. Post-hoc tests for pairwise comparisons concerning perceived level of participation resulted in a significant difference between the consultative setting and the individual/participatory setting ($p \leq 0.003$) and consultative setting and collective/participatory setting ($p \leq 0.019$). The participants that have only been interviewed generally perceived a significantly lower level of being able to participate in the model creation process. For the perceived method expert's contribution, we found that participants in the consultative setting rated the method expert's contribution significantly higher than those in the collaborative/participatory setting ($p \leq 0.038$). Thus we accept hypotheses H1 and H3. We must reject our hypotheses concerning differences in the domain expert's perceived contribution (H2) and ownership feelings (H4). We also explored possible differences in the perception of the contribution by other domain experts but did not find any difference.

According to our correlation analysis (see Table 2), we can accept the hypothesis H5 about a relation between perceived level of participation and PO whereas collective and individual PO were examined separately. We accept H6 only with regard to the relation between perceived individual contribution and collective PO. We reject the hypothesis H7 about a relation between perceived method expert's contribution and PO. Significant correlations are marked with two stars for highly significant p-values ($p \leq 0.01$) and one star for significant values ($p \leq 0.05$). According to [3], an effect is low with a correlation coefficient between 0.1 and 0.3, medium between 0.3 and 0.5, and strong with a coefficient greater or equal to 0.5.

5   Discussion

5.1   Summary and Interpretation

In our study, we compared different levels of involvement of domain experts in the creation of a goal model and their influence on the perceived level of being able to participate, PO on an individual and a collective level, and the perception on one's own, other domain experts' and the method expert's contribution.

We found that in a consultative setting where the participants were only interviewed, they indeed felt a significantly lower level of participation. Both in the individual/participatory setting and the collaborative/participatory setting, the domain experts felt a high level of participation with average ratings of 4.7 and 4.5, respectively, with a maximum of 5. In the consultative setting, the participants did not witness the creation of the model. They were just interviewed and confronted with the model in a second meeting. As hypothesized, these participants rated the contribution of the method expert significantly higher than in the collaborative/participatory setting, whereas for the individual/participatory setting there was too much variance to find a clear difference. The high variance might generally be one reason why we did not find further differences, particularly between the collaborative/participatory and the individual/participatory setting. Nevertheless, the analysis gives hint that concerning the perception of participation, ownership and contributions, these two settings are equally strong.

We did not find significant differences concerning the perception of one's own contributions, the other domain experts' contribution and PO, although the descriptive statistics show that there is a tendency for the participatory settings to promote collective PO. Furthermore, the correlation analysis indicates that the perceived level of participation has a significant influence on individual PO and collective PO. So, we can assume that the extent of involving domain experts in the model creation is important for the emergence of PO. It might be considered as an aspect of being in control as is necessary for the emergence of PO [23]. The perception of one's own contribution also seems to have a significant influence on collective PO. We assume that one's own and other's contribution can be considered as joint control, familiarization and investment of resources [23]. The participants seem to generally feel a collective PO rather than an individual PO, independent of the treatment (see Table 1). This is probably because we made them aware of others being involved and the persons that had worked individually may have noticed changes or additions as was reported in another study [13].

The perceived level of the method expert's contribution did not have an effect on the other variables, especially not on PO as we had hypothesized. Based on this result and a former study on model quality [13], we conclude that the support by the method expert has a positive influence on perceived model quality while not corrupting the emergence of ownership feelings.

5.2 Limitations

Our study has some limitations of which we will list those we consider as most important. Our data sample consisted of only 54 participants and the design was slightly imbalanced. For example, a one-factorial ANOVA, as a parametric alternative to the Kruskal-Wallis test, aiming for a small effect ($\eta^2 = 0.2$) with a significance value of 0.05 and power of 0.9 would have required 54 participants, given that each of the three groups comprised 18 persons. Pearson correlation, as an alternative to Kendall's tau for metric data, aiming for a medium effect (0.3) with the same significance value and power would have required at least

112 participants [3]. Thus, a more extensive data set, especially with a balanced sample, would be desirable. Moreover, although we set a modeling task that should have been relevant to the participants, we cannot be sure that everyone was motivated in the same way. Particularly the fact that the participants could not expect any relevant personal consequences from the modeling limits external validity. PO might not have emerged in the same way like in a real company context where employees are involved.

Furthermore, the students acting as method experts did not have experience in modeling projects in a real company. Nevertheless, they were graduate students, currently enrolled for Master studies in Information Management or Business Information Systems. They had been trained in modeling, e.g. conceptual data modeling and process modeling. In pre-tests, each of them was additionally trained and prepared particularly for facilitating the collaborative sessions. Finally, we had to meet the participants virtually due to the pandemic which might have influenced the communication, especially in the collaborative setting. To sum up, we need further research, especially of real company cases, to support our findings. Such research should not only consider subjective measures, but also include more objective measures, e.g. through observing actual contributions instead of a self-assessment. Such measures will, however, mean an increase in effort of data assessment (see e.g. [12]).

5.3   Implications for Practice and Future Research

This study has focused on the participants' perception of participation and ownership feelings. As a next step we plan to analyze the models that have been created with regard to their content and quality aspects. Besides our experimental research, we need to study more real cases that use either of the three approaches compared here. Until now, the published case studies often lack the assessment of variables with which we could measure the participants' individual appraisals of the process and outcome of a modeling project.

Our findings indicate that the individual/participatory and the collaborative/participatory approach seem both stronger than the consultative approach and similar concerning perceived involvement and PO. Nevertheless, while collaborative sessions require more organizational effort and are more challenging with regard to facilitation, the individual approach has the same disadvantages like the consultative, e.g. individual models might contradict each other, so, the method expert will have to negotiate them, probably through several iterations. This can make the process more laborious. Nevertheless, the study confirms the value of actively involving the domain experts in the modeling.

References

1. Bühner, M.: Einführung in die Test-und Fragebogenkonstruktion. 4 ext. edn. Pearson Studium, München ua (2021)
2. Caspi, A., Blau, I.: Collaboration and psychological ownership: how does the tension between the two influence perceived learning? Soc. Psychol. Educ. **14**, 283–298 (2011)
3. Cohen, J.: Statistical Power Analysis for the Behavioral Sciences. Routledge (1988)
4. De Vreede, G.J., Kolfschoten, G.L., Briggs, R.O.: ThinkLets: a collaboration engineering pattern language. Int. J. Comput. Appl. Technol. **25**(2–3), 140–154 (2006)
5. De Vries, M., Opperman, P.: Improving active participation during enterprise operations modeling with an extended story-card-method and participative modeling software. Softw. Syst. Model., 1–28 (2023)
6. Edelman, J.A., Grosskopf, A., Weske, M., Leifer, L.: Tangible business process modeling. In: DS 58-6: Proceedings of ICED 09, the 17th International Conference on Engineering Design. Design Methods and Tools (pt. 2), Palo Alto, CA, USA, 24–27 August 2009, vol. 6, pp. 1–485 (2009)
7. Eitzel, M., et al.: Assessing the potential of participatory modeling for decolonial restoration of an agro-pastoral system in rural Zimbabwe. Citizen Sci. Theory Pract. **6**(1) (2021)
8. Fellmann, M., Sandkuhl, K., Gutschmidt, A., Poppe, M.: Structuring participatory enterprise modelling sessions. In: Grabis, J., Bork, D. (eds.) PoEM 2020. LNBIP, vol. 400, pp. 58–72. Springer, Cham (2020). https://doi.org/10.1007/978-3-030-63479-7_5
9. Field, A.: Discovering Statistics Using IBM SPSS Statistics - North American Edition. Sage Publications, London (2017)
10. Giordano, A.P., Patient, D., Passos, A.M., Sguera, F.: Antecedents and consequences of collective psychological ownership: the validation of a conceptual model. J. Organ. Behav. **41**(1), 32–49 (2020)
11. Gjersvik, R., Krogstie, J., Folstad, A.: Participatory development of enterprise process models. In: Information Modeling Methods and Methodologies: Advanced Topics in Database Research, pp. 195–215. IGI Global (2005)
12. Gutschmidt, A.: On the influence of tools on collaboration in participative enterprise modeling—an experimental comparison between whiteboard and multi-touch table. In: Andersson, B., Johansson, B., Barry, C., Lang, M., Linger, H., Schneider, C. (eds.) Advances in Information Systems Development. LNISO, vol. 34, pp. 151–168. Springer, Cham (2019). https://doi.org/10.1007/978-3-030-22993-1_9
13. Gutschmidt, A., Lantow, B., Hellmanzik, B., Ramforth, B., Wiese, M., Martins, E.: Participatory modeling from a stakeholder perspective: on the influence of collaboration and revisions on psychological ownership and perceived model quality. Softw. Syst. Model. **22**(1), 13–29 (2023)
14. Gutschmidt, A., Sauer, V., Sandkuhl, K., Kashevnik, A.: Identifying HCI patterns for the support of participatory enterprise modeling on multi-touch tables. In: Gordijn, J., Guédria, W., Proper, H.A. (eds.) PoEM 2019. LNBIP, vol. 369, pp. 118–133. Springer, Cham (2019). https://doi.org/10.1007/978-3-030-35151-9_8
15. Heller, F., Pusic, E., Strauss, G., Wilpert, B.: Organizational Participation: Myth and Reality. Oxford University Press (1998)
16. Ionita, D., Kaidalova, J., Vasenev, A., Wieringa, R.: A study on tangible participative enterprise modelling. In: Link, S., Trujillo, J.C. (eds.) ER 2016. LNCS, vol. 9975, pp. 139–148. Springer, Cham (2016). https://doi.org/10.1007/978-3-319-47717-6_12

17. Luebbe, A., Weske, M.: Determining the effect of tangible business process modeling. In: Plattner, H., Meinel, C., Leifer, L. (eds.) Design Thinking Research: Studying Co-Creation in Practice, pp. 241–257. Springer, Heidelberg (2011). https://doi.org/10.1007/978-3-642-21643-5_14

18. Martins, E.: Psychological Ownership in Organisationen: Explorative Untersuchung der Antezedenzen und des Entstehungsprozesses. Rainer Hampp Verlag (2010)

19. Mayhew, M.G., Ashkanasy, N.M., Bramble, T., Gardner, J.: A study of the antecedents and consequences of psychological ownership in organizational settings. J. Soc. Psychol. **147**(5), 477–500 (2007)

20. O'driscoll, M.P., Pierce, J.L., Coghlan, A.M.: The psychology of ownership: work environment structure, organizational commitment, and citizenship behaviors. Group Organ. Manage. **31**(3), 388–416 (2006)

21. Pierce, J.L., Jussila, I.: Collective psychological ownership within the work and organizational context: construct introduction and elaboration. J. Organ. Behav. **31**(6), 810–834 (2010)

22. Pierce, J.L., Jussila, I.: Psychological Ownership and the Organizational Context: Theory, Research Evidence, and Application. Edward Elgar Publishing (2011)

23. Pierce, J.L., Kostova, T., Dirks, K.T.: The state of psychological ownership: integrating and extending a century of research. Rev. Gen. Psychol. **7**(1), 84–107 (2003)

24. Rittgen, P.: End-user involvement and team factors in business process modeling. In: 2012 45th Hawaii International Conference on System Sciences, pp. 180–189. IEEE (2012)

25. Sandkuhl, K., Seigerroth, U.: Participative or conventional enterprise modelling?: Multiple-case analysis on decision criteria. In: 28th European Conference on Information Systems (ECIS), An Online AIS Conference, 15–17 June 2020 (2020)

26. Sandkuhl, K., Stirna, J., Persson, A., Wißotzki, M.: Enterprise Modeling. TEES, Springer, Heidelberg (2014). https://doi.org/10.1007/978-3-662-43725-4

27. Searfoss, D.G., Monczka, R.M.: Perceived participation in the budget process and motivation to achieve the budget. Acad. Manag. J. **16**(4), 541–554 (1973)

28. Stirna, J., Persson, A.: Ten years plus with EKD: reflections from using an enterprise modeling method in practice. In: EMMSAD, pp. 91–100 (2007)

29. Stirna, J., Persson, A.: Typical organizational problems and how participatory enterprise modeling helps. In: Enterprise Modeling, pp. 33–50. Springer, Cham (2018). https://doi.org/10.1007/978-3-319-94857-7_3

30. Stirna, J., Persson, A., Sandkuhl, K.: Participative enterprise modeling: experiences and recommendations. In: Krogstie, J., Opdahl, A., Sindre, G. (eds.) CAiSE 2007. LNCS, vol. 4495, pp. 546–560. Springer, Heidelberg (2007). https://doi.org/10.1007/978-3-540-72988-4_38

31. Van Dyne, L., Pierce, J.L.: Psychological ownership and feelings of possession: three field studies predicting employee attitudes and organizational citizenship behavior. J. Organ. Behav. Int. J. Ind. Occup. Organ. Psychol. Behav. **25**(4), 439–459 (2004)

32. Zhang, Y., Liu, G., Zhang, L., Xu, S., Cheung, M.W.L.: Psychological ownership: a meta-analysis and comparison of multiple forms of attachment in the workplace. J. Manag. **47**(3), 745–770 (2021)

Author Index

© IFIP International Federation for Information Processing 2024
Published by Springer Nature Switzerland AG 2024
J. P. A. Almeida et al. (Eds.): PoEM 2023, LNBIP 497, p. 209, 2024.
https://doi.org/10.1007/978-3-031-48583-1

Printed in the United States
by Baker & Taylor Publisher Services